Tea[...]k

Upper Intermediate Matters

INSTITUTE FOR APPLIED LANGUAGE STUDIES
UNIVERSITY OF EDINBURGH
21 Hill Place
Edinburgh EH8 9DP

INSTITUTE FOR APPLIED LANGUAGE STUDIES
UNIVERSITY OF EDINBURGH
21 Hill Place
Edinburgh EH8 9DP

JAN BELL
ROGER GOWER

Longman

Addison Wesley Longman Limited
Edinburgh Gate
Harlow
Essex CM20 2JE, England
and Associated Companies throughout the world.

© Longman Group UK Limited 1992
All rights reserved; no part of this publication may be reproduced, stored in a retrieval system, or transmitted in any form or by any means, electronic, mechanical, photocopying, recording, or otherwise, without the prior written permission of the Publishers.

First published 1992
Sixth impression 1996

Set in Adobe ITC Garamond Light 10/12pt
and Frutiger Light 8½/10pt

Produced through Longman Malaysia, CLP

ISBN 0 582 04668 8

Authors' Acknowledgements

We would like to thank the following people:

- Marc Beeby, Sara Humphreys and Sarah Scott-Malden for their great ideas and constructively critical comments.
- Pat Mugglestone and Richard Rossner for their support and advice.
- Those people who piloted and/or reported on the materials: Donald Adamson, Sarah Aitken, Belinda Baldwin, David Barnett, Richard (Cook, Olivia Date, Madeleine du Vivier, Kathy Ellis, Alison Goosey, Sherry Johnston, Rob Jones, Joanne Kenworthy, Roy Kingsbury, Chris Lloyd, Helen Naylor, Janet Olearski, Paul Radley, Beverly Sedley, Lindy Seton Winton, Brian Tomlinson and Ann Wills.
- Those people who allowed themselves to be interviewed for our recordings:
  Marc Beeby, Ben Blunt, Dr Simon Brook, Michael Buerk, Cassita Cabral, Sarah Chedlow, Gillie Cunningham, Sheila Dodds, Helen Dunford, Chris George, Lucy Gower, Kenny Graham, Wolfram Hans, Malcolm Hebden, Rieko Hirano, Celia Jeffries, Pat Lodge, Frances Mann, Maria Cristina Pietrogrande, Desmond O'Sullivan, Satish Patel, Jayne Vaughan-Lane, Dick Williams and Yngve Magnusson.
- Our publishers, Kate Goldrick and Gill Negus; our editor Joy Marshall; our designers, Malcolm Booker, Marnie Searchwell and Sharon Sutdiffe; as well as Lynette Corner (permissions editor); Yolanda Durham (secretary), David Briscoe (audio producer), Martine Parsons (production manager), Marilyn Rawlings (art editor), Clare Sleven (cover designer) and Monique Worton (DTP operator) - all at Longman ELT; as well as Desmond O'Sullivan of ELT Publishing Services, for coordinating the early stages of the project.
- The staffs of Bell School, Cambridge and Bell College, Saffron Walden for their support and cooperation.

Contents

Introduction

What is *Upper Intermediate Matters*?

Upper Intermediate Matters, together with *Intermediate Matters*, forms a fully integrated two-part course for adult learners of English. Each level contains twenty units and provides approximately 120 hours of classroom material, taking learners up to a level equivalent to Cambridge First Certificate.

Upper Intermediate Matters builds on the theme-based, multi-syllabus approach of *Intermediate Matters* and gives special emphasis at this level to vocabulary development, grammar revision and extension, pronunciation and writing skills development. A special feature of the book is the integrated nature of the units, which means that the purpose and motivation for speaking and writing and the context for grammar, pronunciation and vocabulary work often develop out of the reading or listening text.

The course is suitable for students on intensive courses as well as those on part-time courses for an academic year. For short intensive courses a split edition of ten units is available.

Components

1 Students' Book and Class Cassettes

The Students' Book consists of twenty units, each providing between four and a half and six hours of classroom work.

Pairs of units are generally linked by a common theme, although each unit has its own topic focus (e.g. Unit 1 focuses on memories, including childhood memories, and Unit 2 on bringing up children). The *Contents chart* at the beginning of the Students' Book (and repeated in the Teacher's Book) gives a breakdown of the topics and the language areas covered in each unit.

Each unit has either a main reading or listening skills focus, which alternates from unit to unit. (The topics in the Workbook are linked to the topics in the Students' Book and if the focus of the Students' Book is on reading, then the Workbook focus is on listening, and vice versa.) However, there is usually both a listening and a reading text in each unit.

There is also grammar revision and extension work, including practice activities; pronunciation work, usually coming out of the text or linked to vocabulary; a VOCABULARY section; a WRITING section and a SPEAKING section.

Three of the units are slightly different in structure to the others in the book. Unit 1 is an introduction to the course and focuses on both fluency in speaking and writing, as well as on awareness-raising in a number of language areas that upper-intermediate students need to revise. It also contains exercises which require students to reflect on their present abilities and learning strategies. Unit 10 is an integrated skills unit, based on a short story, and Unit 20 is a revision unit.

A *Language reference* page is included at the end of each unit (except Units 10 and 20) to provide an easy-to-understand summary of the main grammar areas covered. In some units a summary of pronunciation and vocabulary areas has been included where we feel that this would be useful for students. The *Language reference* page at the end of Unit 1 takes the form of a useful chart summarising the relationship between verb forms and time.

Support material at the back of the Students' Book consists of a pronunciation chart, a summary of the use of different linking expressions, a list of speaking functions, and the tapescripts of most of the recordings on the Class Cassettes.

The two Class Cassettes contain all the recordings used in the Students' Book.

Split editions of the Students' Book (Students' Book A and Students' Book B) are also available.

2 Workbook and Students' Cassette

The Workbook provides support for the Students' Book, and can be used for homework, for further practice in class, or as material to be worked on in a self-access centre.

The Workbook gives extra practice in and extension of the language areas in the Students' Book, including pronunciation. Each Workbook unit contains either a reading or listening text which links thematically to the corresponding unit of the Students' Book.

There is a *Contents chart* at the front of the Workbook (repeated in the Teacher's Book) so that teachers and students can quickly locate what they want to practise.

INSTITUTE FOR APPLIED LANGUAGE STUDIES
UNIVERSITY OF EDINBURGH
21 Hill Place
Edinburgh EH8 9DP

The Workbook is available with or without a key to the exercises. Split editions (Workbook A and Workbook B, with *Key*) are also available.

A single Students' Cassette contains all the recorded material needed for the listening and pronunciation exercises in the Workbook. It allows students to listen to material in their own time, using their own cassette recorders.

3 Teacher's Book

Each unit of the Teacher's Book opens with a summary of material covered in the Students' Book and Workbook. This opening section helps teachers to prepare their teaching and homework programme. It also shows how each unit can be broken down roughly into three cycles of work.
The Teacher's Book then goes on to provide:
- information on the language focus of each unit, including common student problems and errors. (Common student errors are indicated by a preceding asterisk.)
- notes on many of the exercises (except where the Students' Book rubrics are self-explanatory).
- indication of where material in the Workbook can be suitably integrated into the course.
- ideas for further activities.
- tapescripts of all the recordings on the Class Cassettes, as well as an answer key to the Students' Book exercises.

Indexes at the back of the Teacher's Book give the teacher easy reference and access to the language points in the Students' Book and Workbook.

The upper-intermediate student

At this level students are aiming to do more than simply communicate and be understood in English. For example, many of them need to pass some kind of written examination.

The following tend to be some of the characteristics of upper-intermediate students:
- They need to go over much of the grammatical ground that they covered at intermediate level and can feel frustrated as a result.
- Their vocabulary is often limited, particularly in the area of informal colloquial English.
- Their writing is often inaccurate and disorganised.
- They are often not used to reading or listening to authentic language.
- They are often not independent as learners.
- They do not perceive that they are making progress.

One of the main difficulties in teaching an upper-intermediate class is that students will have different abilities, learning styles and levels of motivation, as well as different attitudes to and expectations of learning. There will probably be an imbalance in how good they are at different skills. Good speakers and weak writers may well be in the same class as weak speakers who are good writers. Reconciling these differences is one of the main problems for the teacher.

Guiding principles

These are the guiding principles which we have followed in our attempt to provide an integrated approach and meet the needs of upper-intermediate students.

1 Exposure to interesting material

In order to sustain students' motivation at this level we feel it is important that the material they come into contact with is interesting and challenging. A good choice of unsimplified 'authentic' material makes students feel they are being 'stretched', as well as involved affectively.

We also believe that students do not properly learn to use the language themselves unless they are exposed to and acquire large amounts of native-speaker use. In other words, in order to improve their productive skills of speaking and writing, students need to develop their receptive skills of listening and reading.

As in *Intermediate Matters,* each unit of *Upper Intermediate Matters* is based around a topic and a reading or listening text. These texts address serious social issues such as 'investigative journalism' or human-interest topics such as 'bringing up children'. Both kinds of subjects include provocative issues that demand a personal response and make students want to communicate.

Reading texts include newspaper and magazine articles, poems and stories. Listening texts include 'real-life' interviews, radio broadcasts and a song. Each provides a springboard for much of the language work of each unit and the integrated approach intrinsic to *Upper Intermediate Matters.*

Our overall aim is to appeal to the 'whole learner', which includes both their intellectual abilities and their feelings.

2 Use

It is important that students have the opportunity to use language 'globally' through fluency-based activities, as well as to practise discrete areas of language to improve their accuracy. Speaking and writing activities, which often link naturally to the texts in *Upper Intermediate Matters*, encourage fluency and a creative use of language. Even in practice activities students are encouraged to work collaboratively and thus give themselves the opportunity to discuss things naturally in English. (In monolingual classes students will need to be encouraged to avoid their mother tongue.)

A topic and text-based approach also means that students can put vocabulary, grammar, pronunciation and functional language (such as *asking for and giving opinions*) to immediate active use, in both spoken and written communication.

3 Accuracy

The main topic in each unit also provides a context for controlled practice work in the areas of grammar, vocabulary and pronunciation. Much of the grammar done at intermediate level still needs to be repeated at upper-intermediate level if learners are to achieve greater accuracy and fluency. However, we feel it is important for upper-intermediate students to compare and contrast key grammar points rather than simply to have them re-presented. 'Old' language is therefore constantly recycled and extended in the REVISION and EXTENSION sections of each unit.

If students are encouraged to work grammar rules out for themselves, they are more likely to feel that they are actually making progress and not simply going over old ground. Lots of practice of the grammar, with a focus on oral personalised activities, helps to consolidate what they have learned.

Pronunciation, and particularly word and sentence stress, is an important element of being accurate, and this is frequently integrated into the grammar and vocabulary sections of the units.

4 Vocabulary

Vocabulary work is vital at this level to motivate students who feel that they are on a language-learning 'plateau' and to help them extend their use of language. Where possible, vocabulary is drawn out of the texts and integrated into subsequent activities. Practice exercises include: deducing the meaning of unknown words in context; word building; using dictionaries to find the meaning and pronunciation of words and expressions. At this level it is also important to do more work in the areas of idiomatic language, phrasal verbs, collocation and connotation.

5 Developing learning skills

Hand in hand with a need to expose students to 'authentic material' is the need to develop their confidence in coping with 'real' language. Activities accompanying the texts in the READING and LISTENING sections help to develop such confidence by on-going development of the sub-skills required to listen and read effectively. Attention is also paid to important language-learning skills such as the efficient use of dictionaries and deducing the meaning of unknown words in context.

It is crucial at this level to encourage and develop efficient learning strategies so that students will be able to continue to learn on their own and not be dependent on a teacher. Throughout *Upper Intermediate Matters* students are encouraged to monitor their own work, especially in writing activities, and to pay attention to the process of production as well as the end-product itself.

TEACHING WITH *UPPER INTERMEDIATE MATTERS*

In general, our approach draws on the best of current classroom practice and balances tried and tested approaches with new ideas.

Unit organisation

Each unit is divided roughly into three cycles of work, and (with the exception of Units 10 and 20) conclude with the *Language reference*, which is a summary of the main language points covered in each unit. The first cycle typically focuses on a reading or listening text, which provides the theme of the unit (the input); the second cycle focuses on the revision and extension of an area of grammar; and the third cycle usually focuses on speaking and writing (output). Vocabulary and pronunciation work are usually in the first two cycles.

The structure of many units, then, looks like this.

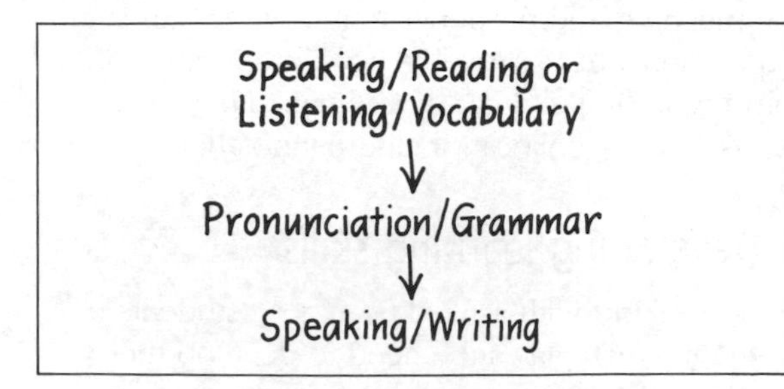

However, there are no rigid divisions between cycles. Material can be cut, re-ordered and supplemented according to the needs of students.

Students may prefer to begin with the *Speaking and Writing* cycle and then move on to the *Revision and Extension* grammar cycle or the *Reading and Listening* cycle. It is also possible to begin with grammar and then go on to practise one or more of the skills.

As previously noted, three of the units have a slightly different format to the rest of the book. Unit 1 is an introductory unit, aiming to introduce students to most of the features of the book. It therefore includes: authentic reading and listening material; learner development activities; grammar revision and fluency activities which the teacher can use for diagnostic purposes. Unit 10 is based on a short story, which means that the three cycles must be done in order. The main focus in all three cycles is on skills practice. Unit 20 is a revision unit, including both language work and skills practice. As in the other units, the three cycles in Units 1 and 20 can be changed, adapted and re-ordered, depending on the needs of the class.

The Workbook extends and balances the Students' Book in that there are extra language practice exercises. These are writing and accuracy-based and might appear to the students as more 'traditional' in style than the more personalised, oral exercises of the Students' Book. There is also further work on pronunciation, vocabulary and writing, and a text-based exercise with a different skills focus from the corresponding unit in the Students' Book.

Methodology

1 Reading

Most of the reading texts are authentic and unsimplified. Texts have been chosen for their general interest and generative nature. Students will feel motivated to read them and then to speak and write about the topic.

The aim of a text-based approach is to expose students to a wide range of language and to develop confidence by systematically giving practice in the main sub-skills. To this end, students are asked to do tasks *before* they read, to motivate them and to give them a purpose for reading (this may be for gist, for specific detail or for interpretation). Such *Before reading* tasks may include prediction exercises, writing questions they would like answered, or simply discussion of the topic. The sequence of reading activities goes from global to intensive, and can usually be done in pairs or groups. Teachers do not, of course, have to use all the activities.

Texts also help students to acquire new language from a variety of natural contexts, as well as to consolidate what they already know. Some texts can also be used as models for students' own writing.

As well as the texts in the Students' Book and Workbook, students should be encouraged to read as widely as they can, e.g. readers, newspapers and magazines.

2 Listening

Much of the taped material has been recorded outside the studio with a variety of different people. Other recordings come from the radio, and there is a well-known song in Unit 20.

If students are not used to listening to real, connected speech in English, they will initially have problems with understanding, because a natural rhythm involves the use of contractions, weak forms, elision and assimilation which students often find difficult to interpret. It is particularly important then that students are aware that listening is a skill which needs developing, and for gist activities they are not normally expected to understand every word.

As with reading, it is particularly important that students are prepared for the text in the *Before listening* activity. While they are listening they should be encouraged to focus only on doing the activity required of them (in the first instance this will be some kind of 'global listening' activity). Later they will be required to go on to exercises which focus on detail and inference. If this staged approach is done as a matter of course, students will soon become more confident.

Other tips for giving support during the listening activities:

- Elicit, brainstorm or teach any difficult words beforehand.
- Use the pause button to stop the tape from time to time to allow students to answer the questions, or to focus on particular features of connected speech.
- Allow students to follow the tapescript while they listen, particularly during the second or third listening, or if the recording is especially difficult.
- Allow students to give their personal response to what they hear (both to the content and the level of difficulty).

3 Vocabulary

Vocabulary is given a high priority in the course and is approached in a number of different ways:

- Words are studied through topics and word fields, with attention being given to connotation, phrasal verbs, idiomatic language, collocation and euphemism. Aspects of word building (e.g. prefixes, suffixes) and synonyms and antonyms are also covered, both in the Students' Book and the Workbook.
- Students are encouraged to deduce and guess the meaning of new words in reading and listening texts from the context and their form.
- Attention is paid to the pronunciation and word stress of new words, as well as to spelling and the link between spelling and sound.
- Guidance is given on how to make the best use of monolingual dictionaries. For this reason, it is advisable to help students to assess and choose a suitable one. The *Longman Active Study Dictionary* is at an appropriate level and includes exercises to help teachers supplement whatever dictionary work is done in class. The *Longman Dictionary of Contemporary English* is a little more detailed and has a Workbook to go with it (see *Bibliography*). Reference is also made in Unit 6 of the Students' Book to the *Longman Lexicon of Contemporary English* (see *Bibliography*). Students will also need advice on a good bilingual dictionary to use.
- Students are encouraged to keep organised vocabulary records as they come across or have their attention drawn to new words and expressions. There is more explicit guidance in *Intermediate Matters*.

Students are encouraged to use vocabulary learned or acquired in each unit in the writing and speaking activities. Opportunities should be created in the classroom to recycle and revise vocabulary.

4 Revision and Extension

The REVISION section of each unit gives students an opportunity to compare and contrast linked and similar areas of language. In Unit 1 the aim is to revise and contrast language which students may feel they have already 'done'. This serves as a useful indication for the teacher as to which areas need more work. To make this challenging for students, a variety of verb forms are linked and compared to different time frames. In Unit 2 a variety of past and present forms are brought together under the heading of 'Habit', and in Unit 4 other past forms are linked through the use of narrative. Students are encouraged to work collaboratively and to discuss their answers. In general, grammar work is seen as a teaching process not a testing device.

The EXTENSION sections introduce and give practice in a 'more difficult' area of language that comes out of or relates to the REVISION section (e.g. the third conditional follows on from the first and second conditional, which students may already use fairly well).

Grammar is dealt with both inductively and deductively, with the emphasis on students being encouraged to work out rules of form and use for themselves and check their answers in the *Language reference*.

Emphasis has been placed on the differences between verb tense and 'aspect' (i.e. progressive or perfective verb forms). Attention is also drawn to the relationship between different verb forms and time.

Each section of language is followed by a range of practice activities. In the Students' Book the emphasis is on controlled and less controlled oral communicative work. In the Workbook there are more accuracy-focused written exercises which can be incorporated into the lesson.

5 Pronunciation

The pronunciation syllabus focuses primarily on connected speech and areas of difficulty such as weak forms, sentence stress and word boundaries, although work on sounds contrast is also included

Many of the exercises come out of the text in the first cycle of the unit or out of vocabulary work. Usually, it is suggested that on-going attention is given to pronunciation rather than devoting specific lessons to this area of language. For example:

- When a word is introduced, practise its sounds and word stress.
- When setting up semi-controlled pairwork, anticipate areas of pronunciation difficulty and practise them.
- In freer activities such as roleplay, or when listening to a cassette, pay attention to the communicative effect of the intonation (e.g. *Does he/she sound bored? Why?*).
- Encourage students to identify their pronunciation problems and work on them by themselves if possible (using a language laboratory or their own cassette recorders). This is particularly important with multilingual groups. Students may like to be referred to books such as *Ship or Sheep?, Sounds English* and *Speaking Clearly,* and teachers will find *Learner English* a useful reference (see *Bibliography*).

Other tips:

- Decide how you will identify the stressed syllable when writing a word on the board and try to be consistent. (In *Upper Intermediate Matters* a prime mark (') is used, as in a dictionary.)
- When getting students to identify stressed words in a sentence make it clear how they should mark this. In *Upper Intermediate Matters* this is sometimes done by putting a box over the stressed word, or by underlining it.
- Decide on the role of the phonemic alphabet (page 149 of the Students' Book). Will you give systematic training in the sounds and link them to the symbols or will you encourage students to use it to help them when they are trying to find the pronunciation of a word in a dictionary?
- Link the sound and spelling of words as far as possible.

6 Speaking

Speaking activities are an integral part of each unit in that in the *Before reading / listening* activities students are frequently encouraged to discuss the topic of the unit and predict what is going to come up in the text. They should also be encouraged to discuss their answers to all activities, including grammar exercises, in English.

Accuracy

As the focus in the REVISION and EXTENSION sections is on accuracy, it is important that errors of language and pronunciation are picked up and corrected, either by the teacher or other students. One technique is to write down any errors you hear and get students to correct them in groups.

Correction can also be turned into a game or communicative activity. See, for example, 'Language auction', 'Snakes and ladders', 'Correcting homework' and 'Mistakes dictation' in *Grammar Games.* There are many other ideas for supplementary practice activities in *Grammar Games* and other books such as *Grammar Practice Activities* (see *Bibliography*).

Many of the practice activities are personalised and open-ended, with students encouraged to talk about their lives and interests.

Fluency

In the SPEAKING section the focus is mainly on fluency and activating vocabulary, so the teacher's role is to monitor how effective students are at communication, and to give feedback on their English (e.g. suggest improvements, give ideas, correct mistakes).

These activities often give the opportunity for students to practise functions such as complaining, disagreeing, showing surprise, etc. and you should refer students to the list of speaking functions on page 150 of the Students' Book.

Some of the activities need careful setting up and clear instructions, and you may want to explain the purpose of each activity to students.

Many activities in the SPEAKING section can be structured in such a way that students practise in 'closed groups' (with ideas for improvement being given by students or the teacher) before they 'perform' to other groups or the whole class. If possible, you could record the 'performance' on audio or video tape.

Freer communication activities such as this can be supplemented by further activities from books such as *Keep Talking* and *Discussions that Work* (see *Bibliography*).

7 Writing

Controlled

In general, written language demands greater planning and more accuracy than spoken language. The WRITING section in *Upper Intermediate Matters* is therefore often controlled and sometimes focuses on reinforcement of grammar areas which are particularly important in writing (e.g. complex sentences, articles, participle clauses), or on organisational work such as linking sentences and clauses together, and writing a summary. It also often focuses on features of layout such as writing a formal letter.

Creative

Other writing activities are more creative and personal (e.g. writing a short autobiography) and focus more on what the students are saying rather than on linguistic accuracy. They often link to the topic or text so that students have a genuine communicative purpose for writing something (e.g. a tourist brochure in a unit on social conventions in different countries).

In general, it helps the writer's 'block' if a writing activity can follow on from a classroom reading, listening or speaking activity in that ideas will already be there and, where possible, it is better if students work cooperatively on writing tasks in the classroom, rather than always taking writing home to be done alone as homework. When setting up a writing task it is helpful to brainstorm ideas about content and language with the class, or get students to exchange ideas in groups.

Students could also do a first draft in pairs or groups, which means that you can actually help students while they are writing rather than simply marking their 'product' afterwards. Students can also learn to check their own and each other's work by using checklists of points to watch out for. It is important that students are made aware of the advantages of this approach, i.e. that if they spend longer on the 'process' of writing, the finished product is going to be improved and any feedback on it much more valuable.

Other tips:

- When marking students' work it is sometimes useful to look only at one or two aspects of their work and indicate errors accordingly. This helps students to improve one problem area at a time (e.g. punctuation or linking expressions) without getting too discouraged. You might also get students to tell you what area of language *they* want you to mark.
- When students have written something they are satisfied with, get them to display it in class for other students to read. This is particularly interesting if it is communicative in some way (i.e. if other students have a genuine reason to want to read it).
- If working in Britain, students could be given a genuine reason for communicating (i.e. a letter of enquiry to a travel agent) and try to get a response.

Acknowledgement

We are grateful to Robert Hill for his suggestions and comments on the language focus of each unit.

Abbreviations

T	Teacher
SS	Students
SB	Students' Book
WB	Workbook
TB	Teacher's Book
GW	groupwork
PW	pairwork

Contents chart (Students' Book)

Unit	Topics	Grammar/functions	Vocabulary
●1●	Memories	Grammar review	Deducing words in context Using a monolingual dictionary
●2●	Bringing up children	Habit in the present Habit in the past *Be/get + used to* (+ *-ing*) Definite article Agreeing and disagreeing	Prefixes and suffixes
●3●	TV and films	Present Perfect Simple and Continuous	Television programmes
●4●	Gambling and other addictions	Past Simple, Past Continuous or Past Perfect? Past Perfect Simple or Continuous?	Verbs and nouns (collocation) Adjectives and prepositions
●5●	Women and work	Question forms Question tags	Work
●6●	Job interviews	Obligation *Make, let* and *allow* Asking for and giving advice	Jobs and duties Using a lexicon
●7●	Forms of transport	Future (*will, going to,* Present Simple and Present Continuous) Changes of plan	Cars Transport
●8●	Space	Future Continuous Future Perfect	Compounds
●9●	Travel	Phrasal verbs	Travel Idiomatic expressions
●10●	Integrated skills		
●11●	The role of journalists	Conditional sentences: first, second, zero *If* or *when* *Wish* + past, *wish* + *would, if only* Pronominal forms	Phrasal verbs: idiomatic and non-idiomatic
●12●	Crime and punishment	Third conditional (past) *Wish* + Past Perfect *Should/shouldn't have done*	Crimes and punishment Law and order
●13●	Wedding customs	The passive Need(s) to be done *Have/get* something done Reflexives	Relationships
●14●	Customs and manners	*-ing* or *to*?	Connotation
●15●	Diets in sport	Quantity Compounds of *some, any, no* and *every* Determiners/pronouns	Homonyms Mixed idioms
●16●	Spectators and sport	Deduction in the present Mixed modals	Sport
●17●	'Life' issues	Reported speech Reporting verbs	Suffixes (adjectives from nouns or verbs) Prepositional phrases
●18●	Ceremonies	Defining and non-defining relative clauses Participle clauses	Word formation Idiomatic expressions Euphemisms
●19●	Mysteries	Deduction in the past	Different sounds Idiomatic expressions
●20●	Integrated skills and language revision		

Pronunciation	Writing
Review of sentence stress Using intonation	Autobiography
Word stress with suffixes Sound: /ə/ Pronunciation chart Intonation of surprise/interest	Personal letter Revising and correcting written work
Weak forms and contractions	Adverbs of degree Strong adjectives Describing a film, play, book, etc.
Sounds: /v/, /w/, silent /w/ Sounds: /p/, /b/	Linking words and expressions: time, addition, contrast, reason, result Narrative
Questions: weak forms and intonation	Sentence patterns Word order Advertisement (job)
Sounds: /æ/ and /ʌ/ Sounds: /ʊ/ and /u:/	Formal/informal language Letter of application (job)
Word linking (consonant-to-vowel; disappearing sounds)	Comparatives and superlatives Advertisement (forms of transport)
Stress in compounds	Complex sentences (linkers and participle constructions) Report, diary or letter to a newspaper
Word linking (vowel-to-vowel, words ending in '*r*')	Indefinite article Personal letter Travel experiences
Sounds: /ʃ/, /tʃ/, /dʒ/	Grammatical and lexical linking words Letter of opinion
Shifting word stress Contractions/stress in conditional sentences	Summary writing Comparing factual and emotional language
Sounds: /ɒ/, /ɔ:/ /əʊ/	Description from notes
Corrective (contrastive) stress	Tourist brochure
Intonation of lists Sound: /l/ (*file*/*light*)	Attitude words Dialogue
Homophones	Formal letter of complaint
Word stress in adjectives Pronunciation of the letter *a*	'For and against' essay: organising and linking ideas
Intonation of relative clauses Word stress: words ending in *-ion*	Description of a scene
Weak forms and contractions	Newspaper article

Learning strategies (Unit 1)

Evaluation of speaking abilities, and discussion of activities
Correction of grammar
Discussion of strategies for learning vocabulary

Contents chart (Workbook)

Grammar	Vocabulary	Pronunciation
Form and function; functional English; verb forms and time; revision	Plurals; describing people	Words from the text: phonemic transcription; word stress
Review of the present; habit in the past; *used to (do)* or *be used to (doing)?*; the definite article	Prefixes; word building; compound nouns	
Present, Present Perfect or Past?; duration; Present Perfect Simple or Continuous?	Entertainment; intensifying adjectives; adjectives and prepositions	Silent letters
Sequence of tenses; Past Perfect Simple or Continuous?; narrative forms	Phrasal verbs; common errors; verbs and prepositions; places	
Mixed question forms; less direct and reported questions; question tags; word order	Men and women; synonyms and antonyms	Question tags
Obligation; advice	Collocation; medical terms	Connected speech
Talking about the future; future time expressions	American English; prepositional phrases; collocation; forming adjectives and adverbs	
Future Continuous or Perfect?; future review; complex sentences	Words often confused; prepositions of time; idiomatic expressions; compound adjectives	
Review of the article; *could / (was/were) able to / managed to; used for; as/like*	Phrasal verbs; animals	
Present, Present Perfect or Past?; question forms; modals of obligation; future forms	Word building; prepositions; phrasal verbs; definitions	Dictation
Mixed conditional forms; *wish* and *if only*	Collocation; phrasal verbs; word association	Dictation
Past conditional and *wish; wish* and *if only*; criticisms (*should (not) have*)	Crime and punishment; nouns and prepositions	
The passive; pronouns; *have (get)* something done	Idiomatic expressions; newspaper headlines	
Verb + object + *to* + base form; *-ing* or *to*?; expressing preferences	Connotation; ambiguity; proverbs	
Quantity; compounds of *some, any, no, every*; *each, another, both, either,* etc.	Numbers; idioms	Words with the same spelling
Modals; reference words	Word building; similes; foreign words and phrases	
Reported speech; direct speech; reporting verbs	Adjectives and nouns; synonyms and antonyms; phrasal verbs	
Defining relative clauses; defining and non-defining relative clauses; participle clauses; adjectives ending in *-ing* and *-ed*	Word building; prepositional phrases; confusing words	Vowel sounds
Review of verb forms; conditionals; *wish*; modals; spot the errors; which is correct?	Colloquial language; test your vocabulary	

Memories

Students' Book

General theme: childhood.
Unit topic: memories.

SPEAKING: talking about childhood.
SPEAKING REVIEW: evaluating strengths and weaknesses in speaking; talking about preferred classroom activities.
LISTENING: interview with Gloria Estefan.

GRAMMAR REVIEW: verb forms as related to time; terminology; mixed verb forms.
PRONUNCIATION REVIEW: sentence stress; stress and intonation.
READING: extracts from autobiographies.

VOCABULARY REVIEW: deducing words in context; using a monolingual dictionary; strategies for learning vocabulary.
WRITING: autobiography.

Workbook

READING: extract from a novel: a description of a teacher.
PRONUNCIATION: words from the text; marking word stress.
GRAMMAR: form and function; functional English; verb forms and time; revision grammar.
VOCABULARY: plurals; describing people.
WRITING: personal description.

Aims of Unit 1

The first unit is a diagnostic unit and aims to get SS to:

a) revise and reflect on grammar and pronunciation.
b) speak and write, with the aim of getting to know other SS in the class as well as for the T to get an idea of the SS' level.
c) listen to and read authentic language.
d) think about learning skills such as deducing words in context; using dictionaries; identifying syllables, etc.
e) reflect on and discuss their learning strategies and needs (e.g. for speaking and vocabulary).

Language

The language focus of this unit is different from other units in that it does not deal with one specific language point. Instead, it aims to give a general overview of verb forms which SS will already be familiar with at this level, and to:

- highlight the flexibility of verb forms in English by making SS aware that tense does not always relate directly to time.
- get SS to identify structures and verb forms and relate them to grammatical terminology.

There are also activities in the SPEAKING and GRAMMAR REVIEW sections which require SS to use a range of verb forms and structures. These will help the T diagnose areas of weakness.

Common problems

At this level, SS will feel that they already 'know' a lot of the grammar covered in this book. However, they are often unable to use it fluently and/or accurately.

English verb forms

One of the biggest problems for learners is the use of the English verb form system. Strictly speaking, English has only two tenses — the present (simple) and the past (simple). For this reason, we refer to other related structures which use auxiliaries (e.g. Present Perfect) as verb forms. Note that in English various verb forms (e.g. Present Continuous or will + base form) are used to talk about future time.

Tense, time and aspect

One misapprehension that learners often have is the belief that there is a one-to-one correspondence between tense and time. However, tenses do have different uses. The Past Simple, for example, can refer to a past event: *We went away last weekend.* but it can also have a hypothetical meaning, which is essentially timeless: *I wish I had a bigger house.* or it can even refer to the present: *Did you want to see me?* (For other examples see the *Verb forms as related to time* chart on SB page 9.)

As well as having to decide whether English verb forms refer to present, past or future time another major problem for SS is 'aspect' – the changes in meaning which occur when verb forms are made progressive (*I'll be going home at...*), or perfective (*He has gone home.*). Aspect is looked at in later units.

SPEAKING

This activity has two main aims — to encourage SS to mingle and find things out about each other, and to get them using language, specifically past forms and expressions of habit, which are focused on in Units 2 and 4. The activity therefore serves as a useful diagnostic tool for the T.

• **Exercise 1** Introduce the topic of childhood by drawing SS' attention to the photographs and getting them to divide them into different ages, e.g. babies, toddlers, school-age children, adolescents. The words in the box may need to be explained, and are meant to stimulate, not constrain SS, so if they want to use other words, this should be encouraged. This activity could be done as a class, rather than a group activity. SS (and the T) could also bring in their own childhood photographs, and try to guess which photograph relates to which student.

• **Exercise 2** This activity might best be done by 'modelling' it first, i.e. by writing some of your own memories on slips of paper, giving them out, and asking SS to ask you questions about your notes. Make it clear that they should be writing only *notes* when they do it, not complete sentences. Language expected to come up will include past forms, including those of habit. Resist the temptation to correct at this stage, although in feedback it may be worth pointing out that there are other ways of talking about habit in the past which will be looked at later. If you make notes of mistakes or 'gaps' in the SS' speaking these could then be written up and SS could try to identify the errors. (This activity could be included in the SPEAKING REVIEW section which comes next.)

SPEAKING REVIEW

Ideally, do this immediately after the SPEAKING section.

• **Exercises 1 and 2** At this level it is important that SS reflect on their oral performance, and are self-critical. Sometimes SS are unsure about what 'good speaking' involves so it helps to break down the skill into specific areas, and raise awareness of which of these areas SS are particularly strong and weak in. Make it clear that pronunciation involves stress and intonation as well as producing correct sounds. In Exercise 2 encourage SS to draw on their past experiences of learning languages, and perhaps give your own experiences, too.

You could follow up these activities by giving advice on how SS can help to achieve their aims (e.g. project work, talking to native speakers, use of the language laboratory self-access centre for pronunciation work, and special classes). Discuss with them the idea of monitoring either their own or a friend's speaking, and suggest recording it where possible. Possibly show SS a list of the mistakes they made in the SPEAKING section, and get them to correct them.

LISTENING

Before listening

If SS do not know the singer Gloria Estefan, you may prefer to do this as a class prediction exercise using the photo as a stimulus ('*What do you think she does for a living?*'). If SS know her, ask questions such as '*What nationality is she?*' (e.g. American, but her mother was Cuban.) '*Do you know the names of any of her songs?*' (e.g. 'Don't wanna lose you') Possibly play one of her songs as a lead-in. Alternatively, play a song as follow-up.

Listening

• **Exercise 1** This is a gist listening activity, so try to dissuade SS from panicking about detail, especially if they are not used to 'real listening'.

• **Exercises 3 and 4** SS need to listen in more detail for the answers to these questions, so it is a good idea to do this in a language laboratory if you have one. Some of the questions may require SS to guess the meaning of vocabulary they don't know, such as *passed on*, *a burden*, and *genes* in Extract 2, before checking in the dictionary. You could explain *PhD* (a *Doctor of Philosophy*, which is a degree of very high rank) and *Master's* (a post-graduate degree).

If SS have had problems with the listening, let them listen to the whole interview again reading the tapescript at the back of the SB at the same time.

• **Exercise 5** SS may like to bring photographs of their family to class.

GRAMMAR REVIEW

• **Exercise 1** PW? SS might well be used to other terminology (such as the Present Progressive), or come across it in grammar books, so elicit other terms or give alternative versions.

• **Exercise 2** This is an awareness raising exercise. It sensitises SS to, or reminds them of, the fact that English tenses or verb forms can be used to talk about different time frames (e.g. the Present Continuous can refer to the future as well as to the present). This is a good opportunity to explain the reasons why much of the grammar which SS may feel they have 'done' in intermediate coursebooks comes up again at upper-intermediate level.

You may want to incorporate discussion of the *Verb forms as related to time* chart on SB page 9 into the lesson.There is more work on verb forms and time in the WB.

• **Exercise 3** PW/GW? You could do this as a kind of competition. The aim of this exercise (and Exercise 1 above) is to check that SS and the T use the same terminology. One of the reasons for this will be to encourage greater independence — so that SS will be able to use the *Language reference* or a grammar book more effectively, and be able to correct their own writing more easily. Again, this is an opportunity to introduce or elicit alternative terminology (e.g. *to* + base form).

• **Exercise 4** This exercise is light relief from the more analytic exercises earlier. However, it is also a useful diagnostic tool for the T, and could introduce SS to the idea of self- or peer-monitoring. The activity should be done individually at first and then the statements can be discussed in pairs or groups, as a way of the SS getting to know each other better. It could be turned into a game with SS writing their sentences on slips of paper. The slips could then be mixed up within the group and placed face down on a table. Each S turns up a piece of paper and the 'author' of the sentence should talk about what is written.

Other ideas for activities using 'unfinished sentences' can be found in F. Klippel, *Keep Talking* and C. Frank and M. Rinvolucri, *Grammar in Action* (see *Bibliography*).

In this part of the lesson you might also like to discuss SS' strategies and experiences in learning grammar; introduce grammar books you think are useful to them; talk about the use they can make of the *Language reference* at the end of each unit in the SB; talk about what grammar is covered in the book and how this is practised in the WB.

In the WB there is a Revision grammar exercise and work on Functional English, which could also be integrated into the lesson.

PRONUNCIATION REVIEW

Sentence stress

This is intended as a 'fun activity'. It serves as an introduction for those SS who have not thought about sentence stress in English, and as revision for those who have. The listening phase could be followed up by oral practice in pairs. It is an opportunity to remind SS that English, unlike many other languages, is a stress timed language, with the stress tending to be on content words such as verbs, nouns, adjectives, etc. and that non-content words are weakened. More work on this is done in Unit 3. (Contrastive stress is looked at in Unit 14.)

Stress and intonation

Again, this is aimed mainly at recognition and awareness-raising, although SS might like to practise the sentences afterwards. Make it clear to SS that a 'monotonous' intonation can be interpreted by native speakers as boredom or rudeness.

There is an exercise on word stress in the WB.

READING

These texts link back to the childhood theme in the SPEAKING section at the beginning of the unit. They also include a variety of past forms which are focused on in Units 2 and 4.

• **Exercise 1** An alternative way of doing this would be to get different SS to read different texts and to report back on what they are about. The exercise is intended to focus on gist reading, so SS should be discouraged from getting bogged down with vocabulary. Perhaps ask them how difficult they found the reading, and, if necessary, suggest ways of improving their reading speed and confidence (e.g. you could start a class library, or encourage SS to borrow books from an English library or self-access centre). Ask SS if they can think of any other novels that talk about childhood, and personalise the context of the extracts by asking them if they have had a similar experience to any of the writers.

• **Exercise 2** This requires more detailed reading, for which SS will need to find the meaning of the words they don't know. Encourage them to deduce the meaning in context first. Note that the VOCABULARY REVIEW section, which follows, gets SS to deduce the meaning of *snap*. You could integrate this exercise if the word comes up. Alternatively, if they are unable to deduce in context, allow SS to use monolingual dictionaries and then focus on strategies for using such dictionaries afterwards (also to be found in the VOCABULARY REVIEW section).

Recommend a monolingual dictionary such as *Longman Dictionary of Contemporary English* that SS can use. Possibly bring forward the discussion on the pros and cons of bilingual dictionaries (see the *Learning vocabulary* exercise in the next section).

VOCABULARY REVIEW

The first part of this section (*Deducing words in context* and *Using a monolingual dictionary*) could be integrated into the READING section above when SS need help as to how to cope with an unfamiliar word. At this level it is very important that SS are aware of strategies for dealing with difficult words in authentic texts, such as deducing meaning from the context, or deducing the meaning or grammatical function from the word itself (e.g. from prefixes or suffixes). It is also vital that SS gain confidence in using dictionaries efficiently. Perhaps encourage SS to use books such as *Longman Dictionary Skills Handbook* (see *Bibliography*) on a self-access basis, or incorporate their use into class time.

• **Exercise 2** Note that students are required to produce /snæpt/ and not just the definition /snæp/ from the dictionary extract. This is an opportunity to introduce SS to the Pronunciation chart on SB page 149 and show them how to use it. How much time you spend on this in class will depend on the motivation and the aims and abilities of the SS. Most adult learners perceive how useful it is to be able to find out about the pronunciation of a word without being dependent on the T.

There is practice in phonemic transcription in the WB.

• **Exercise 3** You could include other new words which SS may have come across while reading the texts in the previous section.

This exercise leads on to the *Learning vocabulary,* which asks SS to think about how they keep vocabulary records, and the different strategies they use for learning new words. It might be appropriate to give them some help and ideas here (see *Intermediate Matters* for more on this). Perhaps a system of weekly vocabulary tests or games could be built into your lessons, so that SS have an opportunity to revise new words and expressions regularly.

WRITING

Autobiography

• **Exercise 1** Tell SS that they are going to write an autobiography about their early life. Start with a discussion to elicit ideas of the sort of things they might include in it. Refer them back to both the listening and reading texts earlier in the unit for ideas (e.g. Gloria Estefan's memories of her grandmother or Clive James's experience with the dog. If they have done the *Reading* in the WB this may give them some ideas for describing one of their family, teachers or friends). Build up a list of ideas, either in groups or as a class.

• **Exercise 2** Give SS time to make notes and plan their writing. Be available to help as needed.

• **Exercise 3** Discuss with SS the importance of checking their written work before they hand it in. Encourage them to use dictionaries (e.g. for spelling and vocabulary), grammar books or the *Language reference* page at the end of each unit in the SB. The idea of SS correcting their own mistakes using symbols is specifically looked at in the WRITING section of Unit 2.

To give SS motivation for writing out the 'final version' perhaps tell them that the autobiographies will be put on the classroom wall for others to read, with or without the author's name on it.

Tapescripts

RECORDING 1

Extract 1

INTERVIEWER: So where would you say your motivation comes from?

GLORIA ESTEFAN: Well, I'm just a survivor, Number 1 and I'm a very positive person. I always try to look at the good side of things and try to, no matter what experience it is, only concentrate on how it could be better or what I can do about it. If there's a problem I'll try to look for a solution and if there's no solutions then I just won't worry.

I: Would you say you were a sort of determined stubborn character?

GE: Very - very determined and I think if you ask my family they'd say stubborn in some ways, when it's something that I really want - when I have a goal that I really want to achieve - I just focus on that one thing and whatever I have to do to get there I'll do it.

Extract 2

I: Do you think that's something you've inherited from your father, because he sounds like quite a tenacious character?

GE: And my mother also. My mother's also very determined. When she came to the States she had a PhD in Education from Cuba and they ripped up all the papers so she had to start over, and she went to the university again and got all her credits again and eventually became a teacher and then got her Master's so, I come - and my grandmother also, she learned to drive when she was seventy-three in the States because my grandfather had passed on and she didn't want to be a burden on anyone, so she also was a very, very strong-willed woman and I guess it comes in my genes.

I: You've mentioned Emilio quite a lot. Would you say he's the biggest influence in your life?

GE: Definitely. My grandmother and Emilio are my two biggest influences. She was a feisty old woman that really did everything that she always ever set her mind to do and she gave me a wonderful example of a strong woman, and in her lifetime - I mean she was, she wanted to be a lawyer when she was nine years old and she never achieved her goal because she had to work for a living in Cuba, but at that time for a woman to want to do that was unbelievable, and her whole life was an example to me. And Emilio who's really helped me blossom as a person. There's never been any jealousy between us. On the contrary he's always tried to do and bring out the most in me and encourage me and motivate me to do more and more things. I'm a couch potato, I really never would have - I'm a very contented human being so I never would have thought well let me go this step further and he really has brought me into the person that I am today.

Extract 3

I: Let's talk about your music. How does it work for you?

GE: I'm not the kind of person that like Diane Warren who worked with me on this album, who gets up every morning at 8 o'clock and all she does is write, cos that's her life. I need some kind of inspiration or an idea or some emotional cue to spur me into writing. My song writing has always been - music to me has always been a very emotional thing. I've been singing since I was three and to me it was my catharsis. I was very introverted and shy so when I wanted to cry or laugh I would just go in my room and sing, and to me that was my way of pouring out my emotions, rather than you know the standard way, and my song writing has turned also into that - into sometimes ideas that I have, cos I love to observe things in life and just sometimes very deep feelings and sometimes the more difficult the feelings the easier it is to write.

RECORDING 2

[See Key.]

RECORDING 3

a) You're Sandra, aren't you?
b) It's cold there in March, isn't it?
c) I'll have a beer, please.
d) A gin and tonic, with ice.
e) You've forgotten your keys.
f) You've lost your keys.
g) She's a lovely person.
h) It's a beautiful garden.

Key

LISTENING

Listening

1
a) 3 b) 2 c) 1, 2 and 3 d) 3

2
b and c

3
a) Very determined (tenacious).
b) Because when she got to the States from Cuba her papers were ripped up and she had to get her qualifications again.
c) At the age of seventy-three. Her husband died and she didn't want to be a burden.
d) A strong will.
e) A lawyer.
f) She had to work (so she couldn't study).
g) Her grandmother's whole life was an example to her.
h) He has helped and encouraged her to do more.
i) A lazy person. (It seems unlikely that she really is because she's achieved a lot).

4
a) inspiration (or an idea, or an emotional cue)
b) a very emotional thing
c) three
d) introverted and shy
e) her feelings are 'difficult'

GRAMMAR REVIEW

1
b) Present Simple; *will* + base form
c) Present Simple (question)
d) Present Perfect
e) Present Continuous
f) Past Continuous
g) Past Simple
h) Present Continuous
i) *will* + base form
j) Past Perfect; Past Simple

2
b) future; future c) future d) present/past
e) future f) past g) present h) present i) present
j) past; past

3
Example answers:
a) my brother *told me that* he had seen
b) we used *to leave* our stockings out
c) they would always *be filled*
d) a long list of *the* presents; one of *the* big stores
e) I remember *believing*
f) If we were lucky, our parents *would take* us
g) we *could* give him
h) we *used to* leave our stockings out
i) in, to, for, on, into, at

PRONUNCIATION REVIEW

Sentence stress

A: I'm just going to phone <u>Mum</u>.
B: Can you ask her if she's coming for a <u>meal</u> on <u>Sunday</u>?
A: What time shall we say to <u>come</u>?
B: Oh, around <u>one</u>, I should think. Tell her to bring the <u>car</u> - I've got some <u>plants</u> for her.

Stress and intonation

b) not sure c) abrupt d) polite e) statement
f) asking for confirmation g) contradiction h) fact

READING

2
a) True b) False c) True d) False e) False f) True
g) False h) False

VOCABULARY REVIEW

Using a monolingual dictionary

1
snap 1.4

2
/snæpt/
The *Pronunciation* chart on page 149.

3
ONE SYLLABLE: 'bark, 'rage
TWO SYLLABLES: 'ruins, up'set, 'pigtail
THREE SYLLABLES: 'tropical, 'traumatise, 'parachute

Cruel to be kind?

Students' Book

General theme: childhood.
Unit topic: bringing up children.

SPEAKING 1: discussion of picture; characteristics of ideal parents.
REVISION AND EXTENSION 1: habits and criticisms (Present Simple; *is always* + *-ing*; *keeps* + *-ing*; *will* + base form); habit in the past (Past Simple; *used to*; *would* + base form).
READING: newspaper article about bringing up children.

VOCABULARY: word building (prefixes and suffixes); suffixes, word stress and the /ə/ sound.
REVISION AND EXTENSION 2: *be/get used to (doing)*; *be* or *get* + adjective / past participle.

SPEAKING 2: agreeing and disagreeing with people; intonation of interest or surprise; having a discussion.
REVISION AND EXTENSION 3: the definite article.
WRITING: personal letter; correcting written work.

Workbook

LISTENING: interview with Pat about bringing up children.
GRAMMAR: review of the present; habit in the past; *used (to do)* or *be used to (doing)*; the definite article.
VOCABULARY: prefixes; word building; compound nouns.
WRITING: dictation.

Language

The language focus of this unit is on habit, and includes revision of present and past verb forms. The aim is not only to revise verb forms and uses that SS are already familiar with (e.g. Present and Past Simple, *used to*), but also to introduce them to different uses of familiar verb forms (e.g. Present Continuous with *always* to indicate irritating habits, *will/would* + base form for characteristic habits). These constructions, as well as *keeps* + *-ing*, are common in everyday spoken English, but SS tend to over-use the Present and Past Simple instead.

To make the unit more challenging for SS at this level the unit also includes work on *to be/get used to (doing)* something (for explicit contrast of *used to do* versus *to be used to doing* see the WB).

The WRITING section revises the definite article, which most SS continue to have difficulties with, particularly in their writing (for work on the indefinite article see Unit 9). The SPEAKING 2 section revises functional language such as agreeing and disagreeing, and practises 'echo questions'.

Common problems

Used to do and be used to doing

Although probably not new to SS, both the 'concept' and the form of *used to* + base form frequently cause problems. The structure is often confused with *to be used to doing*.

1 SS find it difficult to accept that *used to do* is only a past form, and try to use it to talk about the present (**I use to...* or **I am use to...*). They need to be aware that *used to* is a verb and acts differently to *be used to doing*, where there is an adjective (*used*), followed by a preposition (*to*).

2 Many languages have a similar concept to *to be used to* + *-ing* in their own language but often use a base form rather than the *-ing* form. This often causes SS to make mistakes with the form (**I am not used to eat this type of food.*).

3 SS need to be aware that *used to do* is only used for discontinued habits and states, not to talk about how often something was done or how long it took (**I used to visit my aunt three times last month.*)

4 The question and negative forms frequently cause problems (**Did you used to..?*), as well as the pronunciation of *used to* (/ju:stə/) which gets confused with *used* (/ju:zd/) (e.g. *I used a knife.*).

Will and *would*

SS are often unaware that *will* and *would* are used to express habitual behaviour. They also find it difficult to remember that *would* and *used to* are not totally interchangeable, since *would* cannot refer to states (**I would live with my aunt when I was young.*).

The definite article

1 Some nationalities (e.g. the Russians and Japanese) do not use definite articles at all, so tend to leave them out (**Give me book on the table, please.*).

2 Other nationalities (e.g. the Italians and Greeks) use definite articles in a different way, e.g. for generalisations (**I love playing the tennis.*), whereas English does not use them for generalisations.

3 The many rules of use that SS have to learn can be confusing, e.g. using *the* with the names of seas (*the Mediterranean*) but not with lakes (*Lake Victoria*); *the* when talking about buildings (*I am meeting her near the hospital.*) but not when talking about institutions (*He's in hospital.*); *the* for the names of groups of states (*the Netherlands*) but not for countries (*Spain*).

SPEAKING 1

• **Exercise 1** Ask SS what the photograph suggests to them (love, security, happiness?). Get SS to give their views on bringing up children, ask how they think views have changed over the years and what their own parents' attitude is. In a multinational class, cultural differences will mean that there will probably be a lot to talk about, and possibly some quite strong differences of opinion. Since *giving opinions* comes up in SPEAKING 2 later listen out for how well SS do this, and take the opportunity to introduce a few expressions (see the list of *Speaking functions* on SB page 150).

• **Exercises 2 and 3** The aim here is to revise the Present Simple and adverbs of frequency before moving on to less common ways of talking about habit. Perhaps remind SS of the position of adverbs of frequency without making too much of the issue, and possibly move straight on to practise the Past Simple and adverbs of frequency (REVISION AND EXTENSION 1, Exercises 2 and 3).

REVISION AND EXTENSION 1

Habits and criticism

• **Exercise 1** Elicit what the pictures are showing before listening to the recording. Ask SS what comments and criticisms they have about their own families. Although intended as a language presentation, the listening extracts are authentic and so the first time SS listen it should be just for gist – to see if they can get the general idea of what the children are talking about. The second time they listen you will probably need to pause the tape at appropriate moments so that they can write down what they hear.

Then elicit what was said and get SS to identify the verb forms and say why they are used. Try to encourage them to use the appropriate intonation with *always* + *-ing*, to show irritation. It might be worth pointing out that *will*, if stressed, can also imply criticism. Maybe jump directly from this to Exercise 4 to give SS practice in criticising and complaining.

• **Exercises 2 and 3** You may wish to leave these exercises out if SS are having no problems with adverbs of frequency. However, if you feel that they need more practice you could extend Exercise 2 by getting SS to write a couple of sentences about other SS in the class, using these adverbs. Listen how SS pronounce the endings /s/, /z/ and /ɪz/.

• **Exercise 4** Telling each other about irritating habits could be done as GW, or as a class 'mingle'. Other irritating habits could include singing in the shower, borrowing each other's clothes, not cleaning the bath, leaving lights on, etc.

There is also a general review of ways of talking about the present in the WB, which could be integrated at this stage. Alternatively, the exercise can be set for homework and discussed in class. There are lots of other ideas for revising the Present Simple in P. Ur, *Grammar Practice Activities*, M. Rinvolucri, *Grammar Games* and C. Frank and M. Rinvolucri, *Grammar in Action* (see *Bibliography*).

Habit in the past

• **Exercise 1** Use the photograph to see if SS know who Bob Geldof is and why he is famous. (He comes up again in Unit 11.) In discussing what he says you could refer back to SPEAKING 1 and contrast the views expressed by the Indian tribe with the disciplinarian attitudes of Geldof's father. Perhaps ask SS who they think the 'priests' are that Geldof refers to, and why they are important. Tell them that Geldof is Irish, and that many Irish people are Roman Catholics.

• **Exercise 2** After SS have underlined the verb forms discuss with them the different ways of talking about habit in the past. You could show how the use of *would* links with *will* in *Habits and criticism* above. Either draw SS' attention to the form of *used to* and *would* at this stage (see the *Language reference* section at the end of the unit in the SB) or wait until the fluency activity in Exercise 3. It might also be worth highlighting at this stage the pronunciation of *used to* (/ju:stə/), with its unexploded plosive and schwa and the contracted form of *would* (*I'd / he'd*).

There is an exercise specifically contrasting the uses of *used to* and *would* in the WB. If SS start getting confused with *be used to* + *-ing* you could quickly explain the reason for the confusion (e.g. one *used* is a verb whereas the other is an adjective) but leave practice until later in the unit.

You could refer SS back to uses of *used to*, *would* and Past Simple in the READING section of Unit 1.

• **Exercise 3** Extra revision on verb forms to talk about habit could be done if SS compiled a questionnaire about experiences of childhood and asked other people in the class to complete it. This would be particularly useful for question forms (e.g. *How did your parents use to punish you when you were naughty?*).

READING

• **Exercise 1** This exercise asks SS to predict, and can be done in pairs. The text is about an Italian mother's (rather negative) opinions of British parents, so it might be worth asking SS (especially if they are in Britain) if they have any opinions or experiences of the British as parents.

• **Exercise 2** This is a gist reading activity, so it is important to get the SS to read quickly and for them not to get bogged down by unfamiliar vocabulary. You may first need to explain *boarding schools*. Allow time for SS to discuss their answers in pairs.

• **Exercises 3 and 4** SS may need to go back to the text in order to locate the answers to these questions.

Other vocabulary which may come up or to which you want to draw SS' attention: *prevalent, reserve, bear the brunt of, thrive, appalling, hooliganism, shunned, proffered, gulps, bewail.* The vocabulary work could be done in class if there is time (e.g. deducing in context before checking in a dictionary). Alternatively set this as a homework task. Make sure SS are keeping vocabulary records and making a note of new words. If discussion about keeping vocabulary records hasn't come up before (see suggestions in Unit 1), now is a good opportunity.

• **Exercise 5** The reading texts are intended to stimulate SS to speak. The activity could be extended, if required, by giving SS the opportunity to ask other people their views on bringing up children. If possible, it would be interesting to ask a variety of different nationalities their opinions and then report back on the similarities and differences.

VOCABULARY

Word building

Guessing the meaning from prefixes

• **Exercise 1** Probably not all the words SS think of will include prefixes (e.g. *improve*). Make sure they understand what prefixes are and their function before going on to the next exercise.

• **Exercise 2** PW? This could be followed up by an exercise where you give SS some nonsense words, using prefixes. SS then have to guess what the words would mean if they existed (e.g. *reget, dewrite, undersleep, bidaily*). There is more work on prefixes in the WB.

Using suffixes

• **Exercise 1** SS should brainstorm the missing words on the chart before looking them up in a dictionary. Ask them to tell you how many syllables there are in each word and to identify the stressed syllable. Encourage SS to get into the habit of marking the stressed syllable whenever they write down a new word, and agree on the system to use for marking word stress (i.e. putting a prime mark (') before the stressed one). Build up on the board a list of typical endings for adjectives, nouns and verbs, and make sure SS make a note of them for future reference.

• **Exercise 2** Make sure you rub the list of typical endings off the board before doing this exercise. This is a good opportunity to see how many of the typical endings SS remember.

Suffixes, word stress and the /ə/ sound

• **Exercises 1 and 2** This is an opportunity to draw SS' attention to the *Pronunciation* chart on SB page 149 and to show them how to work out how a word is pronounced. For homework SS could practise writing their names using the phonetic symbols.

• **Exercise 3** Make it clear to SS that vowels in unstressed syllables tend to be weak (usually the /ə/ sound).

REVISION AND EXTENSION 2

Be / get used to (doing)

• **Exercises 1 and 2** SS are encouraged to work out the meaning and form of *be used to* + *-ing* for themselves, and contrast it with *used to* + base form (looked at earlier in the unit). There is practice on contrasting the two forms in the WB.

SS are also asked to work out the difference between ***be** used to* and ***get** used to*. They can check their answers in the *Language reference* section at the end of the unit in the SB before going on to practise the structure in Exercise 2.

Some example answers for Exercise 2 are:

a) getting up early; wearing formal clothes;
b) being asked for your autograph; never being able to go out looking scruffy;
c) sharing a bathroom; being tidy;
d) eating less; taking more exercise.

Be or get

Make it clear to students that they are focusing on *be* or *get* with an adjective or participle (not *be/get used to doing*).

SPEAKING 2

Agreeing and disagreeing with people

• **Exercise 1** Quite a lot of the activities in this unit have required SS to give their opinions. This exercise focuses on agreeing and disagreeing. As this will be revision for most SS encourage them to use different levels of formality with the appropriate intonation.

Intonation: interest or surprise

'Echo questions' may be new for some SS. They may need guided practice in this area before going on to the discussion in the next section.

As far as grammar is concerned SS need to remember to invert the subject pronoun and the auxiliary (e.g. *I am against … **Are you**? I can't understand … **Can't you**?*). If there is no auxiliary, SS need to substitute *Do* or *Did* (e.g. *I object to … **Do you**? I used to go … **Did you**?*). (N.B. the 'rules' of 'echo questions' are similar to those of question tags, revised in Unit 5.)

SS also need to practise the intonation of 'echo questions', exaggerating where necessary, and making sure the voice goes up at the end to indicate surprise or interest.

Having a discussion

Obviously SS should be encouraged to give opinions, agree, disagree and use 'echo questions'. Remind SS that at this level it is essential to use the new language they have learned and stretch their English if they are to improve at all. The activity could be extended into a kind of game, where each group thinks of a contentious statement, and invites another group to agree or disagree, giving reasons.

REVISION AND EXTENSION 3

The definite article (*the*)

Writing is very important at this level, especially if SS are to go on to do exams such as the Cambridge First Certificate, and, in our experience, SS' misuse of the definite article is a big contribution to poor writing. If revision and awareness-raising of the basic rules is done at an early stage of an upper-intermediate course SS can then be encouraged to continually monitor their work with reference to the guidelines offered in the *Language reference*. It could be argued that SS do not *learn* the rules associated with the definite article as such but acquire them by continual practice.

WRITING

Personal letter

• **Exercises 1 and 2** The purpose of this activity is two-fold: to remind SS of the format and organisation of a personal letter, which it can probably be assumed they have already done before, and to introduce them to a checklist of points which they can refer to while monitoring their own written work.

Exercise 2 is a more difficult activity, so it is best done as PW.

• **Exercise 3** This is an attempt to make SS think about their own areas of weakness and to prioritise areas for improvement. Try to encourage SS to set themselves personal 'goals' (e.g. to work on their spelling and word order).

• **Exercise 4** This exercise could be done in class or at home, with a friend or alone. The important thing is that SS do a draft, check what they have written and then rewrite, if possible with a communicative purpose. There are more ideas in R. White and V. Arndt, *Process Writing* (see *Bibliography*).

Tapescripts

RECORDING 1

Extract 1: Lucy

My mum's always playing opera music in the car with the windows right down and it's really embarrassing. And I just hope I never see anyone I know when we're driving through town. And she plays it really loud. My father will never cook anything but sausages and spaghetti - which gets a bit boring as Mum's never around because she goes to work.

Extract 2: Ben

Thomas is the worst, I reckon. He plays his music too loud and he always gets his own way when he's watching the television. If I want to watch something he always wants to watch another and then - cos he's bigger than me - he always seems to get his own way.

Thomas keeps coming into my bedroom and taking things or borrowing things - so if I've been out somewhere I'll come home and sort of find the lid off something or something's out of place and I know that somebody's been, like Thomas, has been fiddling with things or trying to work out how to use it or switching on the television and lying on the bed and all sorts. He's got his own television in his room but he often watches mine for some funny reason. And now he always keeps coming in there without asking and that really annoys me.

RECORDING 2

Extract 1: Lucy

1 My mum's always playing opera music in the car with the windows right down and it's really embarrassing.
2 My father will never cook anything but sausages and spaghetti - which gets a bit boring.

Extract 2: Ben

1 Thomas is the worst, I reckon. He plays his music too loud and he always gets his own way when he's watching the television.
2 Thomas keeps coming into my bedroom and taking things or borrowing things.

RECORDING 3

1

A: Well, personally, I'm strongly against mixed education.
B: Are you? Why?
A: If you ask me, kids learn much better in single sex schools. They can concentrate better.
B: Do you think so? I'm not sure I agree with that, actually.

2

A: I think that old people's homes should be closed down! People should look after their old relatives themselves.
B: So do I! I couldn't agree more.

3

A: As far as I'm concerned the police should be allowed to carry guns. It's too dangerous, otherwise.
B: Absolute rubbish! I disagree entirely.

RECORDING 4

A: Well, personally, I'm strongly against mixed education.
B: Are you? Why?

Key

REVISION AND EXTENSION 1

Habits and criticism

1

a)

Extract 1 (Lucy) pictures b) and c)
Extract 2 (Ben) pictures a) and d)

b)

EXTRACT 1
1 always playing opera music in the car
2 will never cook anything

EXTRACT 2
1 plays his music too loud . . . always gets
2 keeps coming into my bedroom

c)

always + -ing; keeps + -ing

2

always → usually → often → sometimes → occasionally → rarely/hardly ever → never

Habit in the past

1

a) priests, father
b) Examples: obedience, discipline

2

'I used to loathe the priests and my father and their systems of authority. I would refuse to cooperate in any way. He (my father) was not, in retrospect, a heartless man. He merely carried with him the values of his age. But they were not values that I shared.'

READING

2

a) 1f), 2c), 3e), 4b), 5d), 6a)

3

a) Italy
b) coldness
c) committing crimes against children
d) happy
e) football hooliganism

4

a) They are unwelcome and rarely seen.
b) She can't understand why the children have to go when they are so young. She thinks it is done because of tradition.
c) That they are excellent parents, but must be unusual.

VOCABULARY

Word building

Guessing the meaning from prefixes

2

b) reprint c) insensitive d) defrost e) undress
f) bilingual g) underpaid h) imperfect

Using suffixes

1

ADJECTIVES	NOUNS	VERBS
en'joyable	*en'joyment*	en'joy
'beautiful	'beauty	*'beautify*
wide	*width*	*'widen*
'patient	*'patience*	-
sweet	*'sweetness*	*'sweeten*
'terrified	*'terror*	*'terrify/'terrorise*
'dusty	dust	dust
'generous	*gene'rosity*	-
'special	speci'ality	*'specialise*

2

a)

warmth (n); tenderness (n); famous (adj); national (adj); experience (n); horror (n); regularity (n); crowded (adj); education (n)

Suffixes, word stress and the /ə/ sound

2

a) tenderness b) national c) horror d) experience
e) enjoyable

3

a) Suffixes *are not* stressed.
b) The /ə/ sound is always *unstressed.*

REVISION AND EXTENSION 2

Be or *get?*

a) get dressed / get ready
b) gets angry
c) 's used / has got used
d) get engaged
e) 's divorced
f) get lost
g) 'm ready

SPEAKING 2

Agreeing and disagreeing with people

1

1 mixed education
2 looking after old people
3 arming the police

2

b)

So do I! I couldn't agree more.
I'm not sure I agree with that, actually.
Absolute rubbish! I disagree entirely.

REVISION AND EXTENSION 3

The definite article (*the*)

1

I live in ~~the~~ Brazil, where *the* weather is very hot and *the* people are very nice. . . .

I love ~~the~~ music and last year I began learning to play *the* guitar . . .

Next year I hope to go and study in *the* United States.

2

a) books b) the books c) Poverty d) stamps e) Europe
f) the Alps g) the baby h) the violin i) school
j) breakfast k) the hospital l) China m) the money
n) Money o) rugby p) the President's q) The elderly

WRITING

Personal letter

1

a)

Pedro has written to his friend Claude to thank him for taking him to the airport, to pass on his news and invite him to go to Boston.

b)

o/p 14th May (should come after the address)
ʎ (word missing) the
vf to take me
g in
p I'm
sp grateful
vf met
wo we enjoyed talking together very much
v At the moment / Now

2

b)

g in
v meet/get
ʎ the
vf talked
p England
g to come
v tell her
g I want her to write to me
ʎ *(p)* teacher, too
sp address
v Best wishes / Love
pg don't
wo I will stay here
p Brazil

TV or not TV?

Students' Book

General theme: addictions.
Unit topic: TV and films.

LISTENING AND SPEAKING: listening to and discussing a Roald Dahl poem; listening to an argument about watching television; connected speech: stressed words and weak forms.
REVISION AND PRACTICE: events up to the present: Present Perfect.

EXTENSION AND PRACTICE: present result: Present Perfect Simple and Continuous.
VOCABULARY: television (e.g. *soap operas*).

SPEAKING: planning a TV schedule.
WRITING: describing a film, play, book, etc.

Workbook

READING: magazine extracts about people's addictions; vocabulary in context.
VOCABULARY: entertainment; intensifying adjectives; adjectives and prepositions.
GRAMMAR: Present,Present Perfect or Past?; duration; Present Perfect Simple or Continuous?
PRONUNCIATION: silent letters.
WRITING: dictation.

Language

The focus of this unit is on the Present Perfect, which is a very difficult area for many SS. It has been assumed that SS at this level will already be familiar with the different forms of the Present Perfect, but are rarely able to use them appropriately in context. The aim of this unit is to bring together Simple and Continuous uses, and, rather than 're-presenting' them, to encourage SS to be analytical and work out differences in meanings for themselves. These different meanings are:

- past experience which is relevant now, specific time not mentioned (e.g. *He has never seen snow before.*).
- unfinished past time (e.g. *I've been living here for six years.*).
- present results of past events (e.g. *They've been playing football so they're filthy.*).

There is also a focus in the unit on questions with *How long* and time expressions such as *for* and *since*.

The biggest problem for SS is understanding why the Present Perfect is used rather than the Present Simple or the past forms. An essential point for SS to grasp is that the choice is dependent on how the event is seen; whether it is seen as a definite past time, psychologically distanced from the present (in which case the Past Simple is used), a completed action where the time the event occurred is not important, or an event continuing into the present (in which case the Present Perfect is used). SS also have to be clear about when the continuous 'aspect' is used (e.g. *He's been running.*) rather than the perfective 'aspect' (e.g *He has run six miles.*) (i.e. the continuous form is more often used for an action in progress, a temporary or an uncompleted event). It is also important that SS see the Present Perfect essentially as a *present* verb form which refers to the past.

At this level an understanding of the importance of 'aspect' in English is essential. It will come up again in Unit 4, which deals with the Past Continuous and the Past Perfect Continuous, and in Unit 8, which looks at the Future Perfect and Future Continuous.

Common problems

1 The Present Perfect Simple is often used in English to talk about past experiences which are relevant to the present, and where the specific time the event occurred is not important. In most European languages, however, the Present Perfect form can be used to talk about definite past time, where the Past Simple is used in English (**I have been there yesterday.*).

2 In some languages the Present Perfect equivalent is formed with *be* instead of *have.*

3 To talk about something which began in the past and continues until the present most languages use the present tense (**I am in Britain since two months.*).

4 Many SS get confused between *for* (to refer to a period of time) and (*since* to refer to a specific point of time).

5 'Aspect' will be a particular problem for those nationalities which don't have continuous forms. There might also be problems with understanding or remembering which verbs don't take the continuous (i.e. 'state' verbs such as *see*).

6 SS often have problems with consonant clusters in ***haven't*** and ***hasn't*** and the fact that the contracted form of, for example, *he has* is the same as *he is* (*he's*). They also tend to forget that *been* (e.g. *he's been running*) is usually weak (/bɪn/).

LISTENING AND SPEAKING

• **Exercise 1** Before listening and reading find out if SS know anything about Roald Dahl, and the books he wrote. As well as being a very popular writer of children's books (this extract is the opening of a poem, the 'Oompa Loompas' Song', taken from *Charlie and the Chocolate Factory*), he also wrote collections of short stories for adults (such as *Tales of the Unexpected).*

You could play or ask SS to read the first four lines of the poem first and get them to guess what reasons the writer is going to give for not letting children near a television set. Then SS can listen to the rest of the text and say whether they agree or not.

This poem is really intended for fun, and as an introduction to the topic of TV addictions. It is important not to spend too long on it, as there is another substantial listening text to follow. Although much of the vocabulary is focused on through the questions, you could also get SS to try and guess words like *install, idiotic, hypnotized, tot.* The poem could be preceded by a quick personalisation of the topic, i.e. asking SS how much TV they watch, etc. Revision of past habit could also be integrated here by asking SS about how much television they used to watch when they were children.

If there is time SS might enjoy reading the poem aloud. It is useful for SS to practise rhyming the words at the end of each line, and to see if they can get the rhythm.

• **Exercise 2** This listening text is quite long – encourage SS to listen to it for gist and give them time afterwards to discuss in pairs which of the arguments Gillie mentioned. They might need to listen again to check their answers.

• **Exercise 3** You could ask SS either to predict or try to remember Mark's arguments before they listen again.

There is quite a lot of vocabulary which can come out of this listening text. For example, the names of different kinds of TV programmes (*soap operas, cartoons, adverts*). Note that these words also come up later, in VOCABULARY. There is also recycling of the phrase *couch potato*, from the Gloria Estefan interview in Unit 1, and expressions such as *load of rubbish*, and *educational stuff.* Possibly open up the discussion into a general one about whether there is too much sex and violence on TV, or whether TV should be more educational. (These issues come up again in the SPEAKING section.)

It might also be worth giving SS time to write down expressions the two people used to disagree with each other (useful revision from Unit 2), either by listening again or listening and reading the tapescript at the same time (*Oh, come on!; Course they do.; That's nonsense; That's complete rubbish,* etc.).

Connected speech

• **Exercises 1-4** The aim of these exercises is to make SS realise which words are generally stressed (i.e. 'content' words such as *reading*), and what happens to unstressed words (i.e. they are contracted or made weak). To help them with Exercises 1 and 4 point out that some stressed words carry a 'main stress' and others a 'secondary stress'. It is not always easy (or important) to discriminate between the two. Explain that when the auxiliary comes at the end of a sentence (*Yes, I do*) it is stressed.

REVISION

Events up to now: Present Perfect

• **Exercise 1** Use the picture to elicit who Nureyev is, and anything SS know about him. The answers to the questions depend on the SS understanding various uses of the Present Perfect, so ask them how they knew the answers to the questions. (Note that the answers to b) and d) are *Don't know.*)

• **Exercise 2** There is an opportunity in c) to revise differences between stative and action verbs, e.g. ask SS which of these sentences is correct, and why: *I am having my lunch.* or *She is having a new house.* There is more work on choosing between Present, Present Perfect and Past forms in the WB.

• **Exercise 3** This exercise practises asking questions, using *How long* and *How many times*, in either the simple or continuous form. More practice on this area with *for* and *since* comes in the next section, and also in the WB.

PRACTICE

• **Exercise 1** The aim of this activity is to get SS to mingle and speak to each other, and to provide both cued practice of the target structure (e.g. *Have you ever had dancing lessons?*, etc.) and an opportunity for less cued questions (e.g. *How long have you been having them? Where did you have them?*, etc.), which gives SS more freedom to choose between the Simple Past, Present Perfect Simple or Continuous. You may need to explain what a *Turkish bath* is (i.e. a health treatment for the body where one sits in a hot steamy room).

The 'mingling' activity needs setting up carefully in that SS need to be clear that they need to:

- find someone who has done something on the list;
- ask this person any relevant information;
- make notes using the model in the book;
- do the same thing for five other people.

SS should then transfer this information to individual slips of paper without giving the person's name. It would be a good idea for the T to give out these slips of paper to make notes on (perhaps with the headings on).

In groups, SS could then put all the slips of paper together and try to guess who the people are. Alternatively, the T could collect them all and read out the information, to see if anyone can guess who the people are. The T could also follow up this activity by having a team game where each team has to guess if the information on a slip of paper is grammatically correct. If it is not they should correct it.

• **Exercise 2** Encourage SS to correct each other's notes. You could follow this up by handing out various English newspaper headlines to SS in groups and asking them to invent a story based on the headlines (e.g. *Treasure found in forest).* This would not only get SS to use the Present Perfect but also require use of narrative forms (which come up in Unit 4) and the passive (Unit 13). This could be very useful for diagnostic purposes.

EXTENSION

Present result: Present Perfect Simple and Continuous

• **Exercise 1** The aim of this exercise is for SS to think about the use of the perfective as opposed to the continuous aspect by contrasting the focus on completed events (*so far he's watched…*) with a focus on an action in progress which may or may not have finished (*he's been watching…*). SS need to be made aware of the nature of the continuous form, with its focus on (temporary) actions in progress, which may or may not be completed. Point out that present result (*his eyes have gone square*) can also be expressed by using the present (***He's tired** because he's been working all day / he has just finished work.*).

• **Exercise 2** PW? This exercise gives more practice in the difference between the Present Perfect Simple and Continuous forms, depending on whether the focus is on the action in progress (Continuous) or the completed activity (Simple). There is more practice in the WB.

PRACTICE

• **Exercise 1** This exercise provides freer practice of the Present Perfect Simple and Continuous. There are several different ways of doing the exercise. SS could work individually and match the two columns, and then ask each other questions in pairs, or it could be done as a class activity.

• **Exercise 2** This exercise focuses on the meaning and use of time expressions. A personalised way of extending it would be to ask SS to select one or two of the words in the box and write sentences about their own life. You could also follow up the activity by getting SS to write sentences using definite time expressions such as *ago, yesterday, in January* (in which case they will have to use the Past Simple).

VOCABULARY

Television

Note that some of the words will have already come up in the LISTENING AND SPEAKING section earlier in the unit. An extra activity which would follow on from this would be for the T to take a television schedule from the newspaper and get SS to match the programmes to the categories in the box (e.g. *documentaries*) and make a note of any programmes which are not covered by these categories. Another possibility would be for SS to write down their favourite programme in each category (e.g. *soap opera: Neighbours*) and compare as PW or GW, or do a class survey on what the most popular programmes (the names or categories) are. There is related vocabulary work on entertainment in the WB.

SPEAKING

Planning a TV schedule

• **Exercise 1** This activity is a simulation which will encourage SS to give their views on the role of television, and use some of the vocabulary which has come up in the unit. Instead of dividing the class directly into groups there could first be a class 'brainstorming activity' on different kinds of television programmes they know, and to what extent those programmes are educational or simply entertaining.

• **Exercise 2** Feedback on the group discussion could be done in different ways. As suggested in the SB each group could simply appoint a spokesperson to report back, and then the class votes on the best proposal. Alternatively, there could be a small panel, to include the Controller, who asks the spokesperson the group's views on various issues.

WRITING

Describing something you've seen or read

The aim of this section is to provide revision of adjectives and adverbs and link the writing task with the theme of the unit. Although few SS will need to write a formal review in real life, SS often want or need to describe things they have seen or read, either in letters, or as part of an exam.

• **Exercise 2** The main aim here is to revise adjectives and adverbs through a piece of descriptive writing. This exercise would work well if it referred to a film the class had seen together, or a book or reader everyone had read, because then a) and b) could be done as a class discussion. SS will already be familiar with most of the adverbs of degree in the box, but they do not often use them. They also often forget that adverbs are used with verbs and other adverbs. This exercise is a good opportunity to do revision on irregular adverbs.

It would be useful in e) to practise the stress and intonation of expressions such as *absolutely dreadful*. There is more work on intensifying adjectives in the WB.

• **Exercise 3** Unless SS have all written a review of the same thing it might be nice to display them and ask SS which film, play, etc. they feel tempted to see after reading the review.

Tapescripts

RECORDING 1

The most important thing we've learned,
So far as children are concerned,
Is never, NEVER, NEVER let
Them near your television set -
Or better still, just don't install
The idiotic thing at all.
In almost every house we've been,
We've watched them gaping at the screen.
They loll and slop and lounge about,
And stare until their eyes pop out.
(Last week in someone's place we saw
A dozen eyeballs on the floor.)
They sit and stare and stare and sit
Until they're hypnotized by it,
Until they're absolutely drunk
With all that shocking ghastly junk.
Oh yes, we know it keeps them still,
They don't climb out the window sill,
They never fight or kick or punch,
They leave you free to cook the lunch
And wash the dishes in the sink -
But did you ever stop to think,
To wonder just exactly what
This does to your beloved tot?

RECORDING 2

GILLIE: Oh, come on! It kills the imagination. I mean, you've heard that term 'couch potato' - I mean, people sit there like vegetables.

MARK: I disagree. No, I disagree. What - and anyway, what would they be doing if they weren't doing that?

G: Well, probably sport, activities, I don't know, but it's . . . so addictive. I mean, they just sit there day after day, night after night and I'm sure it causes bad behaviour in kids.

M: I disag . . . how can - there's no - there are no statistics to prove that, absolutely none. On the contrary, it's a - it's a way of bringing people together. I mean, it's the only time families get together - they sit round - round the TV. It's a friendly, relaxing presence.

G: How can you say families get together?

M: But they do. It brings people together, it keeps kids off the street, keeps them entertained.

G: They don't communicate.

M: Course they do. Family life goes on around it. It's just there - it's just on. This is a very middle-class view, you know, I mean it's like saying that - it's like saying that people would be reading if, if they weren't watching television. Well there's no evidence to show that.

G: I'm sure they would. And instead of reading, instead of playing musical instruments what are they doing? They're sitting in front of this television with no intellectual quality at all - a load of rubbish.

M: That's - that's nonsense - that's absolute nonsense. I mean, there are lots of good programmes on. All you've got to do is be selective. All you've got to do is act with a little bit of judgment. I mean there's a lot of educational stuff broadcast - there's a lot of stuff that you can learn from and if you watch sensibly you can learn a great deal.

G: Yes I know, but I mean, I've got kids - kids like adverts, kids like soap operas, that's what kids want. I mean, you sit them in front of an 'educational programme', they're not interested.

M: Yes, but if you will use the television as a babysitter then that's what's gonna happen, isn't it? I mean, you're just using it to occupy your kids. And all right, while we're on the subject - soap operas. Now soap operas, a lot of people say they're rubbish - no doubt you would - but they can be very educational. They - they bring up all kinds of social issues - they teach people about AIDS, they're engaged in the world.

G: That's complete rubbish, Mark. Come on! People spending three to five hours every evening watching television - watching things like soap operas, you cannot tell me that they're going to intellectually advance themselves.

M: Now that's not fair. We're not saying that they're watching three to five hours of soap operas.

G: And one thing that really upsets me is the amount of violence on television and I'm sure that has an effect on children. I'm sure it makes kids aggressive.

M: How? How?

G: Well, I'm sure they watch - you know, they watch things like Kung Fu or whatever, and I'm sure they just try and imitate it - even cartoons. Tom and Jerry - very violent. The whole cartoon's based on violence.

M: Are you saying that kids are in some way manipulated by this violence? They have the capacity to distinguish between fact and fiction. They know that Ninja turtles are fictional - they know that Tom and Jerry cartoons are fictional.

G: Well, they're out there playing it!

M: Well, what's the matter with playing it? That's fine.

G: But they're actually copying this, they're actually imitating this aggression, as if aggression equals good.

M: Oh come on, come on! Kids are far too sophisticated to assume that - to be affected by the violence in some way. They know it's storybook stuff.

G: Well, I'm not convinced. I mean I don't think they do distinguish that much between fact and fiction - see, what they see on television to them is real, you know. I mean fairies are real to children, Father Christmas is real, you know . . .

M: So you're saying that when they watch - they think Ninja turtles are real? Come on, come on, what sort of kids have you got? I mean . . .

G: No, I really believe they do!

Ninja turtles and Tom and Jerry: TV cartoon characters.

RECORDING 3

And instead of reading, instead of playing musical instruments what are they doing? They're sitting in front of this television . . .

RECORDING 4

[See Key.]

RECORDING 5

[See Key.]

Key

LISTENING AND SPEAKING

1

a) Not letting children near the TV set, or not installing one at all.
b) The TV.
c) *gape, stare*
d) *loll, slop, lounge about*
e) They are shocking ghastly junk.
f) It keeps them still and lets you get on with things.

2

Points put forward: a), c), d), f), g), i)

3

There are no statistics to prove TV causes bad behaviour in kids.
TV is a way of bringing the family together.
TV keeps the kids entertained and off the street.
There is no evidence to show people would read if they weren't watching TV (it's a middle-class view).
There are lots of good programmes to watch if you are selective. You can learn a lot.
Soap operas can be educational.
Children can distinguish between fact and fiction (they know cartoons aren't real).
Children are too sophisticated to be manipulated by violence on TV.

Connected speech

1

Example answers for **a)** and **b)** (but note that *playing, musical* and *sitting* also have secondary stress):

And instead of reading, instead of playing musical instruments what are they doing? They're sitting in front of this television.

3

Not normally stressed: pronouns, prepositions, auxiliary and modal verbs, articles.

4

a)

Example:

A: Do you agree that television can become addictive if you're not careful?
B: Yes, I do. Some people are able to be selective and only watch the things that they really want to, but I'd say that the average person just switches it on out of habit and is glued to it all night – just switching from channel to channel until they find something they like.

REVISION

Events up to now: Present Perfect

1

a) Yes.
b) Don't know. (We don't know exactly, we only know it was when his mother was ill.)
c) No.
d) Don't know.

2

a) ii)
b) i) (It stresses the fact that his dancing has been a continuous process.)
c) ii) (In this context, *have* is a 'state' verb and therefore does not take the continuous form.)

3

a) How long has Nureyev been dancing?
b) How long was he with the Kirov company?
c) How long has he been (living) in the West?
d) How many times (How often) has he been back to the Soviet Union?
e) How long did he dance with Margot Fonteyn?

PRACTICE

2

a)

Example answer:

Police have not yet found the nineteen-year-old university student who vanished (while she was) on her way to a lecture last week.

Police all over the country have been looking for her for three days but haven't had any useful information yet which would help them with their inquiries. They have already interviewed the girl's boyfriend and her flatmate. If anyone has any information, please phone 081-223765.

3

Example answer:

Film star Jane Carman had a romantic wedding in the south of France yesterday. So far this has been her sixth marriage! Apparently she divorced her last husband – pop star Tim Sullivan – because he didn't show enough affection to her cat! Carman has recently made / been making a new film in Hollywood with her first husband. She has now decided to give up acting.

EXTENSION

Present result: Present Perfect Simple and Continuous

1

a) His eyes have gone square. (Present Perfect Simple)
b) He's watched . . . (Present Perfect Simple)
c) . . . he's been watching TV all day. (Present Perfect Continuous)

2

a) I've *decided*
b) She's *been writing*
c) She's *written*
d) He's *borrowed*
e) Have you *heard*
f) Have you *been watching*
g) I've *torn*
h) I've *studied*
i) I've *learned*

PRACTICE

1

b) 6 'I've been having a drink with the boss.'
c) 7 'She's failed her driving test again.'
d) 8 'It's been raining.'
e) 5 'I've been running.'
f) 9 'She's just come back from holiday.'
g) 1 'He's been talking all day.'
h) 3 'I've broken it.'
i) 2 'I've been on a diet.'

2

a) Have you really read that book *already?* That was quick!
b) I've been eating very little *recently.*
c) They've finished most of it but they haven't painted the hall *yet.*
d) She's been in her room *all day* studying.
e) Yes, he's *just* arrived. I can hear his car.
f) They've *nearly* finished their homework. They'll be ready in ten minutes.
g) He's only interviewed five of them *so far* but he's going to see the others tomorrow.

VOCABULARY

Television

a)

1 a wildlife programme
2 a quiz show
3 a children's programme
4 a soap opera / a drama series / a film

WRITING

Describing something you've seen or read.

1

a)

the plot - paragraph 2
the performances - paragraph 3
whether they recommend the film or not – paragraph 5
the background to the film - paragraph 1
the film in general - paragraph 4

b) The Present Simple – for dramatic effect.

c)

Laura: passive; innocent; vulnerable
the husband: obsessive; convincing; sinister; rich; handsome
the film in general: not original; well-observed characters
the plot: feeble; spooky; entertaining
the town Laura moved to: small; delightful

2

d)

Example answers:
riveting – very interesting
hilarious – really funny
terrifying – very frightening / scary
packed – very full
thrilled – really happy
brilliant – really good
dreadful – very bad
astonishing – really surprising

But I can't do without it!

Students' Book

General theme: addictions.
Unit topic: gambling.

READING: magazine article about a teenager addicted to gambling.
VOCABULARY: verbs and nouns (collocation); adjectives and prepositions; sounds: /v/, /w/ and silent /w/.
SPEAKING: discussing addictions and obsessions.

REVISION: Past Simple, Past Continuous or Past Perfect?
EXTENSION: Past Perfect Simple or Continuous?; sounds: /p/ and /b/.

WRITING: linking expressions: time; addition, contrast, reason and result.
SPEAKING AND WRITING: talking about and writing a story from pictures.

Workbook

LISTENING: radio programme about Las Vegas.
GRAMMAR: sequence of tenses; Past Perfect Simple or Continuous?; narrative forms.
VOCABULARY: phrasal verbs; common errors; verbs and prepositions; places.
WRITING: linking expressions.

Language

The aim of this unit is to revise narrative forms: the Past Simple, Continuous and Perfect. Additionally, there is a focus on the Past Perfect Simple in contrast to the Past Perfect Continuous. This contrast is similar to the Present Perfect Simple and Continuous distinction in Unit 3.

It is assumed that SS already know the form of these narrative verbs and can use them reasonably well in isolation. The use of the Past Simple for completed actions, events and situations, and the Past Perfect for talking about the past before the past will probably not be too much of a problem. The problems come when SS have to choose which form to use, in particular when to use the continuous form.

This unit pays special attention to the different uses of the narrative verb forms and gives SS an opportunity to try them out by writing a story. It also looks at some typical collocational problems which SS have with verbs and nouns (e.g. *to* ***lose*** *a game* ; not **to lose a bus* or **lose time,* meaning *waste time*). Although collocation cannot be 'taught' it helps to raise SS awareness of the problems and the need to learn which words go with which.

Common problems

Past Simple and Continuous

1 Some SS may still be using the Present Perfect instead of the Past Simple to talk about definite past events (**I have seen Tim yesterday.*)

2 When speaking, most SS will still make mistakes with irregular past forms and the pronunciation of *-ed* endings. These still need revising.

3 When to use the continuous form rather than the simple or perfect form may still be a problem for some SS, especially for nationalities such as the Scandinavians or Russians, whose languages do not have a continuous form.

4 SS still need further practice in using the weak forms of *was* and *were* when using continuous forms.

5 SS need to be reminded that 'state' verbs do not take the continuous form.

Past Perfect Simple and Continuous

1 Some SS over-use the Past Perfect. Some, for example Turkish speakers, use it in situations where the event is a long way from the present (**I had seen this place 20 years ago.*) and others use it where a Past Simple form would be more appropriate (**When I had turned the corner I saw my boss.*).

2 SS still sometimes forget to use a past participle (**I had already went.*).

3 The difference in pronunciation between *I'd walked* and *I walked* is often difficult for SS to hear.

4 There are problems with the 'aspectual' nature of the continuous form (see *Language* above) so many SS avoid using it.

Sounds: /v/ and /w/; /p/ and /b/

1 Some nationalities (e.g. Germans and Turks) have only one phoneme for /v/ and /w/, which means that *woman* is often pronounced as *voman*, or *wan* is said instead of *van*.

2 Some nationalities (e.g. Arabic speakers) hear /p/ and /b/ as the same phoneme, so will often say things such as *a pig blace*. Other languages (e.g. Portuguese) do not aspirate /p/ in initial position, so this sounds like /b/.

READING

Before reading

- **Exercise 1** PW? Although the word *gambling* will probably not be known by SS it can easily be understood from the pictures, which show different types of gambling. Get SS to use the pictures as a stimulus to talking about what forms of gambling are popular in their own countries, and their views on it. However, be careful, as this may be a sensitive subject for some SS, and in many countries a lot of gambling is illegal. Try to elicit the expression *addiction* or *addicted to*.

- **Exercise 2** GW? You could put the best questions on the board to provide a focus for the skim reading which follows. Notice that the text gives a lot of exposure to narrative forms, which are the language focus of the unit. It also recycles expressions of past habit from Unit 2 (*...he **kept** pestering me; I **used to** spend...; I**d** go into the arcade...*).

Reading

- **Exercise 1** Give SS a time limit to dissuade them from getting bogged down with other information. Dissuade them from using dictionaries too much, since there is also a vocabulary activity to follow. However, you might need to explain expressions such as *bowling alley* and *arcade*, and clarify the difference between *borrow, earn* and *steal*.

- **Exercises 2 and 3** These could be done in groups, perhaps as a competition to see who can find the answers the most quickly.

- **Exercise 4** SS should be encouraged to look carefully at the context to guess the meaning of these words and expressions. They could then either try to explain the meaning in English, in the L1, or use the dictionary to check their guesses.

- **Exercise 5** Apart from being an opportunity for a speaking activity, this exercise gets SS to use the narrative forms which are focused on later in the unit. (You could, of course, jump from this exercise to the REVISION section on the Past Simple, Continuous and Perfect on SB page 28.) Question forms are also revised here, and revision of the pronunciation of *-ed* endings could also be brought in.

Note that there is a listening text in the WB on gambling in Las Vegas.

VOCABULARY

Verbs and nouns (collocation)

- **Exercises 1 and 2** This is an opportunity to introduce SS to the idea that many words in English naturally go together (or 'collocate'). Exercise 2 revises some common verbs that SS often mistakenly associate with certain nouns, often because of L1 transfer. You could ask SS other things that you *drive, say, lose* and *rent*. After trying to do Exercise 2 in pairs SS could then check their answers in a dictionary.

- **Exercise 4** This is a useful way to revise some of the most important collocations with verbs such as *do, make, have,* etc. SS may well have met many of these already in isolation. However, try to avoid 'overloading' SS with too many nouns which are of limited use.

Encourage SS to add collocations when they put new words in their vocabulary book.

Adjectives and prepositions

There is an exercise on verbs and prepositions in the WB. Stress to SS that they should always try to learn the preposition(s) at the same time as the adjective (or verb/noun, etc.), and keep records of this.

Sounds: /v/, /w/

• **Exercises 1 and 2** Notice that the example sentence comes from the previous exercise. You could 'model' the sounds first, in an exaggerated way so that SS can see the position of your lips and teeth as you make both sounds, before they try doing it themselves. (Get them to give comments on each other's pronunciation.) It might help if for /w/ they try putting their lips in a 'kissing' position, and for /v/ they try putting their top teeth on their bottom lip.

• **Exercise 3** An opportunity to revise looking up pronunciation in a dictionary. Make sure SS try to work out the rule first.

SPEAKING

The SPEAKING section opens up the theme of addictions from gambling into other topics such as eating chocolate and smoking. Use the pictures as a stimulus for SS to think of other common addictions or obsessions that they know about (e.g. having lots of showers, exercise, coffee, alcohol). The activity could be extended so that SS do a survey on what people in the class, school or community at large feel that they are addicted to. This could then be written up as a survey report. Alternatively, discussion of the pictures could be developed into a roleplay in pairs: one student pretends to be one of the people illustrated, and the other student is a reporter who is writing a magazine article on the subject.You could link in the reading texts from Unit 3 of the WB which look at other addictions.

There is another SPEAKING section at the end of the unit, so do not to spend too long on this one.

REVISION

Past Simple, Past Continuous or Past Perfect?

• **Exercise 1** The aim is to make sure that SS are clear about the differences in use between the different verb forms which they have met in isolation at the intermediate level. When looking at the timeline make it clear that X and • represent a *point* in time and the wavy line is a *period* of time. Perhaps follow this up by looking at the part of Section 4 in the *Language reference* (SB page 31) beginning 'As with all continuous forms...'.

• **Exercise 2** It is extremely important to get SS to talk about the reasons for their answers, so that they are clear about how the choice of a particular form can affect the meaning of a sentence. For example, in a), c) and e) there may be more than one possibility, but it gives the sentence a slightly different meaning.

• **Exercise 3** PW? This is a 'production' exercise, to follow on from the previous 'recognition' exercise. Again, it is a good idea to get SS to justify their answers and perhaps make them aware of other possibilities.

There is more work on narrative forms and sequence of tenses in the WB.

EXTENSION

Past Perfect Simple or Continuous?

These exercises focus on when the continuous form is used. Emphasise to SS that the same principles apply in the past as they do in the present and future. You could remind them of work done on the Present Perfect Simple and Continuous in the previous unit. In Exercise 2 SS need to be able to explain why certain sentences are not possible. For Exercise 3 tell SS that they are required to use a variety of past forms, not just the Past Perfect.

Sounds: /p/, /b/

The example sentence in Exercise 1 contrasts the 'voiced' /b/ with the 'unvoiced' /p/ sound. They are both bilabial plosives but SS may find it helpful to 'feel' the voicing in /b/ by putting their hands on their throat.

WRITING

Linking expressions

Time

Although SS will understand the meaning of these time expressions they often use them inaccurately in a sentence and make mistakes when choosing the appropriate past verb forms. SS write a sentence personal to them and then discuss it with someone else. It is a good idea for the T to model a couple of personal examples. Afterwards, SS can try to correct each other's sentences or feedback can be done as a class.

In the WB there is an exercise which gives extra practice in joining sentences together using time expressions.

Addition, contrast, reason and result

• **Exercise 1** Before SS do this exercise it may be a good idea to clarify what 'addition', 'contrast', 'reason' and 'result' mean and match the words in the box to each category. Help by giving examples using the first two words (e.g. *Since it is raining I'm going to stay in.; The car isn't there. Therefore they are probably out.*) before SS are asked to give similar examples with the other words.

The exercise then gives extra practice of this. Show SS when the linking word or expression can go in a different place in the sentence.

• **Exercise 2** This exercise emphasises the importance of the correct linking word, as it affects the meaning of what comes next. It is intended as a 'fun' activity and could be extended by asking SS to think of one or two more sentences which could be 'added to' using linking expressions (e.g. *She said, 'I love you' and....*).

Refer SS to the list of *Linking expressions* on SB page 150 and remind them that they can consult this list whenever they are checking or redrafting a piece of writing.

SPEAKING AND WRITING

• **Exercise 1** This is a fluency activity. Impress upon SS that there is more than one possibility – they should use their imaginations and try to be creative. They should look at the pictures in pairs, make notes on their ideas and then perhaps share these ideas with a group or with the class.

• **Exercise 2** Get SS to use some of the intensifying adjectives and adverbs from Unit 3 to 'colour' their story. They should try to include a range of past forms. This activity could be done individually or in pairs.

• **Exercise 3** You could get SS to exchange their work with someone else to check. If you look at it yourself tell SS whether there are any mistakes with narrative verb forms and/or linking expressions but encourage SS to correct the work themselves. You could then get SS to revise their drafts and write a final version of the story to display on the wall.

Tapescripts

RECORDING 1

a) It's the twentieth anniversary of the war, I believe.
b) Would Vera like a glass of white wine while she's waiting?
c) He's very vain but wonderfully witty!
d) We're waiting for William to drive to work.
e) Why don't you and Vicky go for a walk in the woods?
f) The view from the van window is marvellous.

RECORDING 2

a) Have you got a pet?
b) Do you need a bin?
c) Can you see that cab?
d) I sometimes dream of a beach.
e) Is the cat's name Pen?
f) It's a bill.

Key

READING

Reading

2

a) 13.
b) One of his friends persuaded him.
c) Fruit machines.
d) His paper-round, selling his things, stealing from his parents.
e) The fruit machines became his friends; he felt relaxed.
f) He was feeling upset after splitting up with his girlfriend.
g) He just stopped playing completely; he did it on his own.
h) Yes – he's tempted all the time.

3

a) He was *13* when he started gambling.
b) He's spent *more than £20,000* on gambling.
c) He gambled for *5 years*.
d) He was spending more than *£30* a week on machines by the age of 15.
e) He'd sometimes spend *£20* on a taxi to get to his favourite machines.
f) When he was *16* his parents found out about him stealing their antiques and he left home and got a job.
g) He spent *£700* a month on machines when he was working.
h) He gave up gambling *5 months* ago (he hasn't gambled for 5 months).

4

a) kept on trying to persuade me to try
b) a stupid way to spend money
c) job delivering newspapers
d) miss school
e) eight or nine hours without a break
f) difficult, important/crucial time
g) desperate
h) ended the relationship with
i) made . . . suffer

VOCABULARY

Verbs and nouns (collocation)

1

a) break b) wreck c) smash

2

a) drive: a train, a bus
b) say: goodbye, yes
c) lose: your temper, weight, a game, your patience
d) rent: a car, a house, a boat

4

Example answers:

a) *miss* a bus, an opportunity, someone/something
b) *waste* time, money, your breath, paper
c) *do* your hair, business, the washing-up, your homework
d) *have* a meal, an argument, a party, a good time, lunch
e) *keep* busy, a secret, quiet, a diary
f) *make* the bed, a decision, a mess, a mistake, money

Adjectives and prepositions

1

a) to b) by/with c) on

2

a) of b) at c) on d) about e) at f) in g) at/by h) for

Sounds: /v/, /w/

3

a) wreck; who; whole; wrist b) /r/ c) /h/

REVISION

Past Simple, Past Continuous or Past Perfect?

1

a) 1 Past Simple
2 Past Continuous
3 Past Perfect Continuous
4 Past Perfect Simple

b) the dot = had thrown him out (4)
the wavy line = was living (2)
the arrows = had been gambling (3)
the cross = was 18 (1)

2

a) had written / wrote
b) was howling
c) heard / had heard
d) had taken
e) phoned / had phoned
f) was bringing

3

a) . . . he was smoking again.
b) . . . because I'd run out of tea.
c) . . . she hugged her.
d) After I'd paid for food and rent . . .
e) . . . she was thinking about.
f) As soon as I saw him . . .
g) . . . I was spending / I had been spending more than £30 a week on machines.

EXTENSION

Past Perfect Simple or Continuous?

2

Sentences a), c), d) and f) are not likely.

3

1 happened 2 was coming 3 was 4 managed
5 had been looking 6 was sitting 7 took 8 started
9 asked 10 pointed 11 carried on 12 hadn't said
13 leaned 14 blew 15 was feeling 16 jumped
17 took 18 soaked 19 dropped 20 had put
21 picked 22 put 23 went on 24 had been watching
25 applauded

Sounds: /p/, /b/

1

You use your voice with the /b/ sound.

2

a) pet b) bin c) cab d) beach e) Pen f) bill

WRITING

Linking expressions

Addition, contrast, reason and result

1

a) *As/Since* I had had no sun for ages, I was depressed *so* I went out and booked a holiday.
b) There has been no rain for ages. *Therefore* we have to be very careful how much water we use.
c) *As well as* being mad about computers he gambled on fruit machines.
d) Next year I'm going to learn Russian. I'm going to have tennis lessons and take up aerobics *too*.
e) I hated my school. *However,* I decided to stay on there.
f) *Although* I had no money I went on a shopping spree.
g) *Since/As* it was raining, I decided to stay in.

A rare breed

Students' Book

General theme: work.
Unit topic: women and work.

LISTENING: interview with women who run a garage; connected speech (weak forms in questions).
SPEAKING: the intonation of questions; a questionnaire about men and women at work.

REVISION 1: asking questions.
EXTENSION: subject questions.
REVISION 2: reported questions; less direct questions.

WRITING 1: sentence patterns (transitive and intransitive verbs; direct and indirect objects); word order (with adjectives, adverbs and adverbials).
VOCABULARY: different areas of work.
WRITING 2: job advertisement.

Workbook

READING: magazine article about two women who job-share.
GRAMMAR: mixed question forms; less direct and reported questions; question tags; word order.
VOCABULARY: words associated with men and women; synonyms and antonyms.
PRONUNCIATION: question tags.
WRITING: small ads.

Language

This unit focuses on question forms, including their intonation and weak forms. It revises *Yes/No* questions, non-subject questions, question tags, reported questions and less direct questions using phrases such as *Could you tell me...?* All of these forms were introduced in *Intermediate Matters*. The unit also introduces subject questions such as *Who speaks Turkish?* and, in the WRITING 1 section, revises a number of different sentence patterns (subject + intransitive verb; subject + verb + object; subject + verb + complement; subject + verb + indirect object + direct object; subject + verb + direct object + preposition + indirect object).

SS at this level usually still have problems with question forms and need a lot of practice. In the classroom, SS are used to answering questions accurately but often less used to asking them.

When practising question forms and sentence structure, the T should focus mainly on the problems that arise when SS transfer L1 forms to English.

Common problems

Questions

1 SS use statements inappropriately to ask questions (**You speak Spanish?*). Statements are used in spoken English with a rising intonation to express surprise or to confirm something but they are rarely used to ask for information. Also the statement structure is not used with question words (**Where you are staying?*). However, in many other languages (e.g. Greek and Spanish) spoken questions differ from statements by intonation only.

2 The equivalent of *do* when there is no auxiliary in non-subject questions does not exist in other languages. SS therefore often forget to use it (**How you spell 'collaborate'?*), or use it inappropriately in subject questions (**Who did give you the present?*).

3 A common mistake by some SS is to put more than the auxiliary before the subject (**When was built your house?*).

4 In indirect questions (i.e. reported and less direct questions) SS forget to use the statement structure (**Can you tell me what is the time?*). *Ask* is also a problem in reported questions because it takes an indirect object in most other languages (**I asked to him...*).

5 SS find it difficult to distinguish between subject and non-subject questions (**Who did take my pen?*).

Question tags

1 In virtually all other languages question tags have a fixed form (**verdad?*) or two fixed forms, one for confirmation or correction, the other to invite agreement. In English, the form varies and the intonation is important to the message (i.e. rising = wanting information; falling = expecting agreement).

2 SS are often not aware of the special difficulties on top of the 'rules'. For example:

- The tag after *I am* is *aren't*.
- A positive tag can follow a positive statement to express surprise, interest or anger (*Ah! You've finished already, have you?*).
- After *Let's* we add *shall we* (*Let's go, shall we?*), and after *I'll* we add *shall I?*
- After an imperative we can use a tag such as *will you* or *would you* to tell people to do things (*Close the window, would you?*).
- Sentences containing negative words such as *nothing* are followed by affirmative tags (*Nothing matters, does it?*).
- *Somebody, nobody* are followed by tags with *they* (*Nobody saw you, did they?*).

Sentence word order

L1 word order is so deeply ingrained for most students and differs from language to language that it causes many problems. Also, in many languages, word order is freer than it is in English. These are only a few examples:

1 In many languages (e.g. Portuguese and French) an adverb comes between the verb and its object (**I like very much your brother.*).

2 English is a 'subject-verb-object' language, whereas, for example, Turkish and Japanese are 'subject-object-verb' languages (with a lot of other differences).

3 In written Arabic sentences the verb normally comes first.

LISTENING

Before listening

• **Exercise 1** The aim is to stimulate discussion of stereotypical attitudes about which sex does which jobs and why. Ask SS which sex they expect to do some jobs not pictured (e.g. a plumber, a nanny, an undertaker), or SS work in pairs and list as many jobs as they can under headings *Male, Female, Both.* (Note there is a 'Men and Women' vocabulary exercise in the WB.) In a multinational class many interesting comparisons can be made. The *Listening* focuses on women as garage mechanics, the REVISION 2 section on a male secretary and the *Questionnaire* in the SPEAKING section deals with the topic of gender and occupations in more depth. You could do the *Questionnaire* before the *Listening* and in an adult class ask if SS have had any personal experience of sex discrimination at work.

• **Exercise 2** Get SS to make guesses about which words fill the gaps using the context to help them.

Listening

• **Exercises 1-4** The interview can be used for classroom discussion on sexist attitudes to work. The extracts do not include technical vocabulary (except *body* and *bonnet*). Help SS with some of the idiomatic language if it can't be guessed from context: *rough, on its last legs, humble beginnings, ripped off.* Notice that Exercise 4 focuses more on interpretative questions, and that the *Listening* contains some examples of question forms used naturally. You might use the opportunity to bring forward the revision of question forms or reported speech from SB pages 34 and 35.

Connected speech

• **Exercise 1** Tell SS that weak forms are needed more when the question word is stressed or when the speaker is speaking quickly. Before they practise the weak forms, get SS to listen to the recorded phrases.

• **Exercise 2** PW. SS listen to the recording, then take turns to ask the questions and make up answers. Give SS extra questions (e.g. *How do you do?*), get them to finish the questions in Exercise 1 (e.g. *Who can you see?*), or write and practise questions of their own.

SPEAKING

Intonation

At this level SS should not only recognise polite and not so polite intonation patterns but be starting to try to use them effectively. Point out that a flat monotonous tone is considered impolite, particularly to strangers.

• **Exercise 2** After SS have used the cues in brackets for their questions, they should substitute more ideas of their own. Encourage them to use their imaginations and think of a context for each question. Tell them to start their polite questions (whether asking for information or asking someone to do something) at a high pitch. Advise them to finish their polite questions with a fall-rise. In the example and b) a fall at the end would sound odd and rude and in a) and c) a fall-rise sounds as though you are more interested. It is probably better to treat the exercise lightly and get SS to exaggerate their intonation.

• **Exercise 3** Notice that the intonation falls when the speaker is almost sure and rises when the speaker is not sure.

Questionnaire

This is designed to stimulate discussion on sexist attitudes in relation to work. Possibly get the men to ask men and women to ask women. Below are some ideas for extension.

- Discuss the conclusions as a class comparing the attitudes of men and women in answering the questionnaire.
- Conduct the questionnaire outside the classroom and compare results with the SS' answers.
- Write a survey.
- Build up statistics on e.g. the number of people who think that... etc.

REVISION 1

Asking questions

• **Exercise 1** PW/GW. This exercise can be done orally, but if SS write out the questions they must use the correct punctuation. The exercise covers a range of problem question forms, including question tags. Possibly precede with an exercise where SS match a range of questions (*Yes/No* questions, *Wh-/How* questions and question tags) with their answers. This gives SS a model for the forms they will be revising and focuses on the function of the question-type (particularly difficult for some question words like *Which...?*, negative questions like *Haven't you...?* and question tags).

You could supplement this exercise with exercises from the WB (particularly the exercise on question tags). One way of building extra practice into class time is to get SS to write down their own comprehension questions in future LISTENING and READING sections and ask each other.

• **Exercise 2** This aims to get SS to practise questions in context. Allow for correct alternatives. Get SS to practise their dialogues in pairs. To give further practice, follow up with a game of *Alibi* played like this:

- Decide on the crime.
- Work in groups of three and prepare a detailed alibi for your movements from 6 p.m. to 10 p.m. You did something different at least every half an hour. (Your group can be one person or three different people who did something together.) Memorise your story.
- Each member of your group will now be interviewed separately by at least one of the other groups to find out the details of your alibi (*Where were you at...? What did you do...? What time...?*). The two not being interviewed must not listen to the interviews. If there are any details in the stories which contradict each other your group loses.

EXTENSION

Subject questions

• **Exercises 1 and 2** Since subject questions have no inversion they can be quite confusing. Write a subject question, e.g. *Who drank coffee?*, and a non-subject question, e.g. *Who did Jan pay?*, on the board. Show that a subject question asks for the identity of a subject (answer: *Jan did – Jan drank coffee.*) and so the question word *Who* is the subject and *coffee* is the object. A non-subject question on the other hand asks for the object of a statement (answer: *the shop assistant – Jan paid the shop assistant.*) and so the question word *Who* is the object and *Jan* is the subject.

• **Exercise 3** Useful phrases are: *What causes / happens...? How many people...? Who played / came / discovered...? Which country / mountain...? Whose...?*

REVISION 2

Reported questions

• **Exercise 1** Introduce this exercise by reminding SS of the form of reported questions, taking as an example one of the questions in the *Listening* earlier in the unit (e.g. *What do the women customers think?* → *The interviewer wanted to know what the women customers thought.*). Try a simple mechanical drill, either in pairs or T → S, where the response must begin *She asked me....* Make sure both question word and *Yes/No* questions are included (e.g. *Where's the cat?* → ***She asked me*** *where the cat was. What's the time?* → ***She asked me***... *When did you give it to him? Do you like cheese? Have you seen the film?*, etc.) Alternatively, put one of each question type on the board and illustrate the lack of inversion in indirect questions. However, note that reported speech is dealt with more fully in Unit 17.

The question after the text aims to remind SS of the issues discussed at the beginning of the unit. SS could discuss whether they know any male secretaries and what the advantages and problems might be. Explain *shorthand* and *curriculum vitae,* which are useful vocabulary for Unit 6.

• **Exercises 2 and 3** Other questions could include: *Will it matter that I'm a man? Isn't it strange for a man to apply for this kind of job? What do you do in your spare time?* The questions in the pictures can be used to practise reported questions. After either exercise you could give other questions as cues for SS to transform into reported questions. Exercise 2 could be done in pairs. What Gillian says in Exercise 3 contains three examples of reported question constructions which do not contain the verb *ask* (*Wondering what questions...; kept on about why...; wanted to know how...*). The work in this section is fairly open-ended to allow the T to do as much practice as necessary.

Less direct questions

Less direct questions have the same form as reported questions. Since less direct questions are common in spoken English when we want to be polite or more formal, practise the intonation of one or two examples. Try to make the guessing exercise fun.

There is another exercise on less direct and reported questions in the WB.

WRITING 1

Sentence patterns

All the exercises in this section could be done as PW or GW. Potentially they could be quite heavy as classwork and you might want to split the section up and do it over a number of lessons or set some of the exercises for homework. Possibly as follow up get your SS to refer to the section on 'The simple sentence' in L.G. Alexander, *Longman English Grammar* (see *Bibliography*).

• **Exercises 1 and 2** Some introductory work on transitive and intransitive verbs might be useful. Note that some verbs can be both. A simple exercise would be to write a list of verbs on the board (e.g. *cry, stop, camp, give, rise, smoke, meet*), ask SS to divide them into three groups (T, I or both) and check their answers in the dictionary. Alternatively, do the exercise in J. McAlpin, *Longman Dictionary Skills Handbook* (see *Bibliography*).

• **Exercises 3 and 4** Make sure SS have grasped the difference between a direct and an indirect object before doing Exercise 4.

Word order

In a weak class get SS to read the sections in the *Language reference* before doing Exercises 1 and 2. They then do the exercise in the WB for homework.

VOCABULARY

Work

• **Exercises 1-3** PW/GW. Possibly follow up Exercise 3 with a game where groups brainstorm words associated with the areas of work not practised in Exercises 1 and 2 but referred to in the word puzzle: i.e. office work, law, dentistry. The winner is the group with the most words, or the first group with ten words in each category.

WRITING 2

Advertisement

• **Exercise 2** After all the heavier structural work in the unit make this exercise light and fun. The aim is as much discussion and argument as writing, although you might want to link it to the work on ads in the WB. An alternative activity is to give SS adverts to write non-sexist captions for, or give out a series of adverts and get SS to say which are the least/most sexist.

• **Exercise 3** You could display the ads in the classroom.

Tapescripts

RECORDING 1

WOMAN 1: Well the body's rough. I'd quite like to hear it running really to give a proper opinion on it.

INTERVIEWER: Confirmation about what I suspected: my car was on its last legs, but 'Gwenda's', named after a famous 1920s woman racing driver, is flourishing after humble beginnings last May. But why did three women join up for this venture?

WOMAN 1: Well, we needed a job for a start. We just all got together and opened it up after a lot of planning.

WOMAN 2: There aren't any opportunities for women in the motor trade, very, very few if, if at all and so if we wanted to get work, the only way we were going to get work was to create our own jobs. And the second thing is that we wanted to offer women a service they felt they could trust.

I: Unusual in the first place I suppose to train as a motor mechanic if you're a woman?

W1: Yes, but I think that a lot of women would like to do things that are outside of the traditional things that women normally do and if you've got a car or a motorbike I think it's obvious, that women as well as men would want to maintain them, and that's how we've got started really, from having our own vehicles and wanting to maintain them, which was the most sensible thing to do really.

W2: And that's what we actually hope: to encourage women as well, like if women come here and we talk to them about their cars then maybe they can look at that part another time. We run a class for women as well on maintaining their cars and things.

I: Looking at you now in the middle of your garage and looking at all the grease and oil on your hands, that's often the reason given for women not wanting to . . .

W1: I know but this, this amazing sort of invention: it's called soap and water, and that's what we do at the end of the day, we wash just like everybody else . . .

W2: Heavy lifting - that's the usual one: they don't think we can lift.

W3: The toilet facilities.

W1: Yes, toilet facilities, lack of toilet facilities: we haven't got any facilities for women to go to the toilet.

W2: I think that women actually do a lot of things, carrying shopping bags from town, on and off buses, they do a lot of lifting around the house and they do a lot of dirty work, cleaning, and cleaning ovens and washing floors and things like that. I don't think that it's only mechanics that get their hands dirty. I think women often in the housework get their hands dirty as well.

I: And this partnership feels that women can have an uncomfortable time in garages run by men.

W3: When a woman, a woman car owner driver takes a car to the garage, then she can be told anything basically. I mean I'm not saying that she's necessarily going to be ripped off, but you know she's going to be given a load of explanation that she doesn't understand, doesn't feel able to ask questions as to why and, you know what, what exactly is happening, and I think like that something that's important is that we want to, customers to feel they can ask us so that, you know, we'll offer them an explanation that they can understand.

I: Well, what do the women customers think? Do they feel happy with motor mechanics of their own gender? Linda Emery was waiting for work to be completed on her car.

LINDA: It's a woman's garage and I think the advantage of that is that instead of bringing your car in and not knowing what's happening to it, they actually show you what they're doing, why they're doing it and how it connects up with other things in the car, so it takes away the fright when you lift up the bonnet and don't know what the hell's happening. I think that's, that's the advantage of bringing it here.

I: So you've had more explained to you at this garage than other garages?

L: Oh, absolutely. A hundred per cent more. I mean unless you ask specific questions at another garage which you wouldn't know how to ask anyway because you don't know anything about your car, they won't explain anything to you. All you usually get is the bill and recommendations about further work that needs to be done, and you can't make a judgment on whether it's, it's an emergency thing that needs to be done or whether it can be left for a bit. You have to trust them, and basically I don't trust garages, I think, except for Gwenda's, and I know there that I am getting good advice about my car.

RECORDING 2

What do the customers think?

Who can you . . .?
What does she . . .?
How long have we . . .?
Why do they . . .?
How many are there . . .?
What'll you . . .?

RECORDING 3

a) How does he know what to do?
b) When are we going?
c) Who was that at the door?
d) Where had you been before?

RECORDING 4

1 Can you put the bonnet up?
2 What about the service you've had and the work they've done?

RECORDING 5

a) Is that the bank over there?
b) Do you like coffee?
c) I'm not late, am I?
d) They didn't reply, did they?

RECORDING 6

[B's answers from Recording 7.]

RECORDING 7

A: Where are you from?
B: I'm from Turkey.
A: Have you been to Edinburgh before?
B: No, this is my first visit to Scotland.
A: How long did it take?
B: Only six hours from London.
A: And where are you staying?
B: In a hotel near the centre.
A: How far away is it?
B: Not far.
A: What's it like?
B: It's quiet, but my room's a little small.
A: How did you come?
B: I got a taxi.
A: Whose drink is that?
B: I don't know. It's not mine. I haven't had anything to drink yet.
A: Would you like me to get you something?
B: Yes, please. A lemonade.
A: How do you like it?
B: With a little ice, please.
A: How many languages do you speak?
B: Turkish of course, as well as Arabic and a little English.

RECORDING 8

GILLIAN: Yes, before he went to the interview he was in quite a state really. Wondering what questions they'd ask him. Luckily he's very confident and he's got excellent shorthand. Anyway, when he got there they couldn't believe a man would want to do a job like that. But they didn't ask him anything that people normally ask at interviews. Things like his experience or his reasons for applying. Just kept on about why a man should apply for a job like that. Anyway, to everyone's surprise, he got the job. Of course, when he started work the other secretaries wanted to know how he'd learned to type. But none of them offered to help him. It was sink or swim all the way.

Key

LISTENING

Before listening

2

a) Picture 4: a woman car mechanic
b) 1 car mechanic
   2 female car mechanics
   3 women
   4 secretarial
   5 cars
   6 repairs

3

a) It was named after a famous 1920s woman racing driver.
b) Three women who needed a job got together and opened the business.
c) Women customers like it because they have their car problems explained to them.

Listening

2

a) True b) True c) True d) False

3
Example answers:
a) Three women opened their own business.
b) They needed a job.
c) To help women maintain their own cars.
d) Customers are shown what's wrong and they are told what's happening.

4
Example answers:
She is being ironic. People shouldn't complain that it's a dirty job. All you have to do is wash yourself afterwards. Heavy lifting is the usual argument for saying women shouldn't do the job.

SPEAKING

Intonation

1
a) Question 1 is asking somebody to do something. Question 2 is asking for information.
b) Question 1. The voice starts high.

3
a) almost sure
b) not sure
c) almost sure
d) not sure

REVISION 1

Asking questions

1
a) What do you want me to do? – 5
b) He's an actor, isn't he? – 6
c) Where did you say we should meet? – 7
d) Didn't she tell you her name? – 2
e) What are you going to tell her? – 4
f) What was the film like? – 1
g) Everyone likes her, don't they? – 3

2
A: Have you been here before?
A: How long did it take?
A: Where are you staying?
A: How far away is it?
A: What's it like?
A: How did you come?
A: Whose drink is that?
A: Would you like me to get you something?
A: How do you like it?
A: How many languages do you speak?

EXTENSION

Subject questions

1
Subject questions: a), b), d), e)

2
a) Where *has she gone?*
b) Who *lives* in this house?
c) What *made you* angry?
d) What *did you do* that for?
e) How many students *understand* this exercise?

REVISION 2

Reported questions

3
Gillian's mistakes:
Stephen wasn't confident: he wondered if he was good enough.
He hasn't got excellent shorthand: he wondered if he should learn it.
They did ask him why he wanted to be a secretary and if he had had any experience.
The other secretaries did offer to help him.

WRITING 1

Sentence patterns

1
a) a direct object
b) subject

2
The verbs in b), c) and e) are transitive and need objects.
Example answers:
b) You hit *me!*
c) Alex said he enjoyed *the party.*
e) Children need *love and affection.*

3
a) The indirect object.
b) When the indirect object becomes a phrase with a preposition.

Word order

1
a) 1 b) 1, 2 c) 3 d) 1, 3 e) 2 f) 1

2
a) I usually have . . .
b) . . . a small green German car.
c) . . . sitting quietly in the sun today.
d) When I arrived I . . . horrible hooligans.
e) . . . very intelligent dustman who dances very well.
f) I studied English in a language school in London.
g) . . . recommend a good film for children.
h) . . . drove off quickly last week.

VOCABULARY

Work

2
Finance: credit, shares, investment, capital, interest
Building: drill, spade, hammer, bricks, nails, screwdriver, crane
Photography: darkroom, film, print, negative
Gardening: spade, lawnmower, fork, rake, axe

3
1 **S**TOCK MARKET
2 COURT ROOM (**T**)
3 S**U**RGERY
4 BUIL**D**ING SITE
5 OFF**I**CE
6 FACT**O**RY

Artists and photographers work in a studio.

The perfect interview

Students' Book

General theme: work.
Unit topic: job interviews.

READING: magazine article about how to have the perfect interview.
SPEAKING: job interview roleplay.
VOCABULARY 1: jobs and duties; word building; /s/ and /z/ endings.

REVISION AND EXTENSION 1: expressing obligation (e.g. *must / have to / needn't*); sounds /æ/, /ʌ/, /ʊ/ and /u:/.
REVISION AND EXTENSION 2: asking for and giving advice (e.g. *should / it's time...*).
EXTENSION: *make, let* and *allow*.

VOCABULARY 2: using a lexicon.
WRITING: job application letter; formal/informal language.

Workbook

LISTENING: interview between a doctor and patient.
VOCABULARY: collocation (e.g. *swollen ankle*) and prepositions; medical terms (e.g. *surgeon*).
GRAMMAR: expressing obligation; giving advice.
PRONUNCIATION: connected speech: modals of obligation.
WRITING: job application letter.

Language

This unit is concerned with the functional areas of 'obligation', 'prohibition', 'duty', 'requiring something to happen', 'permission' and 'giving advice'. Most were introduced in *Intermediate Matters* and have been put together here for revision and practice. Many of the ways of expressing obligation involve the use of modal auxiliaries (see Unit 16 for a review of modals). Remind SS that modals express the speaker's opinion at the moment of speaking. You might also need to practise the weak forms of *must* and *have to*. Note that several forms (e.g. *should / ought to*; *have to / have got to*; *needn't / don't need to / don't have to*) can be used interchangeably but that *needn't* is not used in American English. In most cases it is not worth trying to make distinctions. A range of exponents are referred to for 'advice', including the second conditional.

Common problems

Obligation

1 Many SS overuse *must / mustn't*. They underestimate its authority when used in the second and third persons (**You must park your car over there.*) in situations where the imperative (with the appropriate intonation) or *should / shouldn't* would sound less dogmatic. They also use it in situations where *have to* would be more appropriate (**I must wear a uniform at school.*).

2 SS have problems remembering to use *had to* (not *must*) for past obligation. They should also remember to use either *must* or *will have to* when referring to the future as *must* does not change its form.

3 *Mustn't* is often used mistakenly to express an absence of obligation, instead of *needn't / don't need to / don't have to*. This is especially a problem for SS whose L1 is one of the Northern European languages.

4 Although *have to* and *have got to* are more or less interchangeable, beware of SS saying **Do you have got to?*

Make, let and *allow*

1 SS don't always realise that *allow* is often quite formal in contrast to *let.* Also the construction is different: with *let* there is no *to* before the second verb.

2 Common mistakes: **It is not allowed to walk on the grass.* (i.e. the 'impersonal' passive construction is not acceptable in English); **let her to play / let her playing; *made her to wash / made her washing.*

Advice

1 While SS have few problems with which form to choose there are frequent mistakes with the form itself. Common mistakes: **You'd better to go. / *You should to go.*

2 *It's time* is always a problem. It can be followed by an infinitive (*It's time to go.*) or when saying it's time for someone else to do something we use the past tense (*It's time you went.*), even though it refers to the present or future.

3 *Had better* also causes problems: it is a fixed form (**have better*) saying that someone ought to do something and is not a comparative; the negative form is *better not,* not *hadn't better,* but the question form is *Hadn't (I) better...?.* The expression is followed by the infinitive without *to*; the *had* is often dropped in informal speech (*You better go.*).

READING

Before reading

• **Exercise 1** Start by comparing the words *interviewer / interviewee* and by asking SS how many interview situations they can think of (e.g. for a job, before entering a college, seeing a doctor). However, keep back their personal experiences until *Reading,* Exercise 4. Some of the things you *should* do in a job interview in Britain are: be on time, be polite, don't talk too much, listen to the interviewers, dress formally, appear confident and relaxed. Some of the things you probably *shouldn't* do are: get angry with or interrupt the interviewers, seem as if you're bored, show any unpleasant personal habits, etc. You might get some interesting cultural differences in a multinational class.

• **Exercise 2** PW/GW? Help SS with phrases like *a balance of power, apply for, body language, CV* (or *résumé* in American English) and *dress the part.* Note that the text to follow does not contain all the 'reasons' expected in 2a. Some suggestions for reasons which can be derived from the text: *Find out...* because you can anticipate questions you will be asked and ask more informed questions yourself; *Discover...* so that you can prepare yourself and rehearse the interview; *Think positively...* to help give the interviewers confidence in you; *Keep calm...* because it will help to put the interviewers at ease. The exercise should give you the opportunity to see what 'advice' expressions SS use and avoid as well as what mistakes they make.

Reading

• **Exercises 1 and 2** Avoid vocabulary issues at this stage and focus on general comprehension. If SS use dictionaries, Exercise 3 will become redundant. Out of Exercise 1 you could get SS to practise the modals of obligation (*You should discover as much as you can...,* etc.) and then jump to REVISION AND EXTENSION 1.

SPEAKING

Job interviews

• **Exercise 1** Some people say that more than one interviewer is intimidating, others that interviewing should be done by a panel so there can be different points of view. The interviewer sitting behind a desk can also intimidate the interviewee, and if interviewers make notes they're probably not listening. Ask SS what other things make good interviewer practice (e.g. interviewers reading the interviewee's CV and preparing questions beforehand; not accepting interruptions from outside during the interview, etc.).

• **Exercises 2 and 3** The aim of doing these exercises in small groups is to get as many SS as possible to participate. In some classes you might prefer to make two large groups or even do the roleplay as a whole class. Go through the ads first to check the vocabulary, before each group chooses one. (*Shiatsu* is a Japanese form of relaxation therapy.) You or SS could bring in your own ads. The activity should be fun, but at the same time it is important that SS take it seriously and really try to get the job and evaluate the worth of the other applicants.

VOCABULARY 1

Jobs and duties

• **Exercise 1** Possibly ask SS to bring in pictures of people doing the jobs. You could extend this into a game where SS give definitions for jobs and other SS have to guess what the jobs are.

• **Exercise 2** This is an opportunity to revise /s/ and /z/ in Present Simple third person singular endings.

• **Exercise 3** You could get SS to think of other words with the same endings in this word-building exercise (e.g. -ing: *dancing, flying, painting, farming*; -ure: *departure, failure, closure*; -ancy: *hesitancy, expectancy*; -ics: *politics, athletics, electronics, linguistics*; -ry: *dentistry, surgery, chemistry*; -ism: *socialism, Buddhism, sexism*.).

REVISION AND EXTENSION 1

Obligation

• **Exercise 1** Examples that SS will need in Exercises 1–4 are provided. This exercise (PW/GW) gets SS to work out the difference between *should* and *must* (*must* is much stronger in the second and third persons); *must* and *have to* (*have to* is a more 'external' obligation); and *mustn't* and *needn't* (*mustn't* indicates it is important not to do something; *needn't* indicates it is not necessary to do something). Notice that *allowed to* is a more informal way of saying 'permit' (and yet is more formal than 'let') and *supposed to* is used to talk about what people have to do according to the rules (of law or custom) or what is expected to happen. Point out that some of the words and expressions illustrated are followed by the base form of the verb with *to* and some without *to* (e.g. *mustn't* ***do***, but *have* ***to do***). Make sure SS use weak forms, elisions, etc. where appropriate (e.g. *don't have to* /dəʊnhæftə/). Find out how much SS know and use the WB exercises as follow-up.

• **Exercise 3** This focuses on the 'past' of *must* (*had to*) and *mustn't* (*weren't allowed to* or *couldn't*).

• **Exercise 4** PW/GW. First go through the dialogue with gaps and work out which speaker is the organiser (i.e. B) and what the friend's attitude is (i.e. critical). Also ask general comprehension questions (e.g. *Why did they decide to hold the event in April?*).

Sounds: /æ/, /ʌ/, /ʊ/, /uː/

For the /æ/ sound the mouth needs to be open with the tongue down at the front of the mouth; for the /ʌ/ sound the mouth should be less open and the tongue a little higher in the mouth. For the (short) /ʊ/ sound the tongue should be low in the mouth and the lips semi-rounded; for the (long) /uː/ sound the tongue should go up at the back of the mouth with the lips rounded. It is better to show rather than explain how to make the sounds and then get SS to imitate them.

• **Exercises 1-4** These exercises are mainly for recognition but get SS to do some practice. Also SS could test each other by one student saying one of the words and the other student writing down the symbol of the sound they hear.

REVISION AND EXTENSION 2

Asking for and giving advice

• **Exercise 1** Highlight the problems referred to in *Common problems* (above) with regard to *should, it's time...* and *had better*. Also point out the difference between *try* + *-ing* (to test by making an experiment) and *try* + *to* + base form (to make an effort to do something). In informal use *try* + *to* + base form is often replaced by *try and* + base form. Refer SS to the *Language reference* for differences of formality and informality. Note that *should* and *should have* for regret and criticism will be looked at in more detail in Unit 12 and that the second conditional will be looked at in Unit 11.

• **Exercise 3** Suggest a number of possible answers. Don't worry if some of them are more like suggestions (e.g. *We'd better go by tube.*). Exercise b) focuses on ways of reporting advice. (Reporting is revised later in Unit 17.)

• **Exercise 4** You could allow SS to think up other problems to add to the list. In b) make sure SS do discuss the options before giving advice: to increase the amount of practice; to encourage them to think through the problem; and to make the exercise more interesting. An example of advice to the teacher who can't remember names: *We think you should try drawing a plan of the class and writing the students' names on the plan.*

EXTENSION

Make, let and *allow*

• **Exercise 1** Point out that *make her do* means 'insist on / expect her to do' and that *let* and *allow* can be used when we talk about giving permission. (Notice that the speaker also uses the passive construction with *make* when *to* is used.) It might be helpful to tell SS that we can also use *can* or *may* for permission (*Can I...? = Am I allowed to...?*).

• **Exercise 2** Get SS to give reasons for their choice. Highlight the differences in form (i.e. no *to* after *make* and *let*) and say that *allow* is usually more formal than *let*. Make sure SS use the weak form /tə/ in *allowed* ***to***.

VOCABULARY 2

Using a lexicon

• **Exercise 1** Get SS to think of other examples to highlight which words they collocate / do not collocate with (e.g. lifts, bells, switches *work* not *go*; you can make a *strenuous* attempt to do something not a *hard-working* attempt). Also, ask which words in I104 have a positive or a negative connotation (e.g. *laborious* is often negative; *hard-working* is usually positive). Note that *industrious* is often formal and pompous.

• **Exercise 2** Note that all the verbs in the box relate to work. Tell SS the words in the exercise may be verbs or nouns and may need an affix (e.g. *un-*) and that there might be more than one possible answer (e.g. a) *promoted/appointed*).

WRITING

Letter of application

• **Exercise 1** PW/GW. Notice that neither letter is wholly good or wholly bad. (Refer to the Key.) Ask SS which gives the better impression and why and find examples of the strengths and weaknesses of each. Possibly ask them to re-express letter A more formally (after doing Exercises 3–5) and correct the layout of letter B for homework.

• **Exercise 2** More general than Exercise 1. First get SS to brainstorm other things that could be mentioned, e.g. your age, details of where you went to school, the names of people who will give you a reference, your previous experience and the parts of your CV that are most relevant to the application (if a CV is attached). Remind SS that the aim of a job application letter is to demonstrate to the employer you have the skills they are looking for, so add any other information that will help (e.g. interests, ability to work shifts).

• **Exercise 3** Get SS to divide the phrases into formal and informal. Obviously the more formal phrases are the ones you would expect to find in a job application. Ask SS to make a list of other words they would expect to see in a job application (e.g. *experience, qualified, advertised, employment, preference, information*).

• **Exercise 6** Encourage SS to write a CV first. If SS are not going to attach a CV, a lot more information will need to be included in the letter. Get SS to write the letter in note form first (GW?), then write a draft before writing or typing it. If word processors are available they would be very useful. Make sure SS remember who they are writing to, what the employer will need to know and what impression they want to make. Note that there is another job application letter in the WB.

Tapescripts

RECORDING 1

a) sang b) fun c) swum d) match e) bank

RECORDING 2

should, flew
book, foot, food, could, shoe, soon, look, moon, would, blue

RECORDING 3

Every Sunday they made me go to church which I didn't mind too much, I enjoyed it. I had my friends at church. We sang in the choir but I was made to go. Weekends they allowed me to go into town on my own. Sometimes they let me go to a football match when I was twelve or thirteen. They allowed me to go to the youth club. They didn't let me go to the Roman Catholic youth club; I had to go to the right youth club which was our church youth club. They let me go to anything that was sporty that I wanted to do. I was allowed to join the tennis club, I could go swimming on my own. All those things they let me do without anybody with me. I was allowed to go on my own as long as they knew who I was with and when I was coming back.

Key

READING

Before reading

1

a)

In pictures 1, 2 and 4 the people are making a bad impression.

Reading

1

Example answers:

a) should find out something about the company.
b) It's probably a good idea to
c) write a
d) should be assertive, smile, look the interviewer in the eye and give a firm handshake.
e) to be too timid.
f) lean too far over the desk.
g) ask for time to consider their offer.
h) ask questions
i) are over-confident or cheeky.

3

a) leading and controlling
b) place, rank
c) strong
d) drop heavily
e) keep calm and don't get nervous

VOCABULARY 1

Jobs and duties

1

JOB	DUTIES
traffic warden	*controls parking*
electrician	repairs electrical apparatus
undertaker	*arranges funerals*
surgeon	performs medical operations
accountant	*keeps accounts*
pilot	flies planes
solicitor	*gives legal advice*
engineer	designs machines
plumber	*fits and repairs water pipes*
hairdresser	cuts hair
miner	digs for coal

2

/s/: keeps, fits, cuts. The final sound of the others is /z/. Notice: arranges /ɪz/.

3

b) accountancy
c) acting
d) psychiatry
e) journalism
f) architecture
g) economics

REVISION AND EXTENSION 1

Obligation

1

a) must
b) needn't / don't need to / don't have to / haven't got to
c) have (got) to
d) mustn't

3

a) had to
b) weren't allowed to

4

1 shouldn't have
2 had to
3 needn't have / shouldn't have
4 needed
5 had to / needed to
6 weren't allowed to
7 didn't need to
8 should have

Sounds: /æ/ /ʌ/. /ʊ/, /uː/

1

/æ/

2

/ʌ/

3

a) sang b) fun c) swum d) match e) bank

4

book, foot, could, look, would

REVISION AND EXTENSION 2

Asking for and giving advice

1

Sound formal: b), c), g)

3

Example answers:
a) If I were you, I'd get a porter to carry all that luggage.
b) Take my advice and don't buy that bicycle.
c) Try shouting next time!
d) You'd better ask for the manager.

EXTENSION

Make, let and *allow*

1

Example answers:
a) They made her go to church every Sunday.
b) They let her go to a football match and go to anything that was sporty.
c) They allowed her to go into town on her own and to go to the youth club.

2

a) let
b) allowed
c) made

VOCABULARY 2

Using a lexicon

1

a) strenuous b) work c) diligent d) operated
e) demanding f) laborious g) run

2

a) appointed b) applications c) management
d) unemployment e) appointments f) recruiting
g) promotion

WRITING

Letter of application

1

a) The layout in letter A is the correct formal layout and would impress the reader.
b) The paragraphing in letter A is better than letter B with a new paragraph for each point. (Dense paragraphing is difficult to read.)
c) The style of letter A is too informal. (Implies laziness.)
d) The content of letter B is good. (In letter A the writer seems to lack motivation and commitment to the job in references to attitude to present job / liking Surrey.)

2

Example answer:
Don't mention anything which implies lack of motivation or commitment to the job.

3

lovely weather here; do write!; pretty good job; not very happy; must stop now.

4

a) 4 b) 3 c) 1 d) 5 e) 2

5

Example answers:
a) I would like to enquire whether you have any vacancies.
b) I would like to apply for the post you advertised last week.
c) I enclose a copy of the advertisement.
d) I am writing to inform you of a change of address.
e) I would be grateful if you could forward correspondence to the new address.
f) I would be grateful for your assistance.

Crawlers, winkers, flashers

Students' Book

General theme: transport.
Unit topic: different forms of transport.

LISTENING: jigsaw listening about a car accident; connected speech (word linking).
VOCABULARY: transport.

REVISION AND PRACTICE: the future: planned / unplanned (*will* and *going to*; Present Simple and Present Continuous).
EXTENSION: describing changes of plan (*was going to, had hoped,* etc.).

SPEAKING: matching cars with people; preparing a television advertisement.
WRITING: comparatives and superlatives of adjectives and adverbs; magazine advertisement for form of transport.

Workbook

READING: extracts from a book on how to fly a plane.
GRAMMAR: the future (comparing verb forms); future time expressions (e.g. *when, while, until,* etc.).
VOCABULARY: American English (transport); prepositional phrases; collocation (*give, make, change,* etc.); forming adjectives and adverbs.
WRITING: written style (making a text less colloquial).

Language

This unit revises ways of talking about the future using *going to*, the Present Continuous, *will* and the Present Simple – all practised in *Intermediate Matters*. SS need to realise that there is no 'future tense' in English as such (i.e. there is no inflected form of the verb as in, e.g., French).

Different verb forms are used to talk about the future depending on the speaker's relationship and attitude to the future event and whether the event is planned or unplanned (see the *Verb forms as related to time* chart on SB page 9). Note that when we talk about a future event arising out of a present situation (i.e. something already put in motion) we use the Present Continuous or *going to* and that when we express a personal spontaneous decision or make a confident personal prediction at the time of speaking we use *will*. The Future Continuous and Future Perfect are introduced in Unit 8.

In the WRITING section there is revision of comparatives and superlatives of adjectives and adverbs (introduced in *Intermediate Matters*).

Common problems

Future forms

1 In many languages the Present Simple is used to talk about the future (**I write to you tomorrow.*). In English, its use is restricted to talk about fixed events such as timetables.

2 SS underuse the Present Continuous when talking about future arrangements. They also overuse *will*, thinking of it as a 'future tense'.

3 *Going to* and the Present Continuous are frequently interchangeable although *going to* is often used to express determined intentions (*I'm going to keep on trying that number until someone answers.*). However, the Present Continuous is restricted to arrangements (future events that have already been planned and organised). For predictions *going to* is used (*It's going to rain tomorrow.* not **It's raining tomorrow.*).

Comparative and superlative forms

1 SS have problems with when to use *-er* and *more* (*He is more tall.*).

2 *That* is often used instead of *than* (**It is colder* ***that*** *yesterday.*).

3 SS often miss out *the* with superlatives (**He is oldest boy in the class.*). Also SS often say **The most intelligent person* ***of*** *the class.*

LISTENING

Before listening

• **Exercises 1–5** This sequence of exercises is quite extensive (writing → reading → speaking). If short of time, focus on either Exercise 1 or 5.

• **Exercise 2** You could use the picture to talk about the conventions of driving on a British motorway (e.g. you have to overtake on the right), and to elicit some of the vocabulary needed for Exercise 3 (e.g. *lane, slip-road*).

• **Exercise 3** SS might need help with some of the vocabulary (e.g. in American English *motorway* is *expressway* or *freeway*; also *mph, overtaking, swift winks, indicator, blasts, pushy, liberal flashing*). Most can probably be guessed from context and will be useful later in the unit.

• **Exercise 5** c) gives an opportunity to revise 'Obligation' from Unit 6.

Listening

This is a jigsaw listening exercise where two groups listen to different but related information and then come together to share what they know. In a large class, if you have extra cassette players available, it might be better to have more than two groups. If you have only one cassette player, get one half of the class to leave the room while the other half listens. If this is a problem, use a language laboratory instead. If a proper jigsaw listening is impossible, do the *Listening* as a whole class.

• **Exercises 1 and 2** Before listening, get SS to look at the map and predict the most likely cause of an accident on this road. Help SS with any words or phrases they need to know to make sense of the speakers (e.g. *slight hill, bend, overtakes*) but discourage them from worrying about the meaning of every unknown word. (Much of the driving vocabulary – e.g. *overtakes* – is practised later in the VOCABULARY section.)

For 1b) there are several possibilities and SS should ask themselves questions like: *Was the taxi trying to turn left or not? Was the Volvo driver looking round talking to his children? Was the lorry driver trying to stop the BMW from overtaking because the driver was a woman? Was the BMW driver overconfident and going too fast?* For 1e) SS should bear in mind: the person in the BMW is an experienced driver in a fast car; the taxi driver knew the road, her destination and what time she had to be there; everyone wants it to be someone else's fault.

You could extend the listening activity into a group roleplay. In groups of four, three of the group are witnesses and the fourth person is a police interviewer trying to find out what happened. Some suggestions are:

- Witness A thought the taxi was starting to turn left but the Volvo was very far out into the middle of the road.
- Witness B thought the BMW was overtaking the lorry but both were speeding.
- Witness C thought the taxi was going straight on but the driver was making a call on the phone and not concentrating. (This witness thought the Volvo was overtaking the taxi and the BMW was about to overtake the lorry.)

Connected speech: word linking

When native speakers speak naturally they generally do not pause between each word but move smoothly from one word to the next. 'In English, word boundaries are "negotiated" in certain ways; sometimes a linking sound is used, sometimes one sound merges with another, and sometimes a composite sound is used.' (Joanne Kenworthy, *Teaching English Pronunciation*, see *Bibliography*.) This unit focuses on consonant-to-vowel linking and disappearing /t/ and /d/ sounds. Word linking is also focused on in Unit 9.

• **Exercise 2** Show SS the linkage by the mark illustrated in the example or by writing the words so that the speaking boundary does not correspond to the normal written boundary (e.g. *righ ton*). After doing the exercise get SS to practise the phrases.

VOCABULARY

Transport

• **Exercise 1** Ask SS to look at the box and tick words that appeared in one form or another in the LISTENING section (*gear, overtake, accelerator, slow down, indicate*). Get SS to group the words in some way (e.g. nouns and verbs; parts of the car) or brainstorm all the words they know associated with cars. You could extend the exercise by getting SS to label the parts of the car, drawing attention to differences in American English (*bumper* BrE / *fender* AmE; *gear-lever / gear-shift*; *bonnet / hood*; *tyre / tire*; *windscreen / windshield*; *boot / trunk*). There is an exercise on transport words in American English in the WB.

• **Exercise 2** Get SS to make comparisons with their own country. The picture at the top right-hand corner is of a rickshaw, found in countries such as India.

• **Exercise 3** Get SS to brainstorm other words they associate with each of these forms of transport.

• **Exercise 4** This collocation exercise could be followed up by the collocation exercise in the WB.

REVISION

The future

In these exercises the following should emerge:

– We use both Present Continuous and *going to* to talk about 'plans', i.e. things that have been decided before the moment of speaking (but see *Common problems 3* above). You might point out when the Present Continuous is *not* used.
– When we express a personal, spontaneous decision made at the moment of speaking we use *will*. This form is used particularly for 'offers', 'promises', 'warnings', etc. Point out that both *will* and *going to* can be used for 'predictions' but that *going to* is used when the speaker is referring to some evidence in the present situation and that *will* is used when the speaker is making a confident, personal prediction.
– Present Simple is less used to talk about the future than Present Continuous, *going to* or *will*.

PRACTICE

• **Exercise 1** PW/GW. Get SS to compare possibilities and give reasons why they chose or didn't choose a particular form. Extra reinforcement can be found in the WB. Extend the exercise by getting SS to choose two or three of the situations and to write a short dialogue for each (PW)

• **Exercise 2** This exercise is important not only to give SS the opportunity to practise future forms but as a pre-exercise for EXTENSION Exercise 3 below. In a) discourage SS from writing sentences but encourage notes. Possibly put headings on the board: METHOD OF TRAVEL, ROUTE, OVERNIGHT STOPS, LENGTH OF JOURNEY, THINGS TO DO. Get SS to make notes under each heading. Remind them of the language of suggestions (*Let's...; Why don't we...?; What about...?*). Note that in b) *going to* is likely to be needed more often because SS will be talking about plans already made.

EXTENSION

Describing changes of plan

• **Exercise 1** You could personalise the topic of the sentences first (e.g. *Have you been to Venice / Bali? Where did you stay?*). Point out to SS that *going to* can be used in the past (*was going to*) to describe changes of plan. Note the other forms used for the same function (e.g. the Past Perfect and *was thinking of*). Exercise b) contrasts the preposition which follows (*hoping* ***to*** and *thinking* ***of***).

• **Exercise 2** Some SS may be unfamiliar with the tradition of New Year's resolutions (plans for self-improvement that people make in the New Year).

SPEAKING

People and cars

• **Exercise 1** This aims to get SS discussing what our choice of car reveals about us. Ask SS which car they like best and why. You could get SS to think of other types of people and invent a quotation for each (e.g. an old couple: '*It doesn't matter how old a car is as long as it's comfortable, reliable and gets me from A to B.*'; a self-employed photographer: '*I buy a new car every year and make sure I get a good trade-in price on the old one.*').

• **Exercise 2** This is an opportunity to revise the language of giving opinions and agreeing/ disagreeing (see SB page 15).

• **Exercise 3** Remember this is a speaking exercise and SS should keep any writing to notes (and possibly drawings) only. You could introduce it with a video of a car advertisement, getting SS to say what image the advertisers are trying to project and what kind of people they are trying to sell to. Get SS to describe their advertisement (with drawings?) to other groups by mixing up all the groups. If you have video filming equipment you could get SS to prepare a fun mock advertisement.

WRITING

Advertisement

• **Exercises 1 and 2** These revise 'making comparisons' (i.e. comparatives and superlatives of adjectives and adverbs). Get SS to read the *Language reference* before doing them. Draw attention to regular versus irregular forms (*more comfortable* is regular; *worse* is irregular) and spelling problems (*bi**gg**er*). In Exercise 2, remind SS about the use of *than* in comparatives, and the use of *the* (and *of*) in superlatives (see *Common problems* above). Focus on SS' accuracy before doing the fluency work in Exercise 3.

• **Exercise 3** If possible, show SS examples of magazine advertisements to give them ideas. This gives good practice for adjectives and adverbs. Remember the exercise is broadly a 'process writing' activity with the emphasis on drafting and redrafting. However, at the end make good use of the 'product' by getting SS to display the advertisements for everyone to see.

Tapescripts

RECORDING 1

A: Well, I was coming up, coming up a slight hill on the London Road, the slight hill where it approaches the bend and I was doing about, doing about forty, close to the limit and - what time was it? - it must have been, yes, it must have been four, four-twenty I should say. I'd just done a drop and I don't like to get there too early cos they're usually having their tea, so yeah, about four, four-twentyish, and anyway as I say I was coming up this hill and suddenly in my mirror I saw a BMW, and it was flying along and I had to slow down at that point because of the bend. I pushed it down a gear, slowed down for the bend, then suddenly this BMW was overtaking me, flying past. She can't possibly have seen where she was going because I was right on the bend by that point. On top of that it was just beginning to get dark, visibility was pretty poor - I think it was about to start raining as well. Anyway, so I'm coming round the bend, and then suddenly she flies past me, and after that there were just cars everywhere. I think there were a few people around as well but I can't really tell you much more than that.

B: Look, officer, it's what I've already told you. There I was about half-past four, driving perfectly safely. You know I've got a BMW. I had plenty of time. I checked my mirrors, I checked the road, everything was fine. What happened? I started to overtake. No problems. Loads of time to get back in when that stupid lorry driver accelerated. It's typical! That is exactly what happens. He looked in his mirrors and what did he see? A woman driver in a BMW. This is a bit of fun, he thought, and went faster. If it hadn't been for him, everything would have been all right. I would really like to talk to him. Honestly, you have got to disqualify him. He's not safe to be on the roads. I drive thousands of miles every year and I have never had an accident.

C: It was just after four o'clock and I had just picked the kids up from school. I was in a bit of a hurry because I had to get home to make dinner and I was driving along behind this taxi, driven by a lady driver and she had slowed down to turn left and indicated that she was going to turn left, so I had a look at the road ahead and it was perfectly clear and I indicated to overtake her and I was speeding up to pass her, going just over forty miles an hour, when suddenly the other car driven by the woman came screaming round the corner. I tried to avoid hitting her but couldn't, and we touched each other and span into the nearside lane forcing the taxi off the road. There was a chap standing at the side of the road hitchhiking and I'm sure he must have seen everything that happened.

D: Well, what happened was this basically. I was travelling along at about forty miles an hour, the speed limit as far as I know on that road is, is forty. I was travelling along up to collect my fare, further along the Birmingham Road, and it was a fairly clear day, I think the time as far as I remember was about ten-past four, in fact I'm sure it was because I had a fare, my fare was due to be picked up at four fifteen and no problems, you know, going along enjoying the drive, when, when suddenly out of the blue this, this bloke behind, I think, I think in a Volvo Estate, dunno, some sort of estate car, overtakes me. We were almost at the bend. He clearly wasn't concentrating on what he was doing. He was, I think he was turning round at, looking at or talking to his kids. He overtakes and at the same time round the bend this woman comes like a bat out of hell, I think in a BMW or something like that, and the next thing I know I'm in the ditch. It was absolutely incredible. It all happened so fast. Now, you know, there was a turning off to the left. I wasn't, I wasn't indicating left, you, there was no reason why I should be and really it was, you know, it was not my fault. These two maniacs were clearly at fault and you know I'm pretty fed up about the whole thing to be quite honest. I drive a taxi for a living and you know it my car is now going to be off the road for, for weeks if not months and, you know, as I say, I'm fed up and you know you don't expect this sort of thing on, you know, a nice September afternoon, so there you are. That's my story.

RECORDING 2

[See Key.]

RECORDING 3

[See Key.]

RECORDING 4

[See Key.]

Key

LISTENING

Before listening

4

You are not allowed to overtake on the inside or to exceed the speed limit of 70 miles per hour.

Listening

1

a) (See the summary in Exercise 2 below.)
c) Examples of disagreements: the exact time of the accident; whether the lorry speeded up or slowed down; the visibility and the weather; whether the taxi driver was indicating left or not.

2

b) Between four o'clock and four thirty a lorry probably on its way to London came to a very slight hill. There was a bend to the left in the road ahead. A BMW was probably overtaking the lorry when it touched a Volvo coming in the opposite direction. The Volvo was probably overtaking the taxi. The BMW and the Volvo span across the road in front of the taxi and forced it off the road.

Connected speech: word linking

1

a) She can't possibly have seen where she was going because I was right on the bend by that point.
b) If it hadn't been for him, everything would have been all right.
c) It was just after four o'clock and I had just picked the kids up from school.
d) He overtakes and at the same time round the bend this woman comes like a bat out of hell.

2

a)

a) pulls up
b) road accident
c) park outside
d) half of
e) he's out of oil
f) get it off
g) Can I have a bit of Angela's ice cream?

b) Example answers:
a) because I right on
b) If it would have been all
c) just after clock and I kids up
d) overtakes and at like a bat out of

3

a) Mind the car.
b) And in perfect control
c) Next time you're here
d) England lost the match.
e) He must be out of town.

VOCABULARY

Transport

1

1 licence 2 gear 3 clutch 4 steering wheel 5 reverse 6 accelerator 7 brake 8 windscreen 9 slow down 10 run over 11 indicate 12 overtake 13 horn 14 flash 15 traffic jam 16 petrol

3

driver: train, rickshaw, bus
runway: plane
commuter: bus, train
guard: train
aisle: boat, plane
filling station: motorcycle, bus
compartment: train
dining car: train
voyage: boat, hot-air balloon
platform: train, bus
cabin: plane, boat
windscreen: train, motorbike, plane, bus
captain: boat, plane
departure lounge: plane
ticket office: train, boat, bus
boarding pass: boat, plane
pilot: plane

4

get on: train, boat, motorbike, camel, plane, bus
get into: rickshaw, balloon (also car, taxi)
land: plane, boat, balloon
dock: boat
get out of: rickshaw, balloon (also car, taxi)
get off: boat, motorbike, train, camel, train
park: motorbike, bus, rickshaw, camel (also car, taxi)
take off: plane, balloon
board: train, boat, plane, bus

REVISION

The future

1

a) Before the moment of speaking.
b) No difference.

2

Example answers:
a) Picture 2: 'Oh no!' 'Don't worry. I'll help you.'
b) Picture 1: 'What time does our train go?'
c) Picture 3: 'When are you going to have the baby?'

PRACTICE

1

Example answers:
a) Don't worry. I'll lend you some.
b) Look out! We're going to crash!
c) I'm sorry I can't make tomorrow night. I'm having dinner with my mother.
d) OK. I'll write to her now.
e) I'm going to get a new car. I'm fed up with this one.
f) When does the exhibition open? When does it close?

EXTENSION

Describing changes of plan

1

a) She went to Bali.
b) Kari was *hoping to go* to the opera and even *thinking of going* to the ballet.

SPEAKING

People and cars

1

a) Possible answers:
A3, B1, C2, D5, E4

2

a) Possible answers:
a) 4, b) 3, c) 5, d) 1, e) 2

WRITING

Advertisement

1

ADJECTIVE/ADVERB	COMPARATIVE	SUPERLATIVE
big	bigger	*biggest*
good	*better*	the best
comfortable	*more comfortable*	*the most comfortable*
bad	worse	*the worst*
easy	*easier*	the easiest
sophisticated	more sophisticated	*the most sophisticated*
slowly	*more slowly*	*the slowest*
far	*farther*	the farthest
few	*fewer*	*the fewest*
little	less	*the least*
exciting	*more exciting*	most exciting

Anyone out there?

Students' Book

General theme: transport.
Unit topic: space.

SPEAKING: space quiz.
READING: extracts from an encyclopaedia and from a 'popular' newspaper on space travel.

VOCABULARY: compounds (including pronunciation).
REVISION AND EXTENSION: Future Continuous.
EXTENSION 2: Future Perfect.

WRITING: complex sentences (*since, in case,* etc.); participle constructions (*Having lived here for twenty years,...*).
SPEAKING AND WRITING: jigsaw listening (UFO stories); paired interviews; group writing (diary entry and a letter to a newspaper).

Workbook

LISTENING: dialogue based on the book *The Right Stuff* between astronaut and Mission Control.
GRAMMAR: Future Continuous or Perfect?; future review; complex sentences.
VOCABULARY: words often confused (e.g. *path* and *way*); prepositions of time; idiomatic expressions with *world*; compound adjectives (*a ten-year-old boy*).
WRITING: abbreviations (*VAT,* etc.); dictation (horoscope).

Language

This unit extends out of the revision of future forms in Unit 7 and introduces the Future Continuous (sometimes known as the Future Progressive) and the Future Perfect. In the WRITING section there is work on complex sentences, including participle clauses.

The Future Continuous, like other forms of the continuous 'aspect', describes a temporary event. As with other continuous forms, it is not normally used with verbs that describe a state (e.g. perception verbs such as *see*; emotion verbs such as *love*; wishing verbs such as *want*; and verbs of thinking such as *know*). SS need to know there are two main uses of the Future Continuous: to describe something expected to be in progress at a particular time in the future; and to talk about things which have already been fixed or decided. The 'softening effect' of the second of these uses in communication can be difficult to understand. The point is that the Future Continuous takes away the idea of intention and is frequently used when talking politely, especially in questions when we do not wish to seem to be pressing for a definite answer: e.g. compare *'Will you be seeing Mary tonight?'* (have you fixed it up?) with *'Will you see Mary tonight?'* (more of a request). SS need many examples which contrast the *will*-future and the Future Continuous (see *Longman English Grammar,* page 150 and the PRACTICE section in this unit).

The Future Perfect says that something will have been completed by a certain time in the future. Since many examples of the Future Perfect use the word *by* it is important that SS know it means 'before' (*I'll have finished it* ***by*** *Friday.*). Make sure SS see that the 'perfective' aspect of the Future Perfect is the same as that of the Present and Past Perfect (i.e. it refers to something which happened before or leading up to another time or event).

Common problems

Future Continuous and Future Perfect

1 In some languages (e.g. Russian) there is no Future Continuous or Future Perfect (**This time tomorrow I will lie on the beach.* **By the year 2050 we'll live in London for 60 years.*).

2 Many SS use the *will*-future instead of the Future Perfect when the reference to the future is clear (**By the year 2050 we will live here for 60 years.*).

3 Both the Future Continuous and the Future Perfect cause SS problems both with what they 'mean' and with their form. Note the weak forms in, e.g., *we'll have* (/wi:ləv/) *finished,* which make it very difficult to distinguish from *we've finished,* and even *we finished.*

Participle clauses

Clause structure is organised very differently in many languages. Japanese SS, for example, often do not appreciate that English conjunctions combine clauses (**I am going for a walk. Because I want some exercise.*).

SPEAKING

These exercises (optional) are mainly for fun and to warm SS up to the topic. In our experience SS are either very interested in 'space travel' and don't need warming up (the picture will be enough), or need to be encouraged to get interested. Note that only the READING section focuses on the more conventional side of 'space travel' whereas the last part of the unit focuses on UFOs. Alternative warm-up exercises could be:
- Play a song like 'Space Oddity' by David Bowie and ask SS to work out what happens at the beginning and the end of the song.
- Get SS to brainstorm words they associate with space travel (e.g. *astronaut, space capsule, galaxy, orbit, rocket*).

• **Exercise 1** Get SS to brainstorm the names of the planets (*Venus, Jupiter, Uranus,* etc.). Treat the quiz as a competition, giving SS a time-limit. Don't let them look at the answers. Note that question 3 links to the theme of the READING section so possibly extend this during feedback to, e.g. *Would you like to go to Mars? What else do you know about it?,* etc. Get SS to think up five extra questions about 'space travel' and ask each other.

• **Exercise 2** An extra question could be: *If you went on a journey into space for six months what things on Earth would you miss most?*

READING

Reading

• **Exercise 1** Make sure SS understand the instructions. Ask them to do the exercise individually first, then compare answers. Get SS to try to distinguish between the cool, general, more factual style of the encylopaedia (*On a high mountain on Earth, water boils at only 70° C. On Mars...*) and the more story-specific style, with quotes, of the newspaper article (*...Cristiano Batalli, says: 'It is clear that Romanenko was used as a guinea pig'*). You could add an exercise which asks SS to say which text:
- gives general information;
- tells the story of a specific incident;
- gives scientific detail (both do);
- is more interested in individual people.

Incidentally, the La Stampa story which was reported here by the *London Evening Standard* was later denied by the Russians.

• **Exercise 2** This exercise expects more detailed comprehension. Make sure SS realise they are expected to write notes.

• **Exercise 4** This exercise focuses on 'referencing' (words like *his* and *its* which refer to people and things already mentioned in the text). It requires detailed comprehension of the text and shows SS how authentic native-speaker texts are constructed. Other units which include work on referencing are 11 and 16.

• **Exercise 5** Ask SS to group the words into those where the stress falls on the first, the second and the third syllable. Obviously the stressed syllable does not contain a weak vowel. Get them to check their answers in a dictionary. Remind SS of some of the rules of word stress in English (e.g. most nouns and adjectives carry stress on the first syllable; prefixes and suffixes are not stressed; in words of four, five or six syllables the stress is usually in the middle of the word). SS might find it useful to practise reading the words.

• **Exercise 6** This exercise provides revision of linkers and ties in with the work on complex sentences in the WRITING section. You could go straight from this into the WRITING section or hold this exercise until later.

Possibly extend out of the *Reading* into a roleplay (e.g. journalists interviewing Yuri on his return; booking a trip to Mars through a travel agent).

VOCABULARY

Compounds

This series of exercises is self-explanatory. Do all (or some) as PW or GW. Note that compound nouns are normally stressed on the first part but there are exceptions where the first element acts adjectively (see Exercise 4). Where the compound is written as two separate words the primary stress is often on the second word (*lawn 'tennis*) - but not always (*'golf club*). Tell SS they are not expected to remember which are one or two words and if necessary they can use a dictionary. Note that when a compound adjective (e.g. *first-'class*) comes before a noun it usually carries equal stress (*He's a 'first-'class musician.*) to allow the main sentence stress to fall on the noun (see Exercise 5). There is an exercise on compound adjectives in the WB.

REVISION AND EXTENSION

Future Continuous

• **Exercise 1** You could introduce this exercise by asking SS one or two personal questions about what they will be doing at a specific time in the future (e.g. *What job do you think you'll be doing in ten years time?*). After the *Listening* ask the SS if they agree with Des's predictions about living under the sea and eating different kinds of food.

• **Exercise 2** Two 'concept' questions to check understanding of the basic meaning of one of the main uses of the Future Continuous. If necessary, bring forward the timeline for the Future Continuous ilustrated in the *Future Perfect* exercise in the EXTENSION 2 section and put it on the board. Highlight the form (*will* + *be* + *-ing*), and remind SS that other modals are possible instead of *will* (e.g. *might* and *should*), depending on the speaker's point of view. Get SS to practise saying the examples using contractions (*I'll be...*).

• **Exercise 3** This exercise focuses on the other main use of the Future Continuous, the 'matter-of-course' use, where the speaker talks about an event that has been fixed up but says it in a way that removes the feeling of personal intention. It contrasts with the personal, spontaneous decision use of *will* which is purposeful and full of intention.

PRACTICE

• **Exercise 1** Since the speaker's attitude is very important in determining which form to use, elicit the context for each example from the SS. This is one reason for getting SS to extend the dialogues. Notice that both uses of the Future Continuous are to be found in the exercise: a) = action in progress; c) and d) = 'matter-of-course'.

• **Exercise 2** This is an 'information transfer' activity. Most examples of the Future Continuous that will come up in this exercise will obviously be of the 'event-in-progress' type. You could give SS 'cue cards' with different jobs on them (e.g. airline pilot; business tycoon).

EXTENSION 2

Future Perfect

• **Exercise 1** Use the 'concept' questions in a) and the timelines in b) to convey the meaning of the Future Perfect. Highlight the form on the board (*will* + *have* + past participle) and remind SS again that *will* can be replaced with other modals (e.g. *should* or *might*) depending on the speaker's point of view at the time of speaking. (Note that *should have* can be used as a Future Perfect as well as for 'past criticism and regrets' – see Unit 12). Get SS to practise the form. Get them to stress the past participle (*found*) and use contractions (*we'll have*) and weak forms (/əv/).

• **Exercise 2** This is a practice exercise, so encourage SS to use the Future Perfect where possible (but not only the Future Perfect). The kind of examples that might come up are: *extended education to everyone; abolished all wars; done away with all poverty,* etc. An extension exercise could be a GW discussion on what changes for better or worse SS think there will be in the next thirty years (e.g. in society, technology, medicine, politics). Then get the whole class to make a list of the conclusions on which they all agree. Note that there is another exercise in the WB. There are also similar interesting exercises in P. Ur, *Grammar Practice Activities* and C. Frank and M. Rinvolucri, *Grammar in Action* (see *Bibliography*).

WRITING

Complex sentences

Complex sentences are made by:

- joining subordinate clauses to the main clause with a linking word: *Whenever it snows in Britain* (subordinate clause), *the railways come to a standstill.* (main clause). *Whenever* is the linking word.
- using participle or infinitive constructions which are subordinate to the main clause: *Being Sunday* (subordinate participle construction), *all the shops are closed.* (main clause).

Both of these types are practised in this section. (Bear in mind that, technically, sentences which have two main parts of equal importance joined together by a linking device such as *and* or *but* or a semi-colon are known as 'compound sentences' not 'complex sentences'.)

Many SS not comfortable with English discourse structure tend to avoid complex sentences and rely on simple sentences. Alternatively, they pile up a series of sentences, joining them with conjunctions which to the native speaker seem randomly chosen. (It is worth remembering that the average English sentence is only about 17 words.)

• **Exercise 1** Possibly start by giving SS the example sentences as two separate sentences (e.g. *It snows in Britain. The railways always come to a standstill.*) and get them to suggest linkers. Look at the sentences and show that the expressions actually link the two parts of the sentence (you might want to avoid the issue of subordinate clauses). Get across the idea that *whenever* means 'every time that'; *in spite of* means 'not paying any attention to'; *in case* means 'because of the possibility' (used to talk about things we do in advance in order to be safe). Refer SS to a good dictionary and the examples there.

Note that:

- *in spite of* is a preposition which is followed by a noun (e.g. *in spite of the rain / in spite of the fact that... / in spite of there being...*). It is similar in meaning to *although* + clause (*although it is raining....*).
- in some expressions *in case* can be similar to *if* (*In case of fire, ring the bell.* = If there is a fire...). However, there is normally a big difference. (Compare: *You should lock the door,* ***in case*** *your house gets burgled.* and *You should phone the police* ***if*** *your house gets burgled.* You lock the door *before* the burglary - it's a precaution; you phone the police afterwards - it's a result.) This sequence of events is important in Exercise 1 if you are comparing *in case* and *even if.*

• **Exercise 2** PW/GW? SS will probably need a lot of help with this construction. Note that it is mainly found in written (rather than spoken) English. Useful reference material is: *Longman English Grammar,* pages 30-3 and/or *Practical English Usage,* sections 454-6 (see *Bibliography*). Refer SS to the *Language reference* or the above reading first, before doing the exercise. There is further work on participle clauses (acting as relative clauses) in Unit 18. There is also another exercise in the WB.

SPEAKING AND WRITING

After the very controlled work on sentence structure in the previous exercise this is more of an integrated skills exercise (from listening → speaking → writing), focusing on fluency. The writing is deliberately 'free' and creative.

• **Exercises 1 and 2** This is a jigsaw listening. You could help SS with some of the vocabulary (e.g. *trembled, wrinkled, heralded, hovering*) by giving out dictionaries. However, they should get the gist of the listening without having to understand every word, and worrying about unnecessary vocabulary. A better strategy might be to ask SS to do the exercise with *no* vocabulary support (except by asking you if they get stuck with important words) and get them to work on the vocabulary with the tapescript and a dictionary for homework. If jigsaw listening is difficult to organise for practical reasons (e.g. if you only have one tape recorder) groups A and B could read the tapescripts instead. You could also get SS to listen to different versions in the language laboratory. Alternatively, get the whole class to work on both texts with the form in Exercise 2 and compare their answers in pairs.

• **Exercise 3** First make sure that each group has listened to the other group's story.

• **Exercise 4** You could pair SS up again, one from each group, and ask them to exchange diary entries and letters. As the exercise is mainly for fun, you might not want them to suggest improvements but simply to read and enjoy them.

Tapescripts

RECORDING 1

[See Key.]

RECORDING 2

DES: Looking fifty years into the future is very difficult indeed, of course. It'll all be very different from the way it is now. I suspect because of overpopulation of the planet we'll be living in places which we're not living now. I think we'll be living under the sea, I think we'll be living on satellites circling the Earth, maybe on other planets even.

In terms of transport I reckon, well I hope anyway, that we'll have found a form of transport that won't pollute the environment quite as much as our present system. And I think, because of pollution and over-population, we'll be eating very different kinds of food from what we're eating today, probably highly-processed food and artificial food.

In terms of work, well I think people will be doing very different kinds of jobs from what they're doing today. I think it's not really possible to predict very much about what work will be like fifty years from now. I'd like to think, though, that people will be working *with* each other rather than *against* each other, in some kind of spirit of cooperation, I suppose.

RECORDING 3

Extract A: Whitley Strieber and the aliens

And then there was the story of the home-loving dad who claims he was experimented on by space alien scientists. Human guinea pig Whitley Strieber suffered a terrifying brain examination as he lay naked inside the hi-tech surgery of the cruel creatures' spacecraft. The writer of the best-selling book *Communion* wants the world to know extraterrestrials are out there - and they're not friendly. Whitley trembled as he recalled his operation millions of light years from Earth.

'I had been captured like a wild animal and it was like they were trying to tame me,' said the 41-year old.

'They performed bizarre medical procedures on me and inserted a thin metal instrument into my brain.'

Whitley claims his outer space tormentors were like giant-sized insects. They were bald, with massive liquid-like narrow eyes, yellowish-brown skin that felt like leather, two holes for nostrils and big, floppy lips.

And to prove his chilling time with the beings actually took place, he agreed to take a lie detector test - and passed!

The New Yorker says his nightmare began when an army of aliens invaded his home while he slept.

He was unable to move as they ripped off his pyjamas, poked him with their wrinkled hands, then took him off to their waiting craft.

'They told me they were going to do an operation . . .'

Extract B: Mrs Coe and the aliens

Yes, the aliens have landed. Only yesterday they stepped out of their spaceship and went for a walk in the park. Three giant creatures twelve feet tall with tiny heads and wearing bluish metallic clothing chose Russia for a very close encounter with the human race.

Their arrival was heralded by a shining ball seen hovering over the local park by residents of Voronezh, 300 miles east of Moscow.

The UFO landed and out came the giants, similar to humans and accompanied by a small robot.

'They went for a walk near their spaceship,' said the official news agency Tass. 'Then they disappeared back inside. Onlookers were overwhelmed with fear that lasted several days.'

The landing was authenticated by staff from the Voronezh Geophysical Laboratory, whose head, Genrikh Silanov, is a respected scientist.

Tass said: 'Scientists confirmed that a UFO landed in the park. They also identified the landing site and found traces of aliens.'

Silanov's men discovered a twenty-yard depression in the park with four deep dents and two pieces of rock.

'They looked like deep red sandstone. But analysis showed that the substance cannot be found on Earth.

There was speculation among UFO experts in Britain that the aliens could have been those that Mrs Coe said landed in her garden last month in a spacecraft which was surrounded by bubbles of light. According to her amazing story the aliens grabbed her by the arms and lifted her up a beam of light into a kind of room. Mrs Coe was reported as saying she felt they meant her no harm and that when she came round she was in her garden and not hurt in any way.

Key

READING

Before reading

1

Headline 4 (*Mars: Man's next base?*) It is less sensationalist, does not seem to be linked to a specific story and seems more factual.

2

All the others come from 'popular' newspapers (except possibly *Space Hero 'A Human Wreck'*). We know this because they refer to less likely stories about 'killer ants', 'twelve feet aliens' and 'UFOs'.

Reading

1

TEXT 1: *Headline 2* (*Space Hero 'A Human Wreck'*)
1A, 2C, 3D, 4F, 5G, 6I, 7J, 8L
TEXT 2: *Headline 4* (*Mars: Man's Next Base?*)
1B, 2E, 3H, 4K

b

a) 4 b) 2 c) 5 d) 1 e) 3

2

Length of journey: takes three years.
Problems of journey: decalcification; heart loses volume; lose blood; muscles lose weight; mental instability.
Problems of living there: thin atmosphere, blood would boil almost immediately.

4
a) it b) their c) his d) Its e) we

5
atmos'pheric, corre'spondent, 'cosmonaut, ex'periments, ex'plorers, i'mmediately, 'physicist, re'quire, 'temperature

6
a) even if / although
b) Nevertheless / Even so
c) Even if / Although / ~~While~~
d) ~~although~~ / while
e) Nevertheless / Even so

VOCABULARY

Compounds

1
Example answers:
a) living room, dining room, sitting room, waiting room
b) dark-haired, light-haired, straight-haired

2
a) first part b) second part

3
b) dining room – A
c) good-looking – B
d) dishwasher – A
e) housework – A
f) old-fashioned – B
g) well-known – B
h) long-haired – B
i) overflow / overwork – A / B
j) wallpaper – A
k) broad-minded – B
l) ashtray – A
m) front door – A

4
a) 'hitchhiker
b) paper 'cup
c) front 'door
d) 'golf club
e) country 'house
f) 'headache
g) lawn 'tennis
h) science 'fiction

REVISION AND EXTENSION

Future Continuous

1
Example answers:
a) We'll be living in places which we're not living in now and we'll be eating very different kinds of food.
b) Not necessarily. We might be.

2
They will still be in progress.

3
a) Sudden decision.
b) Fixed or decided event.

PRACTICE

1
a) What will you be doing ...?
b) I'll give it ...
c) I'll be seeing him tomorrow...
d) Will you lend me...
I'll be going to the bank ...

EXTENSION 2

Future Perfect

1
a) It will be finished.
b) Diagram (ii)

WRITING 1

Complex sentences

1
Example answers:
a) *Since* Anton has no car, it'll take him a long time to get to his parents' house.
b) *In order to* reach the top shelf Rosa stood on a chair.
c) Someone passed me at 50 *even though* there was a 30 mile an hour speed limit.
d) I enjoyed the disco very much *in spite of the fact that / even though* I had to leave early.
e) Greg drove badly, *yet* to my surprise he passed the test.
f) I wouldn't buy you a gold ring *even if* I had the money.
g) Neil likes hot chocolate *whereas* Judith likes coffee.
h) You should insure your jewellery *in case* it is stolen.

2
a) Feeling hot, I took off my overcoat.
b) On waking up, we saw we had arrived in Moscow.
c) Having lit the fire, she sat down and went to sleep.
d) Seeing it in close-up, it doesn't look too bad.
e) Not having eaten oysters before I didn't know what to expect.
f) Although not very well-educated, he was very well-read.

Around the world

Students' Book

Unit topic: travel.

READING AND SPEAKING: magazine article on a visit to a jungle town; planning an adventure holiday.
VOCABULARY 1: travel.
SPEAKING: selling a holiday.

REVISION AND EXTENSION: the grammar of phrasal verbs.
LISTENING: interview with Michael Palin about his trip around the world; connected speech: word linking (vowel-to-vowel; words ending in *r*).

VOCABULARY 2: looking up idiomatic expressions in the dictionary.
WRITING: the indefinite article; personal letter (making arrangements).

Workbook

READING: extract from a travel book about a journey across Tibet; vocabulary in context.
GRAMMAR: definite, indefinite and zero article; *could / (was / were) able to / managed to*; *used for*; *as / like*
WRITING: sounds and spelling; American spelling.
VOCABULARY: phrasal verbs; animals (*a flock of*, etc. and animal noises).

Language

This unit is concerned with the grammar of phrasal verbs. In the WRITING section there is revision of the indefinite article in contrast to definite and zero article (see also Unit 2). To balance the 'heavy' work in these areas there is substantial oral fluency work at the beginning of the unit.

Phrasal verbs are very common in informal English and need to be approached with care when focused on as a teaching item (see *Common problems* below). In many ways the best strategy is to highlight examples as they occur naturally in texts and allow SS to acquire their use slowly. However, many Ts and SS also feel the need for both practice of phrasal verbs as vocabulary items and some explanation of their structural patterns.

Key factors in the mastery of the grammar of phrasal verbs are the efficient use of a dictionary and the examples given there and an understanding of how the phrasal verbs SS already know operate. (Most SS at this level will be able to say things such as *I **put on** my coat.* and *I **get up** at six.* without thinking about the grammar. Using those as examples when looking at the grammar can be very useful.)

Common problems

Phrasal verbs

Given that phrasal verbs are North European in origin, North European SS have fewer problems than other nationalities in using them.

1 Phrasal verbs can have more than one meaning (e.g. *let off* can mean 'excuse from punishment' and 'cause to explode').

2 There are different ways of categorising phrasal verbs as vocabulary:
- those where the verb keeps its meaning and the particle is an 'intensifier' (e.g. *tire out*);
- those where the meaning is literal, i.e. a combination of the meaning of the two words (e.g. *go away*);
- those where the meaning is idiomatic, i.e. it has a different meaning from the two separate parts (e.g. *look after* meaning 'take care of').

The problem for the learner then is not knowing whether they can work out the meaning of the phrasal verb from either or both of the two parts. From the teaching point of view, phrasal verbs in the first two categories can be easily grouped into their constituent parts (e.g. all the verbs where *up* acts as an intensifier, like *hurry up* - see *Intermediate Matters*) but words in the third category are much less easily grouped. In some cases the particle can give a small clue to the meaning (for example, some *down* verbs suggest the idea of 'decrease', such as *cut down* meaning 'do less of something'). However, *down* can also suggest a range of other ideas such as 'failure' (in *let (someone) down* meaning 'fail to help') or 'on paper' (in *take down* meaning 'keep a written record').

3 There are different ways of categorising phrasal verbs grammatically:

- verb + preposition + object (where the preposition links the verb and the object). Some of these are literal (*He* ***listened to*** *the radio.*) and some are idiomatic (*She* ***takes after*** *her mother.* meaning 'resembles'). These are Type 1 in the *Language reference* and often referred to as 'prepositional verbs' (the idiomatic ones are sometimes called 'prepositional phrasal verbs').
- intransitive verb + adverb (*Her car has* ***broken down***. meaning 'stopped working'). These are Type 2 in the *Language reference.*
- transitive verb + adverb + object (*I decided to* ***give up*** *smoking.* meaning 'stop'). These are also Type 2 in the *Language reference.*
- verb + adverb + preposition + object (*I won't* ***put up with*** *your bad behaviour any longer.* meaning 'tolerate'). These are Type 3 in the *Language reference.*

The problem here is that if the structural rules are not understood or acquired naturally then SS can make mistakes with word order. In the combination transitive verb + adverb + direct object the two parts of the verb (the verb and the adverb) can often be separated (***cross*** *a name* ***out*** or ***cross out*** *a name* meaning 'remove by putting a line through'). However, when the object is a pronoun (*she, it,* etc.) the two parts must be separated (***cross*** *it* ***out*** not *****cross out*** *it*). If SS are unsure whether or not a phrasal verb can be split it is safer *not* to split it.

4 In some verb + particle combinations (e.g. *look up*) the particle can function as a preposition or an adverb. In the sentence *He* ***looked up*** *the chimney.* the particle *up* is a preposition and must go before the object (so not **He* ***looked*** *the chimney* ***up***.). In the sentence *She* ***looked up*** *the word in the dictionary. look up* is an idiomatic phrasal verb (meaning 'search for'). Here, the particle *up* is an adverb and can be separated provided the direct object is not a pronoun (*She* ***looked*** *the word* ***up*** *in a dictionary.*). This example is given in the *Language reference.*

5 Collocation is yet another problem. We can say ***get off*** *a bus* but we have to say ***get out of*** *a car* (not *****get off*** *a car*).

Unless you believe in acquisition being the only strategy possible, all of these complications need to be addressed at some time with SS. However, it is probably best to deal with them in small doses over a long period of time (allowing SS to both acquire *and* learn the rules of use) before the SS get to upper-intermediate level. In this unit the idea is to give a review of the grammar, so if your SS are weak it might be an idea to do the work over several lessons and integrate it with the skills work of the unit and the grammar exercises in the WB. Whatever, reassure SS they are not expected to achieve mastery overnight and tell them that even advanced SS have problems!

The indefinite article

The rules for the use of the article are a problem for most SS but particularly those whose first language is a non-European language. Particularly problematic for most SS is the use of the zero article (i.e. no article) when talking about things in general (*Travel broadens the mind.* not **The travel broadens the mind.*). However, many SS confuse the definite and the indefinite article when talking about specific things (**I've got the bad back.*).

READING AND SPEAKING

The focus on this section is the planning of an adventure holiday. SS' travel likes and dislikes will be discussed and a lot of useful travel vocabulary, practised later, should come up.

• Exercise 1 You could start by asking SS which countries they have travelled to, what kind of journeys they made to them (e.g. business trips, package tours) and what kinds of holidays are most popular in their country. Explain the term 'adventure holiday', which will be needed later. Revise *-an* adjectives in relation to countries by getting SS to give you the adjective from the noun including the spelling: e.g. *Peru/Peruvian*; *India/Indian*; *Mexico/Mexican*; *Belgium/Belgian*; *Norway/Norwegian*; *Russia/Russian*, etc. Ask SS the noun of *malarial* (*malaria*) and tell SS what *marauding jaguars* are ('jaguars which move around in search of things to kill').

• **Exercise 2** Using the tape helps create a sense of atmosphere and immediacy. Do not spend too long on the discussion as there is more discussion in Exercises 4 and 5.

• **Exercise 3** Again the main aim is to create an atmosphere. Most of the difficult vocabulary can probably be deduced from context (*Plaza de Armas* – the name of a public square, *threatened, pounced, claws, shrilly, disentangling, crunch*). Guide SS to the meaning using the context (e.g. *What noise do you think cockroaches make under foot?*). Note the alliteration used for dramatic effect: ***s**queaking **s**hrilly / **d**ifficulty in **d**isentangling / **c**ockroaches **c**runch.*

• **Exercise 4** Possibly suggest headings: *Food, Transport, The effect of heat/cold, People*. (Note that Exercises 4, 5 and 6 form a single sequence.)

• **Exercise 5** In e) the term 'traveller' refers to someone who likes adventure holidays and climbing and walking with a rucksack (backpack). Encourage SS to think of the differences between a tourist and a 'traveller', both in the type of people they are and the kind of experiences they have. (Note that second conditional sentences come up in this unit – useful diagnosis for the controlled work in Unit 11.)

VOCABULARY 1

Travel

• **Exercise 1** Essentially this is a collocation exercise (e.g. We talk about a *business trip* not a *business journey*; and we say *stopover in* or *at* but *flying visit to*). The exercise consists of words with a similar meaning which are often wrongly used by SS. The dictionary examples should help. You could start by asking SS to brainstorm a list of words they associate with 'Travel' (e.g. *explore*) and then later tick off those that occur in this exercise. In feedback get SS to give you correct sentences for some of the words which are *not* correct in the exercise, e.g. for *flying visit* in a).

SPEAKING

Selling a holiday

Try to bring some posters and brochures to the class (or get SS to bring them). This will give SS a source of pictures that they can cut up and stick on their own posters. It will also give SS inspiration for their designs. However, do not let them be too restricted by the ideas they see.

• **Exercise 2** Get SS to make a list under each of the main 'selling points'. The language of persuasion and making suggestions will be needed here. (You could elicit some of the *Speaking functions* given on SB page 150.)

• **Exercise 3** Sticking pictures on the posters will work as well (and often better than) drawings.

• **Exercise 4** At the end get SS to display their posters.

REVISION AND EXTENSION

Using phrasal verbs

This section refers to the *grammar* of phrasal verbs. Before the class, you should read Section 1 of the *Language reference* on SB page 68 and the *Common problems* section above. This is because of the inherent difficulties and confusion of this area and because coursebooks and grammar books use a range of terminological expressions and group phrasal verbs into a range of different types. If SS are to be helped rather than further confused, consistency, accuracy and simplicity are essential.

You could start by getting SS to brainstorm phrasal verbs they know and putting some of them in sentences. These sentences can be used as further examples for Exercise 1.

• **Exercise 1** PW/GW. The aim of this exercise is to see how much SS already know. However, first get them to read the introduction to the section and check that they know what a *transitive verb*, a *particle* and an *object pronoun* are. Most classes could read Section 1 of the *Language reference* after doing Exercise 3 but a weak class might need to read it before they start Exercise 1.

PRACTICE

It is a good idea before doing these exercises to go back to the sentences in the previous section, say them aloud naturally and ask SS to listen out for where the stress is in the phrasal verbs. (Is it on the verb, the particle or both?) Note that we frequently stress the particle when it is an adverb rather than the verb, particularly when it comes at the end of a sentence, as in *The travel business is looking 'up.* Then do the first sentence with the SS, getting them to use stress correctly (e.g. *'put out the 'blaze / put the 'blaze out / put it 'out* – though other variations are possible depending on the context).

After these exercises get SS to do the follow-up work in the WB (as homework).

LISTENING

Before listening

Tell SS about the novel *Le tour du monde en quatre-vingts jours* written by the French novelist Jules Verne in 1873. In this novel, Verne recounts the travels of the Englishman Phileas Fogg and his valet Passepartout as they try to get round the world in 80 days. Michael Palin's journey was a 1980's imitation! You could get SS to predict the means of travel Palin used and the problems he would have encountered. You might like to tell SS at this stage that Michael Palin is a TV and film actor who appeared in the *Monty Python* series.

Listening

• **Exercise 1** If necessary, bring in a map to show where the Persian Gulf and the Suez Canal are. It's not necessary to teach any vocabulary before SS listen. Most of the difficult words can be guessed from context and then explored in Exercise 4.

Extra information: in the comic sketch Palin refers to, John Cleese is a dissatisfied customer who returns a 'dead' (but really stuffed) parrot to a pet shop and bangs it on the counter while complaining; and a *St Francis of Assisi scene* refers to the thirteenth-century Italian saint, St Francis, associated with a simple love of nature and often depicted preaching to birds.

• **Exercise 2** In b), make sure SS realise that Palin both liked and didn't like parts of his journey. (Can SS think of things they both like and don't like?)

• **Exercise 4** In a), you could ask SS to think of other words they know with these suffixes (e.g. *relation**ship**, attract**ion**, accur**acy**, exist**ence***). In b), get SS to explore the differences between *nibble, munch, chew* and *bite.* Some dictionaries might not have the informal words in c): *loo* is a word for toilet, acceptable in conversation in most contexts in Britain; *grotty* means unpleasant; and *stroppy* means bad-tempered and awkward to deal with (derived from *obstreperous).*

Connected speech

This part of the section follows on from the work done on word linking in Unit 7.

When native speakers speak naturally they often link words ending in a vowel and words beginning with a vowel by adding a /w/ or /j/ sound. If the vowel at the end of the first word has a rounded lip position like /uː/, as in *do*, the linking sound is /w/, as in *do I* (/duːwaɪ/). If the vowel has a spread or stretched lip position like /iː/, as in *she*, the linking sound is /j/, as in *she asked* (/ʃijɑːskt/).

When words ending in a /r/ sound are followed by words beginning with a vowel the final /r/ sound is often linked to the next word as in *where is* (*whe ris* /weərɪz/).

• **Exercises 1 and 2** If SS don't hear the sound insertion, ask them to listen carefully to the boundary between the words and contrast what they hear with the two words pronounced separately. In the dictation the dialogue is read twice, once without pauses (for comprehension), once with pauses to allow you to stop the tape and the SS to write.

VOCABULARY 2

Looking up idiomatic expressions

With idioms (or 'fixed collocations'), like many phrasal verbs, it is often difficult to work out the meaning from the words they contain.

• **Exercise 1** The aim of this exercise is to help SS get used to using the context to help work out the meaning of an expression. The pictures illustrate a *literal* meaning of *put your foot down, at a stretch* and *bark up the wrong tree*, not an *idiomatic* use, and can be used as humorous contrast. If necessary, guide the SS to the meaning from elements in the context which help them. In a), for example, the definition is given in the phrase *he's got it wrong*.

• **Exercise 2** This exercise focuses on using the dictionary to help with the meaning. Tell SS that when they are looking up a word, the 'key word' they need to find is often the noun or the least common word in the phrase.

WRITING

The indefinite article

• **Exercise 1** This exercise revises the indefinite article. It also requires SS to construct sentences from notes, so ensure they pay attention to sentence length, linking expressions and punctuation. Possibly PW and SS compare their answers in groups. Encourage SS to monitor their future writing for the use of the article.

• **Exercise 2** This exercise revises the contrast between the indefinite, the definite and zero article. Quickly go over any vocabulary (e.g. *bullet train* - the high-speed train in Japan). SS needing further help on the definite article should refer to Section 4 of the *Language reference* in Unit 2 (SB page 17). There is another exercise in the WB.

Personal letter: making arrangements

• **Exercise 1** Introduce the topic of the dialogue by asking (non-Japanese) SS some questions about Japan (e.g. *Do you like Japanese food? What do Japanese people eat for breakfast?*). Ask SS to work out, while they listen, what they can about Helen's character (she is conscientious in relation to her work and generous to her parents), her mother (she is an experienced traveller), her father (he is not as strong as he used to be) and where Helen lives (it is fairly remote). SS might need help with some of the words (e.g. *short-staffed, pretty rough, clubhouse, seaweed*).

• **Exercise 3** You could refer SS to Unit 2 for the layout of a personal letter. The tone of the letter obviously needs to be informal and friendly. As follow-up you might want to do some revision of giving directions using a map (*Go along the road until...*, etc.).

Tapescripts

RECORDING 1

[See Key].

RECORDING 2

MICHAEL PALIN: There was a passenger ferry to Alexandria, there was a ferry down from Suez to Jeddah, after that it was just going on cargo vessels and the most primitive one we went on was the one across the Persian Gulf which had you know no radar, no radio and we were just ... we slept on top of the cargo - (this was the dhow) - under clear skies, this was the dhow.

INTERVIEWER: You say when you were on that that the crew became like your family, in a way, because you were with them for what six, seven days?

MP: Yes, I mean there were eighteen of them and just lived all together on the deck, and I mean you washed together and went to the loo - well, you didn't go to the loo together - but I mean (it's public) everything was open and *al fresco* and so you just you know . . . we needed them desperately, we didn't know - it was unfamiliar territory for us, we had to make friends . . . and they repaid our friendship so well and they were so kind and they looked after us and bring us little mugs of that very sweet tea the Indians like.

I: Did you, did you ever sort of feel a point where you thought, oh just for a bit of privacy, that would be so nice?

MP: Yeah, I did, especially on the dhow when I felt ill. You just, when you're ill you don't want you feel horrible, you feel grotty, you just don't want anyone to see you really, you just want to go away and hide and you couldn't there because it was so hot and there was, you know, you were in amongst all these people, and just you know you weren't fit, you feel you just wanted to be home and in bed. It was as simple as that really.

MP: There was a parrot I met in Hong Kong, in the place called the bird market which is a long, long street full of all manner of birds because in China and Hong Kong it's just this incredible bustle and everything is used, every sort of bit of wildlife is used, and they either use them for song birds or fighting birds - it's very popular - they get birds over from nationalist China who are really stroppy . . . (*noise*) birds like that, and they fight and gamble - people gamble on bird fights (*Oh!*), and there's also, you know the decorative birds, birds, there's birds you can eat and there were these wonderful parrots and one of them bore a distinct resemblance to the parrot which John Cleese used to smack on the counter in the pet shop sketch, and I was talking to it - and this other big bird - I think it was a cockatoo with a great beak was sort of nibbling gently at my trouser leg, so I called the camera over and said 'Oh, look at this' - it's rather nice - you know, St Francis of Assisi scene - Michael surrounded by admiring birds, and it wasn't admiring at all - it wanted to tear my leg off and it actually had to be prised off my trousers with half the trousers in its beak.

I: You've not always travelled in style. I mean you were quite happy to go and sort of use the local rooms and you balanced it with some of the style, five star hotels and stuff. On reflection would you prefer local rooms or the big hotels?

MP: I much prefer local rooms. On reflection, that's the important thing. Looking back, they are terrific. You learn much more from those places and you make friends, but you also take risks, you can have really unpleasant, at the time they can be very unpleasant and very uncomfortable, whereas the five star hotels that we stayed in or four star, three star, were always havens of, so delighted to get to them because they were usually after a hard period of travelling and you could get your things washed and laundered, you could have a hot bath, you know you could have a drink of wine or something like that - I missed my wine, going round the world - and so you know I would say at the time those big hotels served their purpose and kept me going, but the experiences all lie in the sort of the smaller places because they are typical of the country.

RECORDING 3

a) to eat
b) I am
c) she is
d) you ought
e) no other
f) very unhappy
g) who are

RECORDING 4

a) anywhere else
b) we're out
c) more or less
d) sooner or later
e) beer is

RECORDING 5

[See Key.]

RECORDING 6

HELEN: The train gets in about six in the morning from Tokyo. I'll try and meet you at the station but I'm teaching that morning.
MRS BAKER: I'm sure it'll be all right, dear.
H: The trouble is it's very difficult for me to get the time off. They're very short-staffed at the moment.
MRS B: It's all right. It's not as though we're not used to travelling.
H: Anyway, you just get a taxi to the golf course which is where the main road ends. Unfortunately, the taxis don't like going any further because the roads get pretty rough after that.
MRS B: It's all right, we'll walk if it's not too far.
H: Yes. Just leave your suitcases at the clubhouse - the man at reception speaks English - and we'll pick them up later. Anyway don't worry. I'll send you a map showing you the way from there.
MRS B: No problem. It'll be an adventure.
H: Now when you get there, the lady next door will bring you in a real Japanese breakfast: rice, miso soup . . .
MRS B: Miso soup? What's that?
H: It's made from soya beans. It's nice when you get used to it. What else? Mm, grilled fish, pickles, raw eggs beaten with soya sauce and seaweed . . .
MRS B: Raw eggs and seaweed!
H: Yeah, it's great. I really like it now. I know you like exotic foods. Anyway, listen, I'll finish work at about twelve, so have a rest, maybe take a little walk and get a good look at that incredible view we have of the mountain. It's fantastic at this time of the year. It'll be quite safe to walk around. I'll be back about half past.
MRS B: It sounds wonderful. We're really looking forward to it. Unfortunately Dad's legs aren't what they used to be but he can still get about. How long are you going to let us stay?
H: Don't ask such questions. As long as you like of course. I'll drop you a line to explain all this . . .

Key

READING AND SPEAKING

2
The sounds are snakes, parrots, monkeys, a lion, an elephant and flamingoes.

3
Example answers:
a) Poor, deserted, non-threatening.
b) She felt something dig its claws into her neck.
c) Very basic, without light or water, with cockroaches everywhere.

VOCABULARY 1

Travel

1
a) stopover b) trip c) companion d) ruins
e) uneventful f) view g) explorer h) excursions
i) resorts

REVISION AND EXTENSION

Using phrasal verbs

1
The verb is intransitive in sentence c).
The particle can be separated from the verb in sentence b).
The particle and the verb are never separated in sentences a), c) and d). (Note that *look up* in the context of 'getting better' cannot be separated but *look up* in the context of 'search for' can.)
The particle and the verb are always separated in sentence e).

2
a) It gives [T] for transitive and [I] for intransitive.
b) Verbs marked *'infml'*.

3
In a), c), d) and e) the pronoun does not change position.
In b) the pronoun must come before the particle (*I looked **it** up in the dictionary*)..

PRACTICE

1

a) . . . put the blaze out (put it out).
b) . . . went off early.
c) . . . run out of petrol (run out of it).
d) . . . turned the job down (turned it down)?
e) Don't tear that letter up (tear it up)!
f) . . . looks like his mother (looks like her) . . .
g) . . . put up with this situation (put up with it) . . .
h) . . . look into the burglary (look into it).
i) . . . put the meeting off (put it off) . . .
j) . . . put Tom up (put him up) . . .

2

b) Example answers:
2 She's filling in a form (filling a form in).
3 He's doing up his shirt (doing his shirt up).
4 She's come across a £10 note in the street.
5 He's turning off the motorway.
6 She's making out a cheque (making a cheque out).

LISTENING

Before listening

a) Photograph 1: being bitten by a cockatoo in a market in Hong Kong.
Photograph 2: undergoing some kind of comic ceremony / ritual after crossing the international dateline.
b) Photograph 2: (It is the comic certificate proving he had crossed the international dateline.)

Listening

2

a)
Enjoyed: the primitive cargo vessel (?), the crew, cups of sweet tea; the bustle of Hong Kong; the parrots; the local rooms (on reflection); the hotels as a place of calm and safety; the chance to get things laundered; to have a hot bath; to have a glass of wine
Didn't enjoy: the lack of privacy when ill; the fierce cockatoo(?); unpleasant and uncomfortable local rooms at the time
b)
He probably *both enjoyed and didn't enjoy:* the primitive boat; the market in Hong Kong; the modern hotels and local rooms

3

Example answers:
a) . . . he needed their help.
b) . . . he wanted privacy and to hide and be at home in bed.
c) . . . there is a market full of birds.
d) . . . friendly it started to attack him.
e) . . . he preferred local rooms or big hotels.
f) . . . you have more interesting experiences there.

4

a) reflection; resemblance; privacy; friendship
b) spread
c) All except *bustle*.

CONNECTED SPEECH

1

b) /j/ c) /j/ d) /w/ e) /w/ f) /j/ g) /w/

3

a) and **b)**
LUCY: Come_on. Hurry_up! We're_off! Where_are the keys? Is the car_outside?
MIKE: Here_you_are! Why do_you_always get so_excited?
LUCY: Great! Now where_are Mary_and Linda?
MIKE: They wanted to go_out on their_own. They're back_in the_evening.

VOCABULARY 2

Looking up idiomatic expressions

1

a) directing his efforts in the wrong direction
b) for ever
c) without stopping
d) share the cost
e) didn't feel like
f) in your area of interest
g) made a firm decision

WRITING

The indefinite article

1

b) Jo-Anne Campbell is a 24-year-old pianist from a rural part of Australia. She has recently returned from travelling round Kenya in a Land Rover. While there, she met a beautiful African singer called Winnie.
c) Jean-Paul Mitterand is a French-Canadian engineer with a well-known company. He loves unusual adventures and travels everywhere by motorbike. Last year he had a two-month ride round Mongolia.
d) Diyangui Nkama is an Angolan lawyer with a six-year-old child. He had a bad back for years. Earlier this year he stayed in a lodge in a wildlife park in a remote region of India. While there, he needed medical assistance and had to visit a/the local doctor. He made a sensational recovery

2

1 – 2 an 3 – 4 an 5 the 6 – 7 The 8 an 9 The 10 the 11 a 12 the 13 a 14 – 15 – 16 – 17 The 18 a 19 a 20 –

A Family Supper

Students' Book

READING 1
LISTENING 1

READING 2
VOCABULARY: ways of smiling, looking, walking.

LISTENING 2: connected speech (reading aloud).
READING 3
SPEAKING AND WRITING: discussion; writing a letter; planning a film 'trailer'.

Workbook

The aim of this unit is to revise work done in the first nine units of the WB.

READING: 'Strange stories' from a magazine.
GRAMMAR: Present, Present Perfect or Past?; question forms; modals of obligation; future forms.
VOCABULARY: word building; prepositions; phrasal verbs; definitions.
PRONUNCIATION: dictation (stressed words and weak forms).
WRITING: review of linking expressions.

This unit is an integrated skills unit based on a complete short story by Kazuo Ishiguro, *A Family Supper*. All the reading and listening texts in the unit are extracts from this story. There is no explicit grammar focus in this unit, although there is vocabulary and pronunciation based on the text. However, the WB gives revision of grammar, vocabulary and pronunciation, taken from the first nine units. Some or all of this could be used in class if required.

READING 1

• **Exercise 1** Before beginning this unit, find out whether any of the SS have read this story or any other stories by Kazuo Ishiguro. Explain that the unit does not introduce any new grammar but aims to give SS lots of practice in reading, listening and speaking. By this time SS will probably have become much more confident in listening to and reading authentic English texts. Point out the picture and tell SS that fugu, otherwise known as the 'death puffer', is the most poisonous fish in the world, and that it is considered a great delicacy in Japan. Although only special restaurants with highly trained chefs serve it, it still accounts for about 20 victims a year. It might be interesting to discuss with SS the reasons why they think the idea of eating fugu became so popular in Japan after the war (e.g. the idea of living dangerously?).
SS might need help with some of the vocabulary such as *glands, veins, all the rage* and *gutting*.

• **Exercise 2** This activity might lead to some discussion, as the story does not make it clear whether the relationship with the narrator's parents became strained before he went to live in California or as a result of his living there. Get SS to speculate on likely reasons for the deterioration of a relationship between a young man and his parents, and what their own parents' attitudes would be if they chose / had chosen to go and live so far away when they were still quite young. Encourage SS to give ideas about why the narrator might have gone to California. You could ask them why they think he wasn't told how his mother had died (e.g. Did she commit suicide?).

• **Exercises 4 and 5** These exercises require SS to read the text quite carefully. They should be encouraged to give their impressions of the father (e.g. Do they like him?), and speculate on the relationship between the narrator and his father and sister. Note that *tatami* is a rice mat used in Japanese houses.

• **Exercises 6 and 7** These exercises require SS to read carefully and interpret what they are reading. Stress that there might be more than one interpretation. You could ask SS to guess how the story will continue.

LISTENING 1

• **Exercise 1** You could elicit predictions about the pictures before SS listen. This exercise does not require detailed listening. SS could first discuss their answers as PW or GW before reporting back.

• **Exercises 2 and 3** The questions in Exercise 2 are factual ones and those in Exercise 3 require SS to give their opinions. At this point SS are able to check their predictions about why the narrator went to California.

If SS have had difficulty with the *Listening* let them read the tapescript, or listen and read at the same time, before going on to the next reading.

You might want to move from here to the VOCABULARY section. Alternatively, bring in some of the revision work from the WB if you would like to break up intensive work on the text.

READING 2

Again, many of the questions in this section are open to interpretation. You could try to explore what the father means about preferring to be in the airforce rather than on a ship (e.g. Does he mean that he would prefer a dramatic ending to his life?). There is also more opportunity for speculating on what the son did to cause his mother such grief. You could ask SS why they think the father stresses that he has '*A little more time*' (Does he intend to kill himself? Is he ill?). Ask SS whether they think the narrator is 'cold' or hard-hearted in his reaction to the news about his mother's death.

There is scope again here for getting SS to predict the end of the story.

VOCABULARY

Ways of doing things

• **Exercise 1** Some vocabulary is taken from the reading and listening text. Encourage SS to keep 'networks' of similar words (see WB Unit 1) and show them how to find lexical areas such as this in a dictionary or lexicon (see SB Unit 6).

Ask SS to look back at the story and make notes of vocabulary they want to remember. Get them to compare their choice of words with each other.

LISTENING 2

Listening

• **Exercises 1-3** Factual questions in Exercise 1 are followed by interpretative ones in Exercises 2 and 3. In Exercise 3 encourage SS to say the exact words that they believe the character is thinking, e.g. '*That woman looks just like the ghost we saw!*'

Connected speech

• **Exercises 1-3** It is useful for SS to get into the habit of 'thinking ahead' to which words they should stress, but impress upon them that there is no 'one answer' – it depends on the meaning they wish to communicate. Stress the need for practice in this area. You could get SS to work in groups to think about how the first couple of sentences will be said, then exchange views before listening to the tape. Only the main (not the secondary) stresses have been marked.

READING 3

Get SS to discuss what they think happened next and how the story could be continued.

SPEAKING AND WRITING

Discussion

• **Exercise 1** This is an opportunity for debate, and revision of the functions of giving opinions, agreeing and disagreeing. Encourage SS to give examples from their own experience.

• **Exercise 2** SS may refer to the tapescript of LISTENING 1 to remember what Kikuko said.

Planning a film 'trailer'

SS have to decide on the 'key scenes' in the story and thus get a better understanding of what the story is really about. This could lead to some interesting discussions, particularly about the ambiguities in the story. The scenes for the advert could then be acted, mimed or just described. If SS are creative they could design a poster for the film.

Make the complete story available to SS if possible because some SS might want to read the whole story straight through.

Tapescripts

RECORDING 1

'I've been dying for a smoke for the last half-hour,' she said, lighting a cigarette.

'Then why didn't you smoke?'

She made a furtive gesture back towards the house, then grinned mischievously.

'Oh, I see,' I said.

'Guess what? I've got a boyfriend now.'

'Oh yes?'

'Except I'm wondering what to do. I haven't made up my mind yet.'

'Quite understandable.'

'You see, he's making plans to go to America. He wants me to go with him as soon as I finish studying.'

'I see. And you want to go to America?'

'If we go, we're going to hitch-hike.' Kikuko waved a thumb in front of my face. 'People say it's dangerous but I've done it in Osaka and it's fine.'

'I see. So what is it you're unsure about?'

We were following a narrow path that wound through the shrubs and finished by the old well. As we walked, Kikuko persisted in taking unnecessarily theatrical puffs on her cigarette.

'Well, I've got lots of friends now in Osaka. I like it there. I'm not sure I want to leave them all behind just yet. And Suichi - I like him, but I'm not sure I want to spend so much time with him. Do you understand?'

'Oh perfectly.'

She grinned again, then skipped on ahead of me until she had reached the well. 'Do you remember,' she said, as I came walking up to her, 'how you used to say this well was haunted?'

'Yes, I remember.'

We both peered over the side.

'Mother always told me it was the old woman from the vegetable store you'd seen that night,' she said. 'But I never believed her and never came out here alone.'

'Mother used to tell me that, too. She even told me once the old woman had confessed to being the ghost. Apparently she'd been taking a short cut through our garden. I imagine she had some trouble clambering over those walls.'

Kikuko gave a giggle. She then turned her back to the well, casting her gaze about the garden.

'Mother never really blamed you, you know,' she said in a new voice. I remained silent. 'She always used to say to me how it was their fault, hers and Father's, for not bringing you up correctly. She used to tell me how much more careful they'd been with me, and that's why I was so good.' She looked up and the mischievous grin had returned to her face. 'Poor Mother,' she said.

'Yes. Poor Mother'.

'Are you going back to California?'

'I don't know. I'll have to see.'

'What happened to - to her? To Vicki?'

'That's all finished with,' I said. 'There's nothing much left for me now in California.'

'Do you think I ought to go there?'

'Why not? I don't know. You'll probably like it.' I glanced towards the house. 'Perhaps we'd better go in soon. Father might need a hand with the supper.'

But my sister was once again peering down into the well. 'I can't see any ghosts,' she said. Her voice echoed a little.

'Is Father very upset about his firm collapsing?'

'Don't know. You never can tell with Father.' Then suddenly she straightened up and turned to me. 'Did he tell you about old Watanabe? What he did?'

'I heard he committed suicide.'

'Well, that wasn't all. He took his whole family with him. His wife and his two little girls.'

'Oh yes?'

'Those two beautiful little girls. He turned on the gas while they were all asleep. Then he cut his stomach with a meat knife.'

'Yes, Father was just telling me how Watanabe was a man of principle.'

'Sick.' My sister turned back to the well.

'Careful. You'll fall right in.'

'I can't see any ghost,' she said. 'You were lying to me all that time.'

'But I never said it lived down the well.'

'Where is it, then?'

We both looked around at the trees and the shrubs. The light in the garden had grown very dim. Eventually I pointed to a small clearing some ten yards away.

'Just there I saw it. Just there.'

We stared at the spot.

'What did it look like?'

'I couldn't see very well. It was dark.'

'But you must have seen something.'

'It was an old woman. She was just standing there, watching me.'

We kept staring at the spot as if mesmerized.

'She was wearing a white kimono,' I said. 'Some of her hair had come undone. It was blowing about a little.'

Kikuko pushed her elbow against my arm. 'Oh be quiet. You're trying to frighten me all over again.' She trod on the remains of her cigarette, then for a brief moment stood regarding it with a perplexed expression. She kicked some pine needles over it, then once more displayed her grin.

'Let's see if supper's ready,' she said.

RECORDING 2

Supper was waiting in a dimly lit room next to the kitchen. The only source of light was a big lantern that hung over the table, casting the rest of the room into shadow. We bowed to each other before starting the meal.

There was little conversation. When I made some polite comment about the food, Kikuko giggled a little. Her earlier nervousness seemed to have returned to her. My father did not speak for several minutes. Finally he said:

'It must feel strange for you, being back in Japan.'

'Yes, it is a little strange.'

'Already, perhaps, you regret leaving America.'

'A little. Not so much. I didn't leave behind much. Just some empty rooms.'

'I see.'

I glanced across the table. My father's face looked stony and forbidding in the half-light. We ate on in silence.

Then my eye caught something at the back of the room. At first I continued eating, then my hands became still. The others noticed and looked at me. I went on gazing into the darkness past my father's shoulder.

'Who is that? In that photograph there?'

'Which photograph?' My father turned slightly, trying to follow my gaze.

'The lowest one. The old woman in the white kimono.'

My father put down his chopsticks. He looked first at the photograph, then at me.

'Your mother.' His voice had become very hard. 'Can't you recognize your own mother?'

'My mother. You see, it's dark. I can't see it very well.'

No one spoke for a few seconds then Kikuko rose to her feet. She took the photograph down from the wall, came back to the table and gave it to me.

'She looks a lot older,' I said.

'It was taken shortly before her death,' said my father.

'It was the dark. I couldn't see very well.'

I looked up and noticed my father holding out a hand. I gave him the photograph. He looked at it intently, then held it towards Kikuko. Obediently, my sister rose to her feet once more and returned the picture to the wall.

There was a large pot left unopened at the centre of the table. When Kikuko had seated herself again, my father reached forward and lifted the lid. A cloud of steam rose up and curled towards the lantern. He pushed the pot a little towards me.

'You must be hungry,' he said. One side of his face had fallen into shadow.

'Thank you.' I reached forward with my chopsticks. The steam was almost scalding. 'What is it?'

'Fish.'

'It smells very good.'

In amidst soup were strips of fish that had curled almost into balls. I picked one out and brought it to my bowl.

'Help yourself. There's plenty.'

'Thank you.' I took a little more, then pushed the pot towards my father. I watched him take several pieces to his bowl. Then we both watched as Kikuko served herself.

My father bowed slightly. 'You must be hungry,' he said again. He took some fish to his mouth and started to eat. Then I too chose a piece and put it in my mouth. It felt soft, quite fleshy against my tongue.

'Very good,' I said. 'What is it?'

'Just fish.'

'It's very good.'

The three of us ate in silence. Several minutes went by.

'Some more?'

'Is there enough?'

'There's plenty for all of us.' My father lifted the lid and once more steam rose up. We all reached forward and helped ourselves.

'Here,' I said to my father, 'you have this last piece.'

'Thank you.'

RECORDING 3

At first I continued eating, then my hands became still. The others noticed and looked at me. I went on gazing into the darkness past my father's shoulder.

'Who is that? In that photograph there?'

'Which photograph?' My father turned slightly, trying to follow my gaze.

'The lowest one. The old woman in the white kimono.'

My father put down his chopsticks. He looked at the photograph, then at me.

'Your mother.' His voice had become very hard. 'Can't you recognize your own mother?'

Key

READING 1

1

Example answers:

a) There is poison inside the fish (in two bags inside the sexual glands) and this can leak into the veins while the fish is being prepared.

b) Perhaps because people enjoyed living dangerously by trying to cheat death.

c) She had eaten fugu in order not to offend an old schoolfriend, and had died.

2

1 c) or possibly e) 2 e) or possibly c) 3 d) 4 a) 5 b) 6 f)

4

a) No. He used to be, but he has retired (line 24).

b) No, he was a business partner of the writer's father (line 21).

c) True (lines 18–19).

d) No. (See line 45: *Despite our difference in years.* The fact that the sister is still at university would suggest she is much younger than the brother.)

e) No. (See lines 45–6: *my sister and I have always been close.)*

5

a) Picture 2.

b) serious, traditional, proud

6

Example answers:

a) The father and son don't have a very good relationship; they are not very good at talking / communicating.

b) The son had done something to upset his mother, which was probably why their relationship had got worse (going to live in California?).

c) The father and son speak very formally to each other.

d) The father thinks the son had been influenced by others (foreigners? women?).

e) The sister does not get on well with her father.

7

Example answers:

a) Because of foreign influence (lines 25–6).

b) He seems to think it was a matter of principle, and almost inevitable (line 21).

c) He is non-committal – merely saying *I see* (disapproving or not surprised?).

d) To speak more freely?

LISTENING 1

1

a) Watanabe cut his stomach with a meat knife; the well is the place the brother and sister used to believe was haunted; Vicki was the brother's girlfriend in California; Suichi is the sister's boyfriend; the old woman was the 'ghost' the brother saw near the well.

b) the father's future; the mother's death.

2

a) . . . she likes Osaka; she doesn't want to leave her friends there; she is not sure she wants to spend so much time with Suichi.
b) . . . the old woman from the vegetable store.
c) . . . not bringing him up correctly.
d) . . . his relationship with Vicki has finished and there's not much there for him now.

3

Example answers:
a) (ii) He is being ironic.
b) An old woman in a white kimono.
c) Perhaps because she is trying to assert her independence by smoking. She seems to be quite lively, modern-thinking and independent.

READING 2

Example answers:
a) Perhaps to get him on his own.
b) She wanted to resist being told what to do, perhaps, or to avoid taking on a subservient (traditionally female) role.
c) He makes model battleships.
d) Perhaps the father is drawing a parallel between death by battleship or plane and his situation at the moment. He has a choice of whether to 'hang on' or 'commit suicide' as some Japanese pilots used to do in their planes.
e) Not being a more attentive father.
f) She committed suicide.
   One reason for her 'disappointments' was her son's departure to America.
g) He says that she couldn't have expected him to stay at home for ever.

VOCABULARY

Ways of doing things

1

smiling: laugh, grin
looking: glance, watch, gaze, peer, glimpse
walking: stagger, limp, stroll, creep, march, crawl

2

a) glimpsed b) crept c) limping d) glanced e) grinned
f) peered/glanced

LISTENING 2

Listening

1

a) It is the 'ghost' who the son saw in the garden.
b) Fish.
c) The father.
d) The father.
e) The father.

2

Example answer:
The author clearly intends us to think it is fugu.

3

Example answers:
a) 'That's the ghost!'
b) 'You know who it is. Are you rejecting her? / How can you say that?'
c) 'I hope this isn't what I think it is.'
d) 'I'm not going to tell you it's fugu.' OR 'I know you suspect me of cooking fugu so I'm not going to tell you what it is.'
e) 'If you have cooked fugu you should have the most.'

Connected speech

1

Example answer:

At first I continued eating, then my hands became still. The others noticed and looked at me. I went on gazing into the darkness past my father's shoulder.

'Who is that? In that photograph there?'

'Which photograph?' My father turned slightly, trying to follow my gaze.

'The lowest one. The old woman in the white kimono.'

My father put down his chopsticks. He looked first at the photograph, then at me.

'Your mother.' His voice had become very hard. 'Can't you recognise your own mother?'

READING 3

Example answers:
a) Family life.
c) Loneliness; revenge for his wife's possible suicide.
d) 'Please stay here with me. Don't return to America.'

Scoop or snoop?

Students' Book

General theme: media.
Unit topic: the role of journalists.

LISTENING: interview with TV journalist Michael Buerk; sounds: /ʃ/, /tʃ/, /dʒ/.
READING AND WRITING: article about the role of journalists during a famine; grammatical and lexical linking words.
REVISION 1: conditional sentences (zero, first and second); *if* or *when*?

VOCABULARY: non-idiomatic phrasal verbs (e.g. *pick up a pen*); idiomatic phrasal verbs (e.g. *pick up a friend*).
REVISION 2: wanting situations to change (*wish / if only* + past).
EXTENSION: wanting things (not) to happen (*wish / if only* + *would*).

SPEAKING AND LISTENING: interview with MP Clare Short; discussion of privacy laws and the press.
WRITING: letter of opinion to a newspaper.

Workbook

READING: article about press treatment of the 'dingo baby case'.
VOCABULARY: collocation; different meanings of the phrasal verb *go through*; word association.
GRAMMAR: mixed conditional forms; *wish* and *if only*.
PRONUNCIATION: dictation of contracted forms.
WRITING: punctuation and layout of a letter.

Language

In this unit the uses and forms of zero, first and second conditional forms are revised and contrasted. At this level we feel that SS should be encouraged to use modals such as *may* or *might* in the main clause as well as *will* and *would* (e.g. *If I finish in time I* ***might*** *go out.*), and continuous as well as simple forms in the present and past (e.g. *If* ***he's sleeping,*** *I'll go on my own. If the television* ***was working,*** *I could watch that programme.*).

Wish and the past tense to talk about dissatisfaction in the present and a desire for things to be different is also focused on. This structure is linked to the second conditional in terms of meaning (i.e. it refers to a hypothetical situation) and form (i.e. *wish* is followed by the past in the same way as the conditional clause with *if* is in the past) so practice of the second conditional links quite naturally with practice of *wish* + past (e.g. *I wish I were rich. If I were rich, I'd give up my job.*).

Although *wish* and the past will probably be familiar to many SS already, the use of *wish* and *would* to talk about actions or states which people hope will change in the near future (e.g. *I wish it would stop raining.*) may be new to them.

Common problems

Conditional forms

1 SS still have problems at this level with the form of conditional sentences. Many still tend to use *will* after *if* (**I'll come if I'll remember.*) or forget to use the past tense for unreal conditions (**If I have a lot of money, I'd ...*). Some also use *would* in both clauses (**If it would rain, I wouldn't come.*).

2 It is hard for SS to remember when to use the different forms, i.e. that the zero conditional is used for conditions which are usually true at all times; that the first conditional refers to likely results of conditions in the future; that the second conditional is used to talk about improbable or impossible events in the present. If unreal conditionals do not exist in the SS' own language (e.g. Japanese) the 'concept' can be particularly difficult to grasp.

3 SS often over-generalise, and use the simple instead of the continuous form in the first and second conditional (**We won't stay if she eats.* **If it didn't rain,* (i.e. at the moment) *we wouldn't need this umbrella.*).

4 SS often have problems both in understanding and producing the contracted and weak forms of *will* and *would* as well as *was* and *were* in conditional sentences, i.e. *if I* ***were you, I'd*** (/wəjʊaɪd/).

5 Some SS (e.g. Germans) use *if* when they mean *when*, and *when* when they mean *if.*

6 SS often have problems with the meaning of *unless*, and they often follow it with a negative form (**Unless they don't pay they can't come in.*).

Wish + past or *wish* + *would*

1 Some SS think *wish* means *want* (**I wish a cup of tea.*).

2 The difference between *wish* and the past (e.g. *I* ***wish*** *you* ***spoke*** *slower.*) and *wish* and *would* (e.g *I* ***wish*** *you* ***would speak*** *slower.*) is very difficult for SS to understand. They need to be reminded that *wish* and *would* are not used with state verbs (**I wish I would be younger.*).

LISTENING

Before listening

You could ask SS to talk about the pictures before looking at the questions, and elicit words such as *famine, war, nuclear bomb.* Lead in to the questions by asking SS whether they think it is right to take photographs like this while people are suffering and dying.

You might like to tell SS some of the background to the photographs, e.g. that in the Vietnam war (1954 –1975) the Communist Viet Cong (aided by North Vietnam) tried to overturn the government of South Vietnam (aided by the US) and that the North Vietnamese finally won. Lead into the listening text by telling SS that it was Michael Buerk's news report of the 1984 famine in Ethiopia which triggered off enormous financial aid for the famine. Mention that the news report inspired singer Bob Geldof to organise a pop concert in aid of the famine, and this gave tremendous publicity to what was happening in Ethiopia.

Listening

• **Exercises 1 and 2** The aim is to see if SS can first get the gist of what Michael Buerk is talking about before trying to understand what he is saying in more detail. Don't worry too much if SS make mistakes while summarising the extract, provided they understand the main points. Stop after each extract in both exercises in order to get feedback from SS.

• **Exercise 3** If necessary, let SS read the tapescript themselves before trying to guess the meanings of the words, so that they have the complete context. Provide good bilingual or monolingual dictionaries so that they can check their guesses.

The topic (i.e. the role journalists play during disasters) is picked up in the extract of Bob Geldof's autobiography in the READING AND WRITING section, and also in the SPEAKING AND LISTENING section at the end of the unit, where MP Clare Short talks about the invasion into people's private lives by the popular press.

Sounds: /ʃ/, /tʃ/, /dʒ/

• **Exercise 1** Either tell SS how to pronounce the sounds or get them to find the sounds in the *Pronunciation* chart on SB page 149. The /ʃ/ could simply be demonstrated by getting SS to say *Be quiet* (i.e. *Shh*). The sounds /tʃ/ and /dʒ/ are both palato-alveolar fricatives, but /tʃ/ is unvoiced and /dʒ/ is voiced. These sounds cause problems for many SS (e.g. German and Dutch). Get SS to identify all three sounds in the two sentences.

• **Exercises 2 and 3** These exercises practise both recognition and production of the sounds.

READING AND WRITING

Grammatical and lexical linking words

• **Exercises 1 and 2** Refer SS back to the photos on the first page of the unit, and the dilemma about the ethics of taking photos of disasters. Then ask SS to read the text and say whether they agree with Geldof or Lennox. Perhaps refer back to the photo of Geldof in Unit 2.

• **Exercises 3 and 4** Remind SS of the importance of not repeating the same words when they are writing. The words in italics in the text are some of those commonly used to avoid repetition. More work on this will be done in Unit 16. Look out for word repetition from now on in SS' written work.

REVISION 1

Conditional sentences

• **Exercises 1, 2 and 3** These exercises are intended to remind SS about the form and use of the zero, first and second conditional forms. Exercise 3 introduces alternatives to the most common patterns, as well as typical problems with the form (including the use of *unless*). Refer SS to the *Language reference* to check their answers. (There is work on the third conditional in Unit 12.)

PRACTICE

• **Exercises 1 and 2** The aim of these exercises is to get SS to choose the appropriate form to use according to the communicative purpose of each sentence, and to provide further oral practice.

In Exercise 1 although the most obvious choice for all the sentences is the second conditional, the zero or the first conditional could be used in a), b) and d). Point out that *them* is used in sentence b) and *they* in sentence f) to avoid specifying *he* or *she*.

There are more exercises on conditional forms in the WB.

• **Exercise 4** Get SS to compare answers.

VOCABULARY

Non-idiomatic phrasal verbs

In this unit the aim is to make SS aware of how some phrasal verbs can be understood from their component parts but others (non-idiomatic phrasal verbs) cannot. You could ask SS to match the verbs not used in the exercise with their different particles and then make sentences with them.

Idiomatic phrasal verbs

• **Exercise 1** This is a dictation activity, which leads on to the next exercise. Stop the tape as necessary to allow SS time to write.

• **Exercise 2** Get SS to suggest what the meanings of the phrasal verbs in the box are and then decide which of the verbs from the dictation they could replace. There is plenty of scope in the VOCABULARY section of this unit for revision of the grammar of phrasal verbs (see Unit 9).

REVISION 2

Wanting situations to change

• **Exercise 1** This series of 'concept' questions is intended to get behind the meaning of *I wish / if only* + past (i.e. unhappiness with a present state of affairs). Make the link with the second conditional if necessary so that the meaning (i.e. it is an unreal situation, often expressed by a subjunctive in other languages) is absolutely clear, and to give extra revision of the conditional, e.g *If only I had a book to read because if I had I wouldn't be so bored.*

EXTENSION

Wanting things (not) to happen

• **Exercise 1** Point out that if we want to talk about a wish for the future we use *would* + base form of the verb. Give SS examples of state verbs (e.g. *be* or *know*), which do not take *would*, and explain that *would* is only used with 'action verbs' (e.g. *eat* or *speak*), which will possibly change (i.e. *I wish you would eat something* means the person may well eat something in the future).

• **Exercises 2 and 3** Make sure SS use the appropriate intonation when they are complaining about something.

SPEAKING AND LISTENING

Discussion

The topic looks at the question of the right of journalists to pry into people's private lives. Before listening, use the photo of the photographers to elicit views on this topic, or take into class recent newspapers with stories of scandal associated with, for example, royalty or famous people. In Britain, it tends to be the tabloids which do this. Introduce the expression *gutter press* and explain what it means (i.e. newspapers which write articles about sex and scandal, rather than give real news).

• **Exercises 1 and 2** Exercise 1 asks questions about the listening text and Exercise 2 uses the text as a stimulus for discussion. Tell SS that Clare Short is a well-known British Labour Member of Parliament. Point out that in Britain tabloids, such as *The Sun*, are the most popular newspapers, selling millions of copies a day. Ask if the fact that this sells newspapers makes printing such stories valid. You could ask SS which newspaper they read, and why.

In the WB there is a reading text on a notorious 'trial by press' incident (the 'dingo baby case') that could be tied in to classwork if you wish.

WRITING

• **Exercise 1** Make sure SS understand words such as *libel*, *sue* and *damages*. See if SS know what happens in such cases in their own countries.

• **Exercises 2 and 3** This letter is intended as a 'process writing' activity (i.e. the important thing is that SS exchange ideas, discuss how they will organise their letters, and draft the letter together rather than worry too much about following a 'model letter' format). However, you may want to remind SS before they write their final version of how to lay out a semi-formal letter (see Unit 6).

Tapescripts

RECORDING 1

Extract 1
I honestly think that a journalist's job is solely to be a professional recorder of the news, to convey to his audience, or to his readership or her audience, her readership, as clear and accurate and unambiguous a factual account of what's happening as possible. I think it's up to the people themselves when getting as accurate a picture of what's going on as possible, to decide their own point of view and then effect the changes, or effect the help - humanitarian help in the case of a famine, because they have been stirred by an accurate picture of what's going on. I don't think it's a journalist's job to do it. I think it's a propagandist's job to attempt to present things to gain a particular effect one way or another and I don't think journalists should be propagandists.

Extract 2
It's a very difficult question for a reporter. Clearly in a famine situation, and particularly in the 84-85 famine, I felt that it was my job not just to tell the facts of how many people were dead and dying and how many were likely to die and why, but also convey a feeling of what it was like to be there and in a sense, going even further in that particular instance, almost what I felt - what it felt like for me to be there. Now I think in a famine that that was a fair thing to do and a fair journalistic thing to do. It is not the sort of thing that I would do for instance covering a domestic political story where there are, you know, conflicting political views about something. But I think the famine was such a gut human disaster that I felt it needed that extra dimension to try and provide as many extra dimensions to enable people to feel what it was like to be there.

Extract 3
It is terribly difficult because it's very difficult to be an impartial observer - it's very difficult because in those circumstances, because we were European, because you know, we had transport and all that sort of thing people thought we were doctors. And we had people sort of bringing their dying children and saying you know, 'save my child' and under those sort of circumstances one feels as a journalist totally useless - as a recorder of events, what is more useless than that? You know how I wish I'd been better at physics and chemistry and biology and become a doctor or a nurse or an Oxfam worker or something or even somebody who could dig a hole, you know as part of a water project. You do feel, as a journalist, totally useless and it's it has a great impact on you, it's a very depressing feeling merely to be a recorder of events under those circumstances.

Extract 4
Yes. I mean that's bound to be the case, isn't it? I mean, to put it at its crudest if you've got a million people dying of starvation it is a quote great news story, isn't it? On the other hand it has been my experience as a newspaper reporter, radio reporter, television reporter, that while we may feel very sensitive to the crass actions of journalists in disasters it's quite often the victims of disasters and the relatives of the victims of disasters don't have the sort of

sensitivity that we impute to them, particularly people who starving whose interest is merely to focus attention on their particular plight so that help may come. They don't, I think, commonly feel exploited - in that particular way - in a way that we as outside observers might think that this misery was merely being exploited for titillation purposes.

Extract 5
Oh, I think they're absolutely vital, aren't they? I mean there are some extraordinarily talented writers who are able to conjure with their words both the facts and the emotions of occasions like that but nothing can substitute for pictures, and nothing particularly can substitute for moving pictures of what is happening when it is an event. When it comes to famine and war and things of that nature, visual events, I mean the pictures just are so so essential, pictures complemented by words and information and that extra - I mean nothing, nothing can compare with that, not even the most talented writer could possibly have had the same impact with a newspaper story in 1984-85 - or even a radio story - as the television pictures which took you there.

RECORDING 2

a) Look at those chips.
b) Did you watch it?
c) Have a sherry.
d) I think they're cheap.
e) Has he got a big gin?
f) He began to joke.
g) Don't cheer.

RECORDING 3

a) It took her ages to recover from her illness but she's all right now.
b) I'm really excited about my holiday.
c) Don't you think it was an interesting point that Mark made at the meeting?
d) My kids have never learned Spanish but they've acquired it by being on holiday in Spain.
e) I think the ice cream is finished. I'll have to get some more.
f) Tim is exactly like his Dad. He has the same sense of humour.
g) My computer has stopped working. Can you fix it?

RECORDING 4

CLARE SHORT: I say that anything I do in my public life is a matter for scrutiny by the media. If I'm a hypocrite in any way between my private and public life that is to be exposed, if I'm corrupt in any way that is to be exposed. But I am a human being and it isn't right - I mean I have a normal human life. I have a bath. I mean if the *News of the World* put a picture of me in the bath on the front page it would be true that I do have baths but it wouldn't be right. And it's both for me as me the human being but also for all of us. I think this behaviour drags our press and our culture into the gutter. It's nothing to do with investigative reporting, it's just to do with linking everyone up with something to do with sexuality that's supposed to be ideally a little bit hidden and deviant. And I think if we had a privacy law we'd actually help our press out of the gutter and we'd get very much better investigative journalism.

Key

LISTENING

Listening

1
Extract 1: d)
Extract 2: a)
Extract 3: c)
Extract 4: e)
Extract 5: b)

2
Example answers:
Extract 1: accurate
Extract 2: He felt that in this particular situation he should say what it felt like to be there.
Extract 3: He felt useless, and depressed and wished he could help as a doctor or nurse or something.
Extract 4: accurate
Extract 5: He feels pictures are essential if you want to have an impact, however talented the writer is.

Sounds: /ʃ/, /tʃ/, /dʒ/

1
actions /ækʃəns/
journalists /dʒɜːnəlɪsts/
situation /sɪtʃueɪʃən/

2
a) chips b) watch c) sherry d) cheap e) gin f) joke g) cheer

READING AND WRITING

Grammatical and lexical linking words

1
a) Geldof with one of the children Band Aid is trying to help.
b) Geldof isn't there for publicity. He is trying to help.
c) i) visiting politicians
ii) the picture of him with a starving child
iii) the picture of him with a starving child
d) The photographers can take pictures of him in the camp, take pictures of the kids, but not both together.

3
this (line 2): he doesn't want any pictures taken of him with starving children
them (line 3): pictures of visitors with starving children
the Western celebrities (line 6): the politicians
that's (line 8): the picture of Bob with one of the starving children
it (line 11): the picture of Bob with one of the starving children
their (line 13): the children's
we (line 15): the photographers
it (line 17): taking a picture of Bob and one of the starving children
the kids (line 19): the starving children at the camp
the two (line 20): the kids and Geldof

4

a) mine
b) The ones, these
c) then
d) This
e) theirs, one
f) there
g) it

REVISION 1

Conditional sentences

1

a) iii b) i c) ii

If or *when*?

Yes, in ii.

PRACTICE

1

Example answers (see Teacher's notes):

a) If you didn't like your friend's new dress, would you tell her?
b) If your best friend's partner asked you to go out with them, would you go?
c) When you have finished eating, shall we go?
d) If you broke something valuable in your parents' house, would you blame the dog?
e) If you ruled / could rule the world, what would you do?
f) If you could choose an ideal partner, what would they be like?

3

a) When b) If c) If d) When

4

Example answers:

a) We'll probably go out for a picnic tomorrow if *the weather is good.*
b) Remember to turn on the heating if *you get / feel cold.*
c) When the programme finishes, *go to bed. / I'll make the dinner.*
d) Plants die if *they don't get any water.*
e) If you don't give them any water those plants *will die.*
f) Water turns to ice when *it freezes.*

VOCABULARY

Non-idiomatic phrasal verbs

a) Put your coat on. / Put on your coat. (Picture 1)
c) pull them down. / be pulled down. (Picture 2)
g) take your hat off. / take off your hat. (Picture 3)

Idiomatic phrasal verbs

2

a) It took her ages to *get over* her illness but she's all right now.
b) I'm really *looking forward* to my holiday.
c) Don't you think it was an interesting point that Mark *brought up* at the meeting?
d) My kids have never learned Spanish but they have *picked* it *up* by being on holiday in Spain.
e) I think the ice cream has *run out.* / We have *run out of* ice cream. I'll have to get some more.
f) Tim *takes after* his Dad - he has the same sense of humour.
g) My computer has *broken down.* Can you fix it?

REVISION 2

Wanting situations to change

1

a) No.
b) No.
c) No.
d) Depressed, because the woman wants to be able to swim, the man wants to read a book and the boy wants to be at home.
e) The present
f) *If only* is slightly stronger.

3

Example answers:

1 I wish / if only I were/was young again.
2 If only / I wish I could have / had a drink.
3 If only / I wish I could give up smoking / I didn't smoke so much.

EXTENSION

Wanting things (not) to happen

Wish + would

1

a) Both.
b) Base form. No, only 'action' verbs.
c) They want something to change.

2

a) I wish the papers wouldn't write about the Royal Family so much.
I wish the government would build more car parks.
I wish supermarkets wouldn't put sweets and chocolate near the checkouts so that children can see them.

SPEAKING AND LISTENING

Discussion

1

a) Anything to do with her public life deserves to be exposed, for example if she's a hypocrite or corrupt.
b) Linking everyone to sexuality, which has nothing to do with investigative reporting. For example, if they put a picture of her in the bath in the newspaper.
c) A privacy law, which would help the press out of the gutter and mean that we would get better investigative journalism.

Unit 12

Crime and passion

Students' Book

General theme: media.
Unit topic: crime and punishment.

READING: newspaper articles about crimes of passion (jigsaw reading); related vocabulary.
VOCABULARY: law and order; shifting word stress: stress in nouns and verbs.

WRITING: summary writing (comparing factual and non-factual language).
EXTENSION 1: regrets and criticism (third conditional and *wish*); connected speech (conditional forms).

REVISION AND EXTENSION 2: *should / shouldn't (have).*
SPEAKING: discussion of moral issues.

Workbook

VOCABULARY: crime and punishment (types of crimes and names of criminals); nouns and prepositions.
LISTENING: extracts from a radio programme about homicide in Britain; vocabulary in context.
GRAMMAR: past conditional and *wish*; *wish* and *if only*; criticisms should (not) have.
WRITING: summary of an article.

Language

This unit builds on work done in Unit 11 (and before that in *Intermediate Matters*) by introducing the third conditional and *wish* + Past Perfect to talk about unreal situations in the past which often involve regret and criticism. By this level the meaning of the third conditional should be clear to SS. Any problems are usually connected to the form, including the pronunciation.

The unit also practises *should(n't) have*, introduced in Unit 6.

The advantage of introducing and practising these language forms together (third conditional, *wish* and *should(n't) have*) is that they all link semantically and are therefore easily contextualised.

Common problems

Third conditional

1 For many SS the main problem is simply getting their tongues around the construction. There is also a tendency to get the clauses mixed up (**If I would have stayed, I had seen it.*) and the problem of remembering to use the Past Perfect. Other problems include whether to choose the simple or continuous form as well as choosing the correct past participle in both clauses.

2 It is very difficult for SS to recognise the structure in conversation, because of the tendency of native speakers to use contractions and weak forms (*If I'd known, I'd've come.*). It is even more difficult for SS to produce it, so they need plenty of practice!

3 SS have a tendency to avoid using the continuous form and *would* tends to be over-used where native speakers would use a modal verb such as *may/might* (e.g. *If I'd known, I* ***may have*** *phoned.*).

4 In the main clause the use of *would/may*, etc. with *be* is common if the situation is still possible (e.g. *If it hadn't stopped raining, I* ***would still be*** *there now.*).

Wish + Past Perfect

SS at this level have a tendency to get confused with the form of the different *wish* clauses, although the concept is probably clear to them. Just as the present tense changes to the past tense when talking about unreal situations in the present (e.g. *I wish it were summer.*), the past becomes the Past Perfect when talking about unreal events in the past (e.g.*I wish I'd remembered to say goodbye.*).

Should(n't) have

The main problem here will probably be the choice between using the simple or continuous (e.g. *You shouldn't have said that.*, but *It's your fault! You shouldn't have been smoking in the library.*).

READING

Before reading

• **Exercise 1** PW/GW? This is a prediction exercise based on headlines. Tell SS that both the stories are true and encourage SS to speculate about them as much as possible. Notice that both stories focus on domestic violence. You will probably need to explain the meaning of *snapped.*

• **Exercise 3** Perhaps elicit examples of premeditated and unpremeditated crimes, using real-life examples where possible. You could brainstorm words and expressions associated with murder, such as *strangle, shoot, poison,* etc.

Reading

• **Exercise 1** This is a jigsaw reading activity. Tell SS which text to read and get them to discuss their answers in groups after reading the text individually. In this way weaker SS can help stronger ones and all SS will have understood the main part of the story before beginning the information exchange. Tell them not to worry about understanding all the vocabulary (there are exercises on this later), but help with any words which may be necessary for basic understanding of the story. Make sure they understand the questions before they read (i.e. what is a *victim* and *accused*?), and impress upon them the fact that they are taking notes, not writing complete sentences. In c) and d) they may have to make inferences based on the text.

• **Exercise 2** Divide SS into pairs so that they can exchange information. Encourage them to ask any other questions they want answered, based on what they wanted to know in the *Before reading* activity.

• **Exercise 3** Give SS a time limit to read the other story, or set it as a reading activity for homework and do the exercises in the following lesson. The exercises give practice in asking questions. You could ask SS to work out the questions in pairs and then do class feedback.

• **Exercise 4** More work on the language of 'punishment' is given in the VOCABULARY section. You may want to bring this in at this point.

• **Exercise 5** PW? This follows on from work on phrasal verbs done in Unit 11. You could ask SS which phrasal verbs are the idiomatic ones. You may want to point out the nouns made from some of these phrasal verbs (*takeover, handover, breakdown*) and the different stress pattern in phrasal nouns.

• **Exercise 6** PW? You could link this exercise to the next section by getting SS to underline any other words which are new to them, as well as vocabulary connected to law and order.

VOCABULARY

Law and order

• **Exercises 1 and 2** If you think SS have had enough of the texts, a different approach is to give SS the words (on the board, or on cards) in jumbled order, so they can match the word to the sentence. Alternatively, give them the correct word for each sentence but jumble the letters, e.g. a) = *trarse* (*arrest*). Draw SS' attention to collocations such as *plead guilty, on trial.* You could, of course, use the photograph to elicit some vocabulary.

• **Exercises 3 and 4** Exercise 3 could be done as a prioritising activity. Encourage SS to give reasons for their priority and suggest punishments. In multinational classes it would be interesting to compare different types of sentence given in different countries.

In the WB there is another related word-building activity on crimes and criminals.

Shifting word stress

• **Exercise 1** In English many words change their stress pattern according to the grammatical function (e.g. *'import* – noun; *im'port* – verb). The aim of this exercise is to make SS aware of this and to remind them of how to mark the position of the stressed syllable.

• **Exercise 2** PW? Get SS to try reading the sentences aloud in pairs before they decide where they think the stressed syllable is.

• **Exercise 3** Encourage SS to repeat what they heard on the tape and identify which syllable was stressed.

• **Exercise 4** PW? Remind SS how to check the stressed syllable in the dictionary.

WRITING

Summary writing

• **Exercise 1** The aim of this exercise is to get SS to sort out the important facts in a text from what is 'padding', before rewriting it in a shortened form. Make sure SS have time to discuss and justify what they felt was not essential information and then encourage them to prioritise the 'important facts'. There may, of course, be quite valid differences of opinion. For example, they may feel that the fact that Corlett is described as 'mild-mannered' is directly relevant to the crime.

• **Exercise 2** Try to get SS to decide on a topic sentence for each paragraph in the summary, and when they are writing it up remind them to think about linking words and expressions, and to check their work for correct punctuation and grammar.

If the class is in an English-speaking country, you could take the opportunity to compare two different versions of the same newspaper story – a 'serious' one (in one of the 'quality' papers) and a more gossipy one.

There is a similar summary-writing activity for extra practice in the WB.

EXTENSION 1

Regrets and criticism

Third conditional and *wish*

• **Exercises 1 and 2** The aim of these exercises is to focus SS' attention on both the meaning and form of the third (or past) conditional and *wish* + Past Perfect. Refer SS to the *Language reference* to check their answers to Exercise 2. (The answer to 2c) could also be 'Past Perfect'.).

Past hypothesis

It is important that SS realise that the third conditional is not always used for regret and criticism (e.g. *If I'd seen him, I would have told you.*). This exercise also serves as a reminder that other modals such as *may* are possible in place of *would*, and that the main clause can also be formed with the base form of the verb instead of *would have* + past participle (e.g. *If she'd taken that job, she* ***may not be*** *here today.*).

Connected speech

• **Exercises 1-3** The aim of these exercises is to practise weak and contracted forms in conditional sentences. Point out the tendency to contract and/or weaken *had, have* and *would* in conditional sentences, and get SS to repeat the 'model sentence' (*If this had happened here* ...) after listening. You could get SS to divide the sentences into two and practise both parts separately. In Exercise 3 make sure SS are aware that auxiliaries such as *been* and *were* are also weak, and help them not to stress prepositions, pronouns, etc. by getting them to identify and put the main stress on the word which comes before or after (e.g. *I wouldn't even* ***think*** *of it.*).

PRACTICE

• **Exercises 1 and 2** These give more practice in pronouncing the sentences, and link the meaning of the conditional sentences with *wish* (i.e. for unreal past situations).

• **Exercise 3** If you ask SS to give reasons for their regrets they will probably use the third conditional (or perhaps *should have*) quite naturally.

REVISION AND EXTENSION 2

Should / shouldn't (have)

• **Exercise 1** It might be possible to lead in to this exercise by finding an example personal to the SS (e.g. *If you want to pass this exam, what should you do?*).

• **Exercise 5** Possibly use the pictures to elicit what Louise did before focusing on what she *should* or *shouldn't have done*. (e.g. *She packed her suitcase that morning, but she should have packed it the night before.*).

There is another exercise on *should have* in the WB.

SPEAKING

When reading the instructions make sure that SS remember what the meaning of *sentence* is. The main focus in this activity is on fluency and giving opinions, but clearly it is also a good opportunity to revise *should / shouldn't have* and the vocabulary of punishments. The activity should also generate the use of the second conditional (e.g. *I would sentence him to ...*).

You might also be able to link the situations with something that is actually happening or has recently happened in the news.

Tapescripts

RECORDING 1

The police arrested the convict.
The police had to convict him.

RECORDING 2

a) The protest was fairly peaceful.
b) I want to protest.
c) Imports are rising sharply.
d) We need to import more coal.
e) Have you bought your mother a present?
f) They presented him with a gold watch.
g) If you don't work you won't make any progress.
h) He has progressed at an amazing rate.

RECORDING 3

[See Key.]

RECORDING 4

a) If it had been working properly I could have done it.
b) She might have agreed if the job had paid more.
c) If I were you I wouldn't even think of it.
d) He would have had a shock if he'd seen her.
e) I couldn't really go unless the boss agreed to it.

RECORDING 5

SAM: It was all my fault. I mean I wish now I hadn't been so thoughtless. I used to come back late from work, after stopping off at the pub on the way home, and didn't lift a finger to help when I did get home. I should've helped more with the baby and things like that.

FRIEND: Well yes, the main thing if you ask me is that you shouldn't have taken on that new job in London when she'd just had a baby.

RECORDING 6

1 I wish now I hadn't been so thoughtless.
2 I should have helped more with the baby.
3 . . . you shouldn't have taken on that new job.

RECORDING 7

SAM: I know, I mean I'd just collapse in front of the TV and show no interest in what her day had been like or anything, I was so tired. And then there were a lot of other things like we never went out on our own anywhere because I couldn't be bothered to get a babysitter - we never did anything together. I used to shout at the dog, which she loved, all the time. I never really said anything nice to her - I don't blame her for leaving me, actually.

Key

READING

Reading

1

Text A

Example answers:

a) She was strangled.
b) Because of a row over some mustard.
c) She was untidy, thoughtless.
d) He is a perfectionist, houseproud, of 'impeccable character', mild mannered.
e) Three years in jail for manslaughter.

Text B

Example answers:

a) He was stabbed.
b) He was violent to his wife.
c) He was violent, difficult, depressed.
d) He is quiet, well-spoken, non-violent, courageous.
e) Three years probation for manslaughter.

3

Text A

Example answers:

a) What was Corlett found guilty of?
b) How long did it take the jury to decide whether Corlett was guilty or not?
c) How long had Corlett and his wife been married?
d) What were they having for supper on the day of the crime?
e) What did Corlett do when his wife fell down unconscious?

Text B

Example answers:

a) What did Peter use to kill his father?
b) What was Peter like? / What kind of person was Peter?
c) Why did Peter kill his father?
d) Why did his father lose his job?
e) When did he lose his job?

5

Example answers:

a) started doing / taken responsibility for
b) put it down violently / noisily
c) gave it
d) intervened / joined in
e) collapsed / stopped

6

Text A

Example answers:

a) (household) chores
b) craving
c) rage
d) grabbed
e) lenient

Text B

Example answers:

a) a bond
b) half-hearted
c) a burden

VOCABULARY

Law and order

2

a) arrest b) court c) plead d) witness e) jury f) judge

5

a) The person will only be sent to prison if he or she commits another crime within a certain time.
b) The person is free but must be regularly visited by or report to a probation officer.
c) The person is free until their trial but has to guarantee a sum of money that they will appear in court.

Shifting word stress

1

The police arrested the *'convict*.
The police had to *con'vict* him.

2

a) 'protest
b) pro'test
c) 'Imports
d) im'port
e) 'present
f) pre'sented
g) 'progress
h) pro'gressed

4

a), d), e), f) and h) have the same stress pattern for both verbs and nouns.

WRITING

Summary writing

1

a) Example notes:

A They had a row over a tube of mustard.
Corlett was jailed for three years.
He denied murdering his wife.
He was found guilty of manslaughter.
They had been married for 26 years.
Corlett grabbed his wife during the quarrel.
Corlett called an ambulance when she fell unconscious.
Corlett's boss gave him a glowing reference.

B He was a houseproud husband.
He was a 58-year-old balding civil servant.
His wife became ill with asthma.
In 1985 she forgot to send him a birthday card.
They had a supper of sausages, green beans and mashed potatoes at their home in Middlesex.
It was a tube of German mustard.

EXTENSION 1

Regrets and criticism

1

a) True b) False c) False d) True

Connected speech

1

If this had happened here, the boy would have gone to prison.

2

a) If it had been working properly, I could have done it.
b) She might have agreed if the job had paid more.
c) If I were you, I wouldn't even think of it.
d) He would have had a shock if he had seen her.
e) I couldn't really go unless the boss agreed to it.

PRACTICE

1

a)

a) 2 b) 3 c) 4 d) 1

2

a)

Example sentences:

b) If Tom Willis hadn't gone on holiday to Russia, he wouldn't have met Ludmilla. If he hadn't met her, he wouldn't have thrown up his well-paid job.
c) If the World Wide Fund for Nature hadn't set up reserves, tigers might have disappeared completely by now.
d) If Steve Perry hadn't gone to that fish restaurant, he wouldn't have been ill. If he hadn't been ill, he would have played better and his team might have won.

b)

Example answers:

i) I wish I'd never met Ludmilla. If only I had stayed in Britain!
ii) I wish we'd chosen another restaurant. If only I hadn't got food poisoning!

REVISION AND EXTENSION 2

Should/shouldn't (have)

2

Example answers:

a) coming back late from work
stopping off at the pub
not lifting a finger to help at home
not helping with the baby
b) taking the new job in London when she'd just had a baby

3

a)

I wish now I hadn't been so thoughtless.
I should've helped more with the baby. (Sam)
You shouldn't have taken on that new job ... (Sam's friend)

4

Example answers:

You should have shown more interest in what kind of day she'd had; you should have gone out more together; you shouldn't have shouted at the dog; you should have said nice things to her.

5

Example answers:

1) She should have packed the day before.
2) She should have left earlier / gone by train.
3) She should have made sure she knew where she was going. / looked at the map before.
4) She should have gone to the bank the day before.

Unit 13

Just a piece of paper?

Students' Book

General theme: social customs.
Unit topic: wedding customs.

LISTENING: a Gujarati Indian talking about his two weddings to his Swedish wife.
REVISION: the passive.

EXTENSION 1: need(s) to be done.
EXTENSION 2: *have (get)* something done / do it oneself (including reflexives).
VOCABULARY: idiomatic expressions connected to relationships (e.g. *split up with*); sounds /ɒ/, /ɔ:/, /əʊ/.

SPEAKING: discussion on marriage.
WRITING: the story of a wedding ceremony from notes.

Workbook

READING: magazine article about divorce in different parts of the world.
GRAMMAR: the passive; pronouns (reflexive, possessive and object); *have (get)* something done; idiomatic expressions with parts of the body (e.g. *pain in the neck*).
VOCABULARY: newspaper headlines.
WRITING: letter of invitation.

Language

This unit revises the passive and extends into other constructions, like *needs* + *to be done* and the causative (*have/get something done*).

SS at this level should have little difficulty with the form of the passive but will still need help with when best to use the construction in English. They need to realise that it often has the effect of sounding detached and impersonal. In some contexts this is necessary because we are not interested in (or don't know) *who* did something; in others it allows the speaker not to commit themselves personally to something. SS also need help with the tendency in English to use the passive to highlight new information by putting it at the end of a sentence (*The symphony you are listening to was written by Beethoven.*) and also in writing to put longer and 'heavier' expressions at the end of a sentence (*The window was broken by a young boy who lives on the other side of the street.*).

Common problems

The passive and causative

1 SS often confuse the active *be* + *-ing* (*was giving*) with the passive *be* + past participle (*was given*), and the passive *be* + past participle (*was given*) with the active *have* + past participle (*has given*) (**She has given a new watch for her birthday.*). The pronunciation can sound very similar.

2 There are many differences in the form and use of the passive with most other languages. For example, in most languages except English you cannot use the indirect object as the subject of a passive verb (*I was given a lovely watch for my birthday.*). Also some English passives (*I was born in...*) would not be passives in some other languages and some active English verbs, especially verbs of position (e.g. *he is sitting*), might be passives. And the Japanese can make passives for people but not for things.

3 Note that some active verbs (e.g. *sell, wash, need*) can have a passive meaning (*Some jumpers don't wash well.*). *Need* can be followed by *-ing* and have a passive meaning (*Your hair needs washing.*). However, in this unit this use is avoided in favour of *needs to be done.*

4 The word *get* normally implies a change of state (*get married*) – see Unit 2. In the passive it can be used instead of *be* for things done suddenly and unexpectedly (*He got killed by a terrorist.*). In the causative (*have something done*) *get* can be used instead of *have* to imply difficulty (*I finally got my car repaired.*) or to give an order (*Get your hair cut!*). SS will need to learn the limitations of *get* but at this level it is probably better to regard *get* in causative sentences as interchangeable with *have* (*have* or *get your eyes tested*). Also, past participles will still need revising.

5 The causative structure does not exist in some languages (e.g. Greek, Arabic and Japanese).

Reflexives

1 In English there are very few verbs that must be followed by a reflexive pronoun and quite a few where it is optional (e.g. *behave* or *behave yourself*). Also, verbs which have to be followed by a *-self* word when there is no other complement (e.g. *enjoy yourself, hurt himself*) are not followed by a *-self* word when followed by an ordinary object (*I enjoyed the film.*).

2 When the subject and object of a verb are the same person (*She dried herself.*) the verb must be followed by a *-self* word, not an object pronoun (*her*). In Latin languages, reflexive pronouns are the same as the object pronouns (**I cut me on some glass.*) and there may be no distinction between 'ourselves' and 'each other' (**We looked at us.*).

3 Some everyday things we do to ourselves (e.g. *get dressed, get up, sit down*) are expressed with reflexive verbs in some other European languages (**I dressed me.*). However, we can (but rarely do) use reflexives with verbs like *wash, dress, shave* (*He washed and* ... or *He washed himself and...*). For more on reflexives refer to *Longman English Grammar,* pages 82–4 (see *Bibliography*).

LISTENING

Before listening

This section raises the issue of how people from a different culture and background come to terms with the new society they are living in, in this case in relation to weddings and marriage.

It also asks SS to quickly talk about their views on 'arranged marriages'. Overall, it's best to keep the topic fairly light at this stage and not to go into it in depth since the exercise is a warm-up for the *Listening* to follow. Note that the headline is only loosely linked to the photograph. There will be an opportunity later for further discussion.

One possible advantage of 'arranged marriages' could be that couples don't expect too much of each other. One possible disadvantage could be that the parents' social and financial interests may be more important than the couple's emotional needs.

You could ask SS which countries they know have arranged marriages and how the system works. Ask them whether they would like (would have liked) their own marriage to be arranged.

Listening

• **Exercise 1** This is a prediction exercise which gives SS a reason for listening. (Possible answers are given in the Key.) Note that a Gujarati Indian comes from Gujarat, a region in West India.

• **Exercise 2** This is for gist and intensive listening. Get SS to make notes for a) and b) and compare their answers in pairs. Check answers by listening to the extract again.

• **Exercise 3** This is for intensive listening. Stop the tape at the relevant points and possibly encourage PW discussion of the answers.

• **Exercise 4** PW? Notice that the gaps lend themselves to passive constructions, the language focus of the unit. It's probably better not to tell SS this and see how easily and accurately they use them. This will help you decide how much practice work will be necessary later. To give SS time to write, stop the tape where necessary or allow SS to do the exercise in a language laboratory.

REVISION

The passive

• **Exercise 1** You could write the model sentence on the board, ask the SS what the form is (*be* + past participle) and where the stress is. Then elicit a similar sentence in the active (e.g. *My parents arranged my brother's marriage.*) and make a comparison between the active and the passive. Ask *why* Satish used the passive (i.e. because information about *who* arranged the marriage is not relevant here). Point out the weak form (/wəs/) and note there is an exercise on weak forms of the passive in the WB which can be done as follow-up, possibly as homework.

• **Exercises 2 and 3** Since context, purpose and effect are very important in the use of the passive in English, it is worth spending time on these exercises. Note that while the passive is more often used in written language (particularly newspapers, reports, scientific writing, notices and announcements), it can also be used in spoken English (*The train's been cancelled.*). You could get SS to brainstorm a list of common contexts, or take some texts, such as newspapers, to the class to get SS to find examples.

• **Exercise 4** This is a tricky exercise for many nationalities (see *Common problems – The passive*, 2 above). Do as PW? Emphasise that 'new information' is what is perceived to be new in the context by the speaker and that the tendency in English is to put such information at the end of a sentence. Possibly, for each answer, ask SS when one form would be used instead of the other.

• **Exercise 5** The aim of this exercise is freer practice of the passive. Warm SS up by asking what their favourite drink is and if they know how it is made. Make it absolutely clear that SS have to include articles, prepositions, etc. by doing an example with them first. Groups should decide what the expanded notes would be and then write them down before comparing their answers. Notice that *wine* refers to both 2 and 4. Part b) gives SS practice of the question form.

EXTENSION 1

Need(s) to be done

• **Exercise 1** In Britain the post-marriage celebration is called a 'reception' at which friends and family eat and drink. At a traditional wedding, the newly-married couple leave the reception early to go on their honeymoon. In a multinational class SS can make cross-cultural comparisons.

• **Exercise 2** This is an opportunity to practise not only the 'target structure' but the passive (*Have the invitations been sent out?*), as well as the functional language of complaints (*Why haven't you...? I thought I told you...*), excuses (*I was going to do it but...; Sorry, but...*) and promises (*Don't worry, I'll...*). You could do this as a dialogue with the whole class first to practise the functional language. Allow SS to extend their dialogues a little if they wish.

EXTENSION 2

Have (*get*) something done / do it oneself

• **Exercise 1** PW discussion? This exercise encourages SS to work out some grammar rules for themselves. In a) possibly ask SS why. It contrasts the idea of getting somebody to do something for you (*have the video mended*) with the idea of doing it for yourself. It also contrasts the use of a *-self* word as emphasis (*I did it myself.*) with a *-self* word as a reflexive (*I enjoyed myself.*). Although there are differences between *get* and *have* in *have (get) something done* (see *Common problems* above), it might be best to teach them here as interchangeable. At the end of the exercise refer SS to section 3 of the *Language reference*. Some SS might need to do the revision of pronouns in the WB.

• **Exercise 2** This provides practice for Exercise 1. Either elicit a variety of answers orally or get SS to decide on answers in pairs.

• **Exercise 3** This exercise can be done with SS getting up and mingling with each other around the room or by PW and GW. See if SS can draw any conclusions about each other's character (e.g. independent or dependent? Hard-working or lazy?).

VOCABULARY

Relationships

• **Exercise 1** Do this as PW, getting SS to talk about how many of the expressions they know without referring to the dictionary. See if they can add other expressions to the box (e.g. *have a row*).

• **Exercise 2** This exercise helps SS relate the expressions to a context and pay attention to collocation (e.g. note that *love at first sight* is usually preceded by *it was/is*).

Get SS to record the expressions they want to remember in an 'Idioms' section or a 'Relationships' section in their vocabulary records. Possibly ask them if they know any proverbs/clichés about love and ask them whether they believe them (e.g. *The course of true love never runs smooth. Absence makes the heart grow fonder. Love makes the world go round. Money can't buy you love.*).

Sounds: /ɒ/, /ɔː/, /əʊ/

• **Exercise 1** Get SS to practise the sounds in isolation after listening to them. Both the /ɒ/ sound and the /ɔː/ sound are made at the back of the mouth. The lips are rounded with the body (but not the tip) of the tongue raised. However, the /ɔː/ sound is long and the mouth less open than it is for the /ɒ/ sound. If necessary, show SS how the sounds are made and get them to imitate you. In diphthongs like /əʊ/ there is a glide from the first vowel sound (/ə/) to the next (/ʊ/), with the first sound (/ə/) more prominent. If SS have problems get them to make the schwa sound (/ə/) and then tighten the mouth (make it rounder) to get the second sound (/ʊ/).

• **Exercise 3** Other /ɒ/ words are: *dog, olive, wander, promise, watch;* other /ɔː/ words are: *warm, talk, almost, floor, naughty, water;* other /əʊ/ words are: *hope, grow, ghost, oak, show, joke.*

SPEAKING

• **Exercises 1 and 2** The aim is to stimulate discussion on marriage (including weddings and divorce). The first article presents plural marriage in a positive light. (SS might need help with the phrase *juggle their career.*) You could ask SS whether such arrangements are possible in their country and what the advantages and disadvantages are. The second article contrasts marriage with 'living together'. During the GW in Exercise 2, in a mixed nationality class, interesting cultural comparisons should emerge as well as different personal attitudes. Note that e) is not necessarily the same as a plural marriage – it could be going out with another person while married to one person. Try to be sensitive to any personal problems in the class (e.g. SS whose parents have been recently divorced) and encourage discussion of opinion rather than personal experience. Other ways of dealing with the questions in Exercise 2: do them as a survey questionnaire; in a multinational class get 'similar' nationalities to sit together (e.g. catholic Europeans) and then compare their conclusions with other nationalities; ask different groups to focus on different questions.

• **Exercises 3-5** This should be a light-hearted discussion. In a mixed-sex class you could divide the class into male and female groups before each S joins up with someone from the opposite sex for Exercise 4. The 'living together' can of course be within a marriage. Some couples these days prefer a 'personal contract' even in a marriage. (Other things that could be discussed: twin or double-beds; who uses the car and when; who does the gardening; what happens if they disagree about which TV programme to watch; what they do if they get tired of each other, etc.). Note that 'reporting back on disagreements' is more interesting than talking about 'agreements'. Perhaps the rest of the class could make suggestions about how to compromise.

WRITING

Writing from notes

This section could be a jumping-off point for a comparison of different wedding and marriage customs in different countries and for different religions (e.g. Taoist customs in China; Muslim customs in the Middle-East). You could bring in (or ask SS to bring in) books on the subject. In a multinational class you might compare customs of the SS through a questionnaire. Notice that the focus is very much on the process and a sequence of events. This allows for the passive to come up naturally in both the reading (*...is suddenly carried off*) and the writing (*They were collected from the hotel...*).

• **Exercises 1 and 2** These exercises help SS think about how to organise a text which describes a process. Do as PW/GW? You could get SS to summarise the article in note form.

• **Exercise 3** This wedding is obviously very commercial in an American kind of way. Possibly get SS (PW or GW) to talk through the notes first and make sure they understand everything. Then get them to discuss how they will divide their notes into sections before they do a draft. Help them with any difficult vocabulary (e.g. *regular, glossy, tuxedo, limousine, vows*). Remind them to use appropriate linking expressions (e.g. *however*).

• **Exercise 4** You could give SS a checklist so that they can correct their own work before passing it on to another S for 'editing', e.g.

Is all the information included?
Does one thing follow another logically?
Is the writing clear and easy to understand?
Are all the sentences necessary?
Is there repetition?
Do things need to be put into a different order?
Are the links between paragraphs clear?
Does the text communicate effectively?

When SS work on their colleagues' descriptions make sure they react positively to the good points as well as suggesting improvements. Tell them to focus not only on grammar and vocabulary but sentence/paragraph construction and general organisation.

Tapescripts

RECORDING 1

INTERVIEWER: Satish, you've married your wife twice. Can you explain why?

SATISH: Yes, well my wife, Barbrô, she's Swedish and my parents, they are Gujarati Indian, and so we had two ceremonies, one to satisfy my parents' wishes and one to satisfy Barbrô and her parents' wishes.

INTERVIEWER: How did the Swedish ceremony compare with the Hindu wedding?

SATISH: Different . . . very different, in for example length. The Hindu wedding took seven hours, the Swedish wedding in church took maybe thirty-five, forty minutes at the most. The number of people, the Hindu wedding had up towards 800 people, the ritual was very different. In the Swedish wedding I knew what the priest was saying. I knew . . . I could understand every single word. Everybody was listening to what was being said by the priest. In the Hindu wedding ... I was being asked to do things by the priest. The priest would give me the instructions in a language, Swedish or English, that I could understand but the Hindu priest said everything in Sanskrit, which is a very old language, which . . . of which I have no knowledge whatsoever, so that was also very different. We weren't the centre of attention in the Hindu wedding: families were meeting; we were seeing people that we hadn't seen for a long time; perhaps future marriages were being arranged because everybody was dressed very smart, we were all of the same caste there, so there were all these aspects. And one other thing is actually timing; the Swedish wedding I had to get there to the church at five o'clock, I had to get out by a certain time, the car was going to pick us up at a certain time, etcetera. It was very time-oriented. The Hindu wedding, it started when it got round to starting and it carried on and it finished when it finished. There was no time element to it.

INTERVIEWER: Of the two weddings, which was the real one for you?

SATISH: I have to say that they were both because I belong to two cultures, both a Gujarati one and a Western one for want of a word and they were equally important; the first one when I married, when I got married in Sweden was something very important for my wife and her family and my Western friends; and the wedding that I had in Britain with my family there was very, very important to them.

INTERVIEWER: Do your parents share that view?

SATISH: Well, for my parents, the real wedding came when we were in Britain, when we had the Hindu ceremony. Because, for example, when people have a registered marriage according to different . . . according to their Government, their country, this is just seen as a bureaucratic OK, whereas the Hindu wedding is the one that counts for them.

RECORDING 2

INTERVIEWER: Your marriage wasn't an arranged marriage. Is that because you don't believe in arranged marriages?

SATISH: My marriage wasn't an arranged marriage because it wasn't something for me. My, my older brother for example, three years older than myself, his marriage was arranged. He and his wife are very happy, all of . . ., nearly all of my friends who have got married have had arranged marriages and they're also happy in theirs. I'm also happy in mine. It just means that it wasn't for me.

INTERVIEWER: How can you defend arranged marriages to somebody who doesn't believe in them?

SATISH: Arranged marriages have a faith for tomorrow. What I mean by that is, it's not only your feelings, what you feel that day. In a relationship you meet somebody and it's very exciting and you learn to know each other and you do many things together and it's great fun, it's a wonderful feeling. But when those original, when these fresh feelings begin to die off and you still have each other you know a lot of each other. Is that a time then to throw away the relationship and start all over again or can you build upon it? An arranged marriage is where, although you don't have this love for each other you know that your love will develop, you will learn to love, but in fact in an arranged marriage people, the people who meet they know each other before their marriage, or at least their parents know each other's background, your family backgrounds are known, you've been checked out, they know that you are not a bad person or a drunk or somebody who's aggressive or etcetera, and therefore in some ways you know each other before you've met. I'd like to make an important point here I think: an arranged marriage is exactly that: it's arranged, it's not necessarily forced. Some people, of course, I think a minority have had a forced marriage where this person has been told that you're going to marry this other person but in the case of my friends, and my brother who had an arranged marriage, they had met one or two or three people. My brother had met one or two or three girls before he found somebody who he thought 'I am compatible with this person' and therefore it was arranged. My brother didn't have the choice of getting married or not but he did have the choice of marrying the person that he wanted to marry.

INTERVIEWER: How do the courtship rituals differ?

SATISH: Well, an arranged marriage courtship is under supervision. People, the couple that were engaged would, could go out together but it would be a few hours and they'd get back before a certain time, no overnight stays or anything of that kind. It's done so that the, both the bride and groom keep their respect of each other up until the wedding ceremony, the idea being that both will be pure up until the wedding ceremony.

RECORDING 3

/ɒ/ got, /ɔː/ door, /əʊ/ blow

RECORDING 4

straw, throat, sorry, off, thought, over, all, go, open, cough, home, horse

Key

LISTENING

Before listening

Example answers:

a) Because they don't regard their legal marriage in Britain in a registry office as their real one; their real one is the Hindu wedding they have afterwards.
b) Because their parents are keeping them pure for their marriage.

Listening

1

Example answers:

The Swedish wedding was the quickest and very time-oriented (in and out at set times).

There were a lot more guests at the Hindu wedding with families meeting and even arranging future marriages.

At the Hindu wedding Satish and Barbrô were not the centre of attention.

The ritual was very different: at the Swedish wedding the priest spoke in Swedish and everyone understood; at the Hindu wedding the priest spoke in Sanskrit, an old language, which neither Satish or Barbrô understand.

2

a) For Satish both weddings were equally important for different reasons (the Swedish one was for Barbrô and her family; the Hindu wedding was for his family).
b) For Satish's parents the real one was the Hindu wedding; registry office weddings are just a bureaucratic necessity to them.

3

a) He thinks 'arranged marriages' are fine but it wouldn't suit him to have had one.
b) In an 'arranged marriage' although you may not love each other when you marry, love develops over time.
c) Your partner's parents won't let you marry until they've checked that you have a suitable character and background.
d) In an 'arranged marriage' you can't choose whether or not to get married but you can usually choose who you marry from two or three candidates.

4

a) got/was married
b) was asked
c) were being arranged
d) are seen
e) is . . . forced
f) are checked out

REVISION

The passive

1

a) verb *be* + past participle.
b) The past participle is usually stressed; the form of the verb *be* is usually weak.

2

a) A notice on public transport - the passive gives the impression of an impersonal authority and is very formal.
b) In a conversation about a novel - the passive is used to continue the theme (the novel) and new information is highlighted by being put at the end.
c) A politician - the passive is used to shift personal responsibility away from the speaker.
d) Newspaper headline (abbreviated) - we don't need to know who arrested the politician; what is important is what happened to him.

3

a) Because the focus is on what the doer (Gascoigne) does, not what happens to him.
b) Because the focus is on the doer, Dick Francis, not the book.

4

a) The papers were handed to the invigilator.
b) The person who found the wallet was offered a reward.
c) His wife was left a lot of money by an unknown stranger.
d) A trip on the Orient Express has been promised to the woman who cured him of his sickness.

5

a)

1 First, real coffee is made with hot water. The water is then evaporated and the powder which is left is instant coffee.
2 The world's most expensive bottle of wine was sold in London in 1985 for $105,000. It was a bottle of 1787 Chateau Lafite, once owned by the third American president, Thomas Jefferson. When it was opened it was found to be undrinkable.
3 Vintage champagne is made from white grapes grown in northern France and has to be kept for 15 years in bottles before it can be drunk.
4 The process of wine-making was started 4,000 years ago in Egypt. The wine was kept in large pots.
6 In Germany 150 litres (33 gallons) of beer are drunk on average per person a year.

b)

Example answers:
2 What was the world's most expensive bottle of wine? What happened when it was opened?
3 How long does vintage champagne have to be kept?
4 How long has the skill of wine-making been known?
5 How are fizzy drinks made?
6 How much beer is drunk in Germany?

EXTENSION 2

Have (get) something done / do it oneself

1

a) i)
b) The word emphasises the speaker did it. Yes.
c) No, it is a reflexive. The speaker enjoyed him/herself - not anything else.

2

Example answers:
a) 's going to look after him herself.
b) have a tooth out
c) have (get) one made
d) do it ourselves
e) have (get) your eyes tested
f) have (get) it cut
g) made it themselves
h) have (get) one taken
i) myself

VOCABULARY

Relationships

1

a) split up with; fall out about
b) love at first sight; going out together
c) on the rocks
d) going round in circles
e) heart's in the right place; off the deep end

Sounds: /ɒ/, /ɔː/, /əʊ/

2

a) sorry, off, cough
b) straw, thought, all, horse
c) throat, over, open, go, home

WRITING

Writing from notes

1

D, B, A, F, C

2

Example answers:
a) In paragraph A words or phrases which refer back are: the girl's family, in B the girl, in C couples are married, in E the shock reaction, the family
b) Paragraph D is a kind of general introduction to the topic (therefore the opening); paragraph C extends from the topic into another area (and is likely to be at the end).

Mind your manners

Students' Book

General theme: social customs.
Unit topic: customs and manners.

SPEAKING 1: discussion on acceptable public behaviour.
READING: extract from *A Year in Provence* (about people's behaviour in public); corrective (contrastive) stress.

REVISION: *-ing* form or *to* + base form after different parts of speech and after different verbs.
EXTENSION: *-ing* form or *to* + base form after certain verbs which cause a change in meaning (*forget,* etc.).
VOCABULARY: connotation of adjectives.

SPEAKING 2: discussion of national stereotypes.
WRITING: tourist brochure.

Workbook

LISTENING: extract from a radio programme about bad manners; vocabulary in context.
GRAMMAR: verb + object + *to* + base form; *-ing* or *to* + base form after different verbs; expressing preferences (*prefer / would prefer; rather / would rather*).
VOCABULARY: positive and negative connotation of different adjectives; ambiguity (two meanings of *curious,* etc.); proverbs (e.g. *Absence makes the heart grow fonder.*).
WRITING: spelling.

Language

SS will already have come across the *-ing* form of a verb used as a present participle in continuous forms (*She's **running***.). The *-ing* form can also function as a kind of noun – sometimes called a 'gerund' (***Swimming** is fun.*). After certain verbs, when another verb is needed, one can either use the *to* + base form (*I want **to go***.) or the *-ing* form (*He doesn't like **reading***.).

This unit focuses on the use of the *-ing* form as a noun and revises the use of either the *-ing* form or *to* + base form after prepositions (*Before **leaving** ...*), adjectives (*Pleased **to meet** you ...*), question words (*I don't know what **to do***.) and certain verbs. It extends out of work done in *Intermediate Matters* and introduces those verbs where either the *-ing* form or *to* + base form can be used, usually depending on whether the speaker is referring to the past or the future.

Some verbs can only be followed by either an *-ing* form or a *to* + base form (*I enjoy **reading.*** not **I enjoy to read. I hope **to see** you.* not **I hope seeing you.*). Verbs followed by *to* + base form often express a concern with the future (e.g. verbs of hopes, offers and plans). Some verbs can be followed by an *-ing* form or *to* + base form with a little change of meaning (e.g. *I like playing chess.* suggests a general liking of chess whereas *I would like to play chess.* – with *would* – suggests a desire to play chess now.) The verbs which can be followed by either an *-ing* form or a *to* + base form and suggest a big difference in meaning (e.g. *regret, remember*) need a lot of practice (**Don't forget telling her.*).

Common problems

1 After many verbs only one form (the *-ing* form or *to* + base form) is grammatically correct. Because of mother tongue interference SS often mix up the two.

2 SS may need reminding of the spelling rules of *-ing* forms:
– double the final consonant if the final vowel is stressed and written as a single letter, and also if

there is only a single final consonant (e.g. *stop* → *stopping* but *head* → *heading* and *mend* → *mending*);
- the silent *e* disappears in verbs ending in *e* (*give* → *giving*);
- *ie* (*die*) in front of *-ing* becomes *y* (*dying*).

3 In some cases *to* seems to be part of a *to* + base form construction but is really functioning as a preposition and is therefore followed by an *-ing* form (*I look forward to seeing you.; I'm used to riding horses.* – see Unit 2; *I object to you smoking in class.*). Tell SS they might be able to check by putting a noun after the *-ing* construction instead of a verb. If it can be followed by a noun, then *to* is a preposition (*I'm looking forward to lunch.; I'm not used to this weather.; I object to loud music.*).

SPEAKING 1

• **Exercises 1 and 2** These provide a lead-in to the main topic of the unit, i.e. public behaviour in different cultures. Possibly do as PW or GW. SS can generalise about what is acceptable public behaviour in their country. In a multinational class this could be handled as a mingling activity, where SS get up and ask each other, or extended into a questionnaire; some generalisations can then be drawn about which (if any) of the actions are acceptable/unacceptable in *any* country. In classes of one nationality there may be disagreement about what is unacceptable, particularly if SS are from a mix of social backgrounds. Perhaps get SS to make lists of other things that are acceptable and unacceptable.

• **Exercise 3** This exercise personalises the topic for SS. You could ask how many of their answers are also true for other people in the country or whether they are only personal views. Possibly get SS to write a statement which is true for them.

• **Exercise 4** Other example answers in some cultures: a) someone refusing to have anything to drink or someone arriving late; b) good manners: keeping your elbows off the table when you eat; using a knife and fork 'correctly'.

• **Exercise 6** Be careful, particularly in a multinational class. Some acceptable gestures in some cultures are offensive in others (according to writer Desmond Morris, the 'OK and good' gesture in the USA means zero in France, money in Japan and in Tunisia it means 'I'll kill you'!). Desmond Morris's book *Bodywatch* published by Jonathan Cape is a useful source of information for this topic. You could bring forward Exercise 6 from the WRITING section.

READING

• **Exercise 1** This is a prediction exercise and an opportunity to see what stereotypical views SS have of the English and French. Who do SS think will be the more open or more reserved?

• **Exercise 2** This is a gist reading activity of quite a difficult text. Tell SS not to worry about the words they don't know at this stage, though you could explain the difference between *manners* (social ways of behaving) and *mannerisms* (odd ways of behaving that have become a habit).

• **Exercise 3** More intensive reading is expected here. Possible problem words: *damned, snorted, delight, absorbed, nod, ration, confine, thorough, startling, niceties, unencumbered, perilous contortions, grope, handlebars, restrained, demonstrative, pummel, clutches, superficial, blunder, miscalculates, proffered, snobs, congenital, triple.* Get SS to use the context to help guess the meaning of the words before checking in the dictionary.

• **Exercise 4** This is a more interpretive reading focusing on what the language *suggests.* Connotation and attitudes are very important in this text (e.g. *snorted* suggests the friend disapproves; phrases like *squeeze shoulders* and *slap backs* are slightly humorous and suggest that the writer by contrast is more detached). You could get SS to tell you what the different attitudes of the lawyer and the writer are. How do they know? However, if SS find this kind of thing difficult, don't push the point too hard. (Note that there is an exercise introducing connotation in the VOCABULARY section which you could bring forward, as well as a follow-up exercise in the WB.)

• **Exercise 5** The 'gestures' part of this exercise picks up on Exercise 6 in SPEAKING 1. You could quickly revise the parts of the body mentioned in the text (*index finger, waist, palm of the hand, thumb, the little finger*). After listening, give SS the meaning of any words they want to know (e.g. *thrust, caution, agitated metronome, parting*). If necessary, let them listen again reading the tapescript at the same time.

Corrective (contrastive) stress

• **Exercise 1** PW? In English, stress falls on the most important 'content' words (usually verbs, nouns, etc.), according to the 'message' the speaker wants to communicate. If a speaker wishes to disagree with or highlight a difference with what has been said then they can show this by stressing the key word. In the example in the exercise, *father* is stressed because the speaker wants to say *'No, it's not my mother who has been to France. It is my father.'* Make sure SS give reasons for why they have underlined the words.

• **Exercise 2** This exercise checks that SS understand the communicative purpose behind the different stress patterns and gives follow-up practice. It is important that SS realise that being able to use sentence stress flexibly is an important part of being an effective communicator.

REVISION

-ing or *to?*

• **Exercise 1** In this exercise the *-ing* form acts like a noun as part of the subject of a sentence: *Travelling first class* (subject) *is snobbish.* (Note the double *l* in *travelling* in British, but not American English.) Get SS to guess the meaning of the word *snob* or look it up in a dictionary. In Britain it can suggest two types of person: someone who dislikes people from a lower social class and someone who feels he or she has superior tastes. This is a good opportunity to compare British and other cultures in relation to class and snobbery.

• **Exercise 2** You might need to explain *darts* (a pub game) and *Rottweiler* (a fierce dog sometimes kept as a pet). Note in b) iii) that not all verbs are followed by *-ing.*

PRACTICE

• **Exercise 1** Note that in Britain 'high society' does not necessarily mean the most wealthy people: it refers more to the upper classes (with titles like *Duchess* and *Lord*), famous and fashionable people and a 'lifestyle' which includes pony clubs, ballet, etc. SS might need help with some of the words (e.g. *eligible, shed, henceforth, precious few*). Ask SS if there is an equivalent to the 'deb system' (a kind of fashionable 'rite of passage') in their country and what they think of it. Get SS to refer to the 'rules' of when to use an *-ing* form or *to* + base form that they worked out in. Exercise 2 in the REVISION section. They should try to imagine the context while doing the exercise. Get them to compare their sentences in pairs.

As a follow-up exercise tell SS they have been invited to a private party given by the Queen. Get them to discuss what to wear, using *where..., who..., how...*, etc. (to practise *to* + base form after a question word). For practise of the *-ing* form after prepositions there is a good problem-solving exercise called *How could you...* in P. Ur, *Grammar Practice Activities*, pages 146–7 (see *Bibliography*).

• **Exercise 2** Do a quick comprehension check first (e.g. *What does Sophie not like about being a deb? What is she going to do when she 'comes out'? What's she doing tomorrow night?*). Remind SS that some verbs are followed by *-ing* and some are followed by *to* + base form before they do the exercise as PW/GW. The focus of the exercise is on whether an *-ing* form or *to* + base form follows the main verbs, even though other constructions might be possible. Allow SS to use a dictionary to check. Try to get SS to produce different verbs to follow the main verb. Also encourage them to have a section in their vocabulary records for the two types of verb and add to it whenever they can; alternatively, they can add the relevant information to verbs whenever they keep notes. Use the last part of Sophie's interview as a basis for a quick discussion (e.g. *How would you describe Sophie's character? What do you think of the 'deb' system?*).

EXTENSION

-*ing* or *to* ?

• **Exercises 1 and 2** PW? Do a) with SS and elicit the 'rule' (*-ing* refers to the past; *to* + base form refers to the future). Get SS to refer to the *Language reference* to check their answers. There is a follow-up exercise in the WB.

VOCABULARY

Connotation

If SS are to be effective communicators they need to be aware of the attitudinal, evaluative and emotional overtones of words (their 'connotation'). Some words have an intrinsic negative or positive quality (*gross* when referring to people's weight is always negative) which needs to be taught as part of their meaning. Other words can change their meaning according to the attitude of the speaker in a situation.

• **Exercises 1 and 2** These focus on the intrinsic connotation of a word. Get SS to think of other words to add to each box, perhaps referring them to a *Thesaurus*; in Exercise 1 for example: *tubby, corpulent, large, stout, lean, emaciated, gaunt,* etc.; in Exercise 2: *green, callow, aged, elderly, doddering,* etc. Most of these words are likely to be more useful for recognition than production.

• **Exercise 3** GW? This focuses on connotation in context. You could allow SS to use a dictionary. There is a follow-up exercise in the WB.

SPEAKING 2

• **Exercise 1** SS try to guess the nationalities from the pictures and match the pictures with the words in the box. Ask them what other images (words and phrases) they associate with each country. Make it clear that the activity is not meant to be too serious and that disagreement is likely to be more interesting. In b), treat the activity lightly, particularly in a multinational class where SS could accidentally hurt people's feelings. The aim of this and the next two exercises is to get behind national stereotypes, to examine their truths and fallacies, not to reinforce them.

• **Exercise 2** The aim here is to see whether SS will come up with stereotypical images of people from these countries and whether they can predict how people from those countries see themselves. If you have these nationalities in your class it is better to elicit ideas from them first. Most of the speakers are teachers of English. Note that a *favella* is a Brazilian-Portuguese word for a very poor district. Ask SS what things surprised them and contradicted their ideas and which of their preconceptions were reinforced. (If necessary, SS can listen a second time and read the tapescript.)

• **Exercise 3** Other possible questions: *Are national stereotypes dangerous or harmless? Do they affect how you feel when you meet someone from another country for the first time? Are they affectionate and amusing? In what ways are all human beings the same? In what ways are we all different?*

WRITING

Tourist brochure

• **Exercise 1** You could ask SS *which* countries they associate with these customs and manners. Extend by putting a country on the board which is not represented by SS in the class and get SS to brainstorm the customs and manners of that country (not necessary if you do Exercise 2).

• **Exercise 3** This is an opportunity to revise the language of advice. Elicit advice expressions on the board beforehand (possibly before Exercise 1). The reason for adding 'bad' advice to the entry is to give a communicative purpose to Exercise 4 and make it more fun. Use the pictures for ideas and bring in some tourist brochures to help SS get a feel for style. Get SS to cut some brochures up to help them illustrate their writing.

• **Exercise 6** Do as GW?

Tapescripts

RECORDING 1

The instrument of warning and argument is the index finger, in one of its three operational positions. Thrust up, rigid and unmoving, beneath your conversational partner's nose, it signals caution - watch out *attention*, all is not what it seems. Held just below face level and shaken rapidly from side to side like an agitated metronome, it indicates that the other person is woefully ill-informed and totally wrong in what he has just said.

Describing a sudden departure needs two hands: the left, fingers held straight, moves upwards from waist level to smack into the palm of the right hand moving downwards.

At the end of the conversation, there is the promise to stay in touch. The middle three fingers are folded into the palm and the hand is held up to an ear, with the extended thumb and little finger imitating the shape of a telephone. Finally, there is a parting handshake. Packages, dogs and bicycles are gathered up until the whole process starts all over again fifty yards down the street. It's hardly surprising that aerobics never became popular in Provence. People get quite enough physical exercise in the course of a ten-minute chat.

RECORDING 2

a) No, Peter studies in Cambridge. No, Peter studies in Cambridge.
b) No, I bought a new Volvo. No, I bought a new Volvo.
c) No, the play lasted two hours. No, the play lasted two hours.
d) No, she's nearly thirty-three years old. No, she's nearly thirty-three years old.

RECORDING 3

SOPHIE: What's it like being a deb? Well, it's actually quite fun in a lot of ways simply because the kinds of things we do are the sort of things I like doing anyway. I love going to parties and meeting people and having fun and not really having to have a serious conversation about anything, but there are certain drawbacks as well. It is actually quite boring when you're not in the mood having to go out and be polite and friendly, particularly when there's the older generation around. A lot of these parties you get the parents and all of their friends there and sometimes I'm just not in the mood for being a sweet, friendly person, but I think it's probably quite good in, in a way to have to train yourself to be sociable even if you don't feel like it.

The plans I've got for when I actually come out are mainly just carry on having fun actually. I hope that I'll be able to keep up with a lot of the people who I've become friendly with. In fact, I think I might be going on holiday with a couple of people I've met.

My engagements for the coming week, I've actually got quite a full agenda. I'm going to a cocktail party tomorrow night and I'm going along with a friend of mine who's also doing the deb season so it's quite nice, I can go along with her. And then after that I'm going for dinner with some people I've met who've invited me round for dinner. I suppose some people would say we are privileged, because we spend a lot of money and that, that is true. It is entirely a frivolous activity but I, I tend not to worry about that really because it's always been like that. Some people have money and some people don't and those that do might as well spend it.

RECORDING 4

CASSITA: Usually, the Brazilians are lively, outgoing and friendly, easy to get along with, and they, although they have many problems, as you see in documentaries on TV coming from abroad, the poor people in the *favellas*, they seem happy. It's also important to focus the mixed races we have in Brazil especially São Paulo, there are many Japanese already Brazilians and many Italians who are Brazilians, the mixed races makes the race very beautiful.

RIEKO: Well, a typical Japanese person is rather shy and they are not so accustomed to mixing to other people but they are very interested in the news of other countries and so many people like reading newspapers and magazines and seeing movies of other countries.

WOLFMANN: For the foreigner a German seems to be very serious at first glance but I think a German isn't only serious, a German can be very, very funny. He's normally a bit silent. He's not as loud as many people think and he doesn't want to play an important role in the world as many people think as well but he keeps on old traditions.

MARIA CRISTINA: Really, if you are asking me what an Italian is I wouldn't know how to answer because we are coming from such a different kind of countries all together and Italy was made just only last century. And we are completely different for culture, background, even physically different and so I will answer what I feel is an Italian . . . We are very friendly, . . . every foreigner is welcome but we are very, very jealous about what is going to happen or what is our house, our home. Home is completely apart from the public and this is another point that goes together with the fact that we likes clothes because we like how we appear and I would say that for an Italian would be much more important how you look likes than how you are and for this reason I thinks that even if you are wearing cheap clothes, clothes or dress you are very careful about matching the colour or things like that because for an Italian it is very important to be smart, to appear.

YNGVE: What we all have in common in Sweden is that we love the countryside very much and we are used to having a lot of space around us and therefore many Swedes they go to the north of Sweden fishing and climbing the mountains, doing things like that where they can be completely alone for weeks and they just enjoy the silence around them.

Key

READING

1

The people in Provence, unlike the British, come close to you and make physical contact when they meet.

3

a) False b) True c) True d) False

4

a) They are more affectionate to animals than people!
b) They like to make a lot of physical contact when they meet.
c) When the other person's hands are dirty.
d) Kissing, squeezing shoulders, slapping backs, beating stomachs, pinching cheeks.
e) Not performing the right kissing ritual when meeting.

5

a) Picture 1: warning someone to be careful
Picture 2: telling someone they are wrong
Picture 3: talking about someone leaving suddenly
Picture 4: promising to see someone again
b) People get quite enough exercise from talking to each other.

Corrective (contrastive) stress

1

a) Jeremy b) phoned c) Peter

2

Example answers:
a) Does Peter work in Cambridge? Does Peter study in Oxford?
b) Did you buy a second-hand Volvo? Did Mary buy a new Volvo?
c) Did the play last three hours? Did the film last two hours?
d) Is she thirty-three years old? Is she thirty-four years old?

REVISION

-ing or *to?*

1

a) Wearing b) Telling c) Drinking d) Owning

2

a) 'Before going to the opera I think it's important to dress up.'
b)
i) *-ing* form *(Before going)*
ii) *to* + base form *(important to)*
iii) *-ing* form *(enjoys having)*
iv) *to* + base form *(where to exercise)*

Prepositions can never be followed by *to* + base form.

PRACTICE

1

Example answers:
a) to meet people
b) to talk to
c) of doing later
d) of staying here in all this noise
e) to see so many people I didn't know
f) in going for a walk
g) to seeing my parents in the morning
h) to say

2

Example answers:
a) She enjoys meeting people.
b) She intends to go on holiday with some people she met.
c) She has arranged to go to a cocktail party.
d) She wants to carry on seeing the people she's become friendly with.
e) She hopes she'll go on having fun when she 'comes out'.
f) She resents having to go out when she's not in the mood.

EXTENSION

ing or *to?*

1

a) forget feeding ii)
forget to feed i)
b) remembered to send i)
remembered sending ii)
c) regret to tell ii)
regret telling i)
d) stopped to have ii)
stopped having i)

2

a) to wear b) going c) not telling d) laughing
e) to bring f) to tell g) seeing h) to look

VOCABULARY

Connotation

1

fat, obese, portly, gross, bony, plump, skinny, thin

2

youthful, mature, child-like, grown-up, adult

3

a) ii b) i c) ii

SPEAKING 2

1

a) 1 American 2 Australian 3 English

Training diets

Students' Book

General theme: sport.
Unit topic: diets in sport.

LISTENING: interview with 'The Strongest Man in the World'; intonation of lists.
VOCABULARY: homonyms; sounds: /l/; idioms.

REVISION: quantity expressions.
EXTENSION: compounds of *some, any, no* and *every* (e.g. *somewhere*); *each, another, both, either,* etc.

SPEAKING: roleplay on the topic of fitness obsession.
WRITING: attitude words; writing a dialogue.

Workbook

READING: magazine article on trainee Sumo wrestlers; vocabulary in context.
VOCABULARY: numbers; idioms (*break the ice,* etc.).
GRAMMAR: quantity; compounds of *some, any, no, every*; *each, another, both, either,* etc.
PRONUNCIATION: words with the same spelling (homographs).
WRITING: punctuation; lists.

Language

Although quantity expressions were introduced in *Intermediate Matters*, SS at this level still make mistakes and need further practice, particularly with indefinite quantifiers (determiners) such as *some, few,* etc. (Words which tell us exactly how many or how much are thought of as definite quantifiers – e.g. *three, a litre,* etc.).

Common problems

1 For SS the main problem with quantifiers is in deciding which one to choose (**There isn't many cheese left. *I didn't see nothing.*). Unless SS acquire the collocations, to make the correct choice in English they need to know whether a noun is countable or uncountable. Where possible, SS should be referred to a dictionary where the difference is usually indicated by a *C* or *U*. Some words can be both countable and uncountable (e.g. *three onions / some onion*). Note that words that are uncountable in English (e.g. *furniture*) might be countable in other languages. Also some languages (notably Japanese) have no clear singular/plural distinction and therefore no countable distinction.

2 Collocation is very important. We say *some/any/ most / none **of**...* before articles (*some of **the** ...*), demonstratives (*any of **those** ...*), possessives (*most of **my** ...*) and personal pronouns (*none of **us** ...*) but not before nouns (**some of cakes.*). In fact, knowing whether the word is being used as a determiner or a pronoun can affect choice (*There's **no** paper left.* – determiner. ***None** of the guests should leave.* – pronoun; not **There's none paper... *No of the guests...*).

3 The use of *some* can be a problem if SS have been taught that it is only used in affirmative sentences. (It can also be used in requests and offers when we expect the answer *yes* – *Would you like some...?*). Note that *some* has strong pronunciation when used as a pronoun (*some of the milk... No, thanks. I've got some.* /sʌm/) and usually (except in initial position in a sentence) weak pronunciation when used directly before a noun (*some milk...* /səm/).

4 Compounds (*someone*, etc.) can be difficult to use and SS should study the notes in Section 3 of the *Language reference.*

5 *Else* is often avoided by SS. It is a useful word which can follow compounds (*nowhere else*), most question words (*Who else...?*) except *which*, and the words *little* and *(not) much* (*little else...*).

6 Common mistakes with the other determiners in Section 4 of the *Language reference,* mainly due to mother tongue interference are: **The both girls... *Each my children... *Either of the cars are... *I can't too.* (for *I can't either.* or *Neither can I.*) **She ate the whole eggs.* (for *All of the eggs...*) **There are other three people in the house. *Where are the others eggs? *I'd like an other cup of coffee. *I'd like other cup of coffee.*

LISTENING

Before listening

• **Exercise 1** This is a warm-up exercise for the interview with Jamie Reeves in the *Listening.* Find out what mistakes SS make with quantity expressions (the language focus of the unit) by getting them to predict Jamie's weight and diet. (Note that there is another opportunity in the *Listening.*) Also revise words connected with weights and measures. (Some come up in Exercise 2.) You could write their abbreviations on the board and get SS to write down the complete word and check their answers in the Weights and Measures section of a dictionary. The most important words for this unit are *cm* (*centimetre*), *m* (*metre*), *km* (*kilometre*) for linear measurement; *g* (*grams*) and *kg* (*kilograms*) for weight. To make the exercise more challenging, you could add a section on British and American units (e.g. *in / inches*; *ft / feet*; *oz / ounces*; *lbs / pounds*; *st / stones*, etc.), although these systems have mainly been avoided in the unit. (However, note that in the *Listening* Jamie says he is 6 foot 4.)

• **Exercise 2** Check that SS know what a *decathlon* is (a sport in which the athlete must take part in ten events). Revise parts of the body, including those in the *Listening* (*chest, biceps, shoulders, neck, waist, thigh*). Some SS might not know that *lorry* is the British word for *truck* (American). Ask SS to work out from context what *dethrone* and *reigning champion* are.

Listening

• **Exercise 1** You could get SS to underline what seems wrong in pencil first and then discuss reasons for their guesses in pairs.

• **Exercise 2** This is an authentic radio interview with Jamie. By eliciting why various types of food are good or bad for you, check SS know what the following are: *calories, carbohydrates, protein, cholesterol.* Focus mainly on gist.

• **Exercise 3** You could write the words *Breakfast* and *Evening meal* on the board and get SS to make a list of food under each. Let SS listen again to check their answers, possibly while reading the tapescript.

• **Exercise 4** Notice where the stress falls on *compe'tition.* You could extend by getting SS to add other nouns to the endings *-ion, -th, -ness, -y.*

• **Exercise 5** This exercise focuses on the intonation of lists. Notice the voice rises to indicate incompleteness (i.e. there is more of the list to come) and falls to show the end of the list. Ask SS to predict the intonation before they listen to the example. Get SS to exaggerate the activity and make it fun. You could point out the punctuation of lists (i.e. there are usually commas after each item except the penultimate and the last one). Notice there is a WB exercise on writing lists.

VOCABULARY

Homonyms

• **Exercise 1** Homonyms are words with the same spelling and pronunciation but more than one unrelated meaning. For this exercise each pair of SS should have a dictionary to hand. (If necessary, remind SS of the abbreviations for parts of speech: *v, n, adj.*) Get SS to divide up the words in the box between them so that all of them are covered. Each pair (A and B) then decide which two meanings the words they have chosen could have and who will write a sentence to illustrate which meaning. They then check their answers in the dictionary and show the sentences they have written to other pairs.

• **Exercise 2** Note that *board* has several meanings, both as a verb and a noun, and so is a good word to explore in the dictionary. Other words with more than one meaning are: *stand, plane, leave, fine, saw,* etc.

Sounds: /l/

This exercise focuses on recognition rather than practice of the light and dark /l/ sounds. The dark /l/ sound as in *file* usually comes after but not before a vowel. The /l/ sound as in *light* occurs before a vowel. Practise the sounds by getting SS to make the sounds in isolation first. To make the dark /l/ sound the back of the tongue is raised towards the soft palate (the velum). Notice that the tip of the tongue is in the same position for both sounds. (Note that people from some parts of Britain do not use a dark /l/ sound and many Americans do not use a light /l/ sound.)

A selection of idioms

PW? Allow SS to use a dictionary if necessary. Remind them that the way to look up an idiom is to search the idiom for the key word. You could quickly go through and establish the key word for each idiom. As follow-up ask SS to write personal sentences for each idiom (e.g. *I'm fed up with doing grammar exercises.*).

REVISION

Quantity

• **Exercise 1** At this level SS should be familiar with the idea of a difference between *countable* (or *count*) and *uncountable* (or *mass*) nouns. However, there will still be many problems, some of which may emerge in this exercise, such as the fact that a word ending in *-s* (*news*) can be *uncountable* and therefore usually singular. (See also *Common problems.*)

• **Exercise 2** One way of extending this exercise is to shout out a number of nouns and get SS to give you other expressions (***matches*** *– a box of;* ***flowers*** *– a bunch of;* ***flour*** *– a bag of;* ***marmalade*** *– a jar of;* ***toothpaste*** *– a tube of;* ***bread*** *– a loaf of;* ***beer*** *– a can of / a bottle of / a pint of;* ***cornflakes*** *- a packet of,* etc.). This could be varied by having two sets of cards, one with nouns on (*matches* , etc.), the other with expressions on (*a box of...*) and getting SS to match them.

• **Exercise 3** This exercise focuses on recognition rather than production. It highlights the problematic areas in the grammar of quantity expressions and of collocation (e.g. we say *a couple* ***of*** *bottles* not **a couple bottles*). Use for further diagnosis of any problems. You may prefer to do Exercise 4 a) here before doing Exercise 3.

First, get SS to skim read the passage once. Then get them to write some questions to ask each other or ask some yourself. Examples: *Is there any white wine left? Was there much when Diane arrived? What does she think of the red wine?* You could get SS to predict how they think the dialogue will continue in preparation for Exercise 4.

• **Exercise 4** Exercise 4 a) focuses on exploring the grammar and collocational aspects of quantity expressions. It could be done in groups. Get SS to try out the examples (*eggs* and *milk*) on each of the expressions to see if they 'feel' right before checking their answers. (They could use a dictionary instead of, or as well as, the *Language reference.*) Exercise 4 b) gets SS to practise using the expressions in a very controlled way. In some cases more than one answer is possible. You could add some inference questions such as: *What do we know about Jenny, her family and their lifestyle? Guess what Diane thinks of her sister and why.*

• **Exercise 5** This communication gap exercise gets SS to use quantity expressions more freely. Notice that most but not all of what Diane says is untrue. Student B could ask such questions as: *How much food is really in the freezer? How much bread is there?,* etc. SS in need of further controlled practice will find an exercise in the WB.

Other supplementary activities to practise quantity:

1 Kim's game: Let SS look at a collection of items on a table for a short while before covering it up. SS then tell you which items they can remember, using correct determiners. Make sure you mix up the items in varying quantities to get good practice.

2 Each SS writes a shopping list of food they need for the weekend without determiners (*milk, eggs, money,* etc.). They then give their list to another S who should guess the quantities needed and add determiners. The first SS then say whether or not they agree with the quantities suggested, giving reasons (e.g. *I need more milk because my parents are coming...*).

EXTENSION

Compounds of *some, any, no* and *every*

Tell SS that *else* is a very useful word often used after question words (including their compounds). You could write *some other place* on the board and tell SS that native speakers would more naturally say *somewhere else*.

Each, another, both, either, etc.

This exercise gives practice in other determiners (sometimes used as pronouns) which give SS a lot of problems (see *Common problems*). Elicit an example for each of the words in the box, and put it on the board, pointing out any areas of grammar (e.g. after *each* the verb is in the third person singular; instead of saying *Neither does Julia.* you can say *Julia doesn't either.*; you can say *Both my...* or *Both of my...*, etc.). Make the exercise into a game so that the group with the most correct answers wins. (You might get SS to refer to a dictionary and/or a grammar book to check their answers.) Note that there is a further exercise in the WB. You could extend into a discussion on the points raised in the questionnaire.

SPEAKING

• **Exercise 1** This provides some input for the roleplay in Exercise 3. SS might need help with some of the words: *body supplements* (e.g. vitamins, glucose and salts used to increase or replace lost energy), *withdrawal, 'cold turkey'* (the sickness caused when addicts come off hard drugs), *E-numbers* (numbers used to name a particular chemical that is in food), *organic vegetables* (vegetables grown without the help of chemicals). This could lead to a discussion on additives, healthy foods, vegetarianism, etc.

• **Exercise 2** This is the context for the roleplay in Exercise 3. SS might need help with *junkie* (someone dependent on a hard drug) and *steroids* (chemical compounds, including hormones, that many sportsmen use, often illegally, to improve their physical performance).

• **Exercises 3 and 4** You could start by getting each 'character' to brainstorm ideas they can use in the roleplay, i.e. all As, Bs, Cs and Ds discuss them together in separate groups, before dividing into groups of four (A, B, C and D). SS could take some notes but discourage them from writing too much as it is a free-speaking exercise. Possibly elicit some of the 'advice expressions' that Students C and D might use (e.g. *I think you should...; If you don't...; Why don't you...?,* etc.). You might want to record the roleplay on audio or video tape so that Exercise 4 can be a proper review session, but it is often better to keep this kind of activity fairly light and quick so as not to spoil the effect of the roleplay. An alternative strategy is to make notes yourself and give your impressions afterwards.

WRITING

Attitude words

The aim of this section is to make SS aware of attitude words and encourage them to use such words naturally in their informal written English through the writing of dialogue.

• **Exercise 1** SS should 'know' most of these words but not necessarily be able to use them naturally in context. Get SS to skim read the dialogue first and ask some gist questions (e.g. *Where has Debra been? Why does she go? When does she go? Does Eve agree with it? Why not?*). Note that question a) suggests that Eve may be jealous of Debra because she is seeing Tony. Perhaps the other person he is seeing is her! As follow-up (possibly for homework) get SS to write a sentence for some of the more important of the attitude words that do *not* fill the gaps, using a dictionary to help them (e.g. *really, naturally, honestly, frankly*). Notice that there is a punctuation exercise in the WB.

• **Exercise 3** Quickly go over some of the conventions of dialogue writing first (e.g. the use of exclamation marks to suggest strong feeling; the use of contracted verb forms; informal, colloquial language; layout on the page).

Tapescripts

224

RECORDING 1

INTERVIEWER: Have you always been a large and a strong man? Where did you get the idea for instance to go in for competitions of this kind?

JAMIE REEVES: I've always been very big, my parents were very big, so to do this much in the sport I've chosen, obviously like any other sport you've got to be genetically gifted so with big bones, etc. I were very gifted at this and also at 6'4 I'm a very big man anyway. 'The Strongest Man in the World' is a competition which is devised to test all aspects of strength, so to actually become the strongest man in the world you need all-round body strength. It's a kind of question as who's the decathlete of strength, so I try and train all of my body not just certain parts.

I: Give me an idea then of your training regime day to day. What kind of training you have to do.

JR: What I try and do is split me training up into three days: on day one I would do legs and abdominals, on day two I would do chest, shoulders and triceps, and day three I would do back, biceps and front deltoid.

I: What about sports, apart from just training? Do you play any sports to make it more interesting?

JR: I like all kinds of sport but obviously I'm restricted with me training. I like to add a little swimming into me training, maybe do some running, some sprinting, maybe a little football, any kinds of sport. I don't mind. I like all kinds of sport.

I: Let's have a look at diet . . . what you eat in a normal day . . . it would be very different from a person's normal meal, so take me through your normal diet.

JR: My normal diet really consists of just more or less the same food as an average person but I try and eat every three hours and consume about three times as many calories per day, so most of my food is just good all-round balanced food but maybe three times as much.

I: So give me an idea of your breakfast, your lunch and your dinner, what you actually eat.

JR: It differs from day to day what I actually eat but what I try and do is consume thirty grammes of protein every three hours, good balanced carbohydrates, greens for irons and minerals and water for body clearance but in general just more or less the same as a normal person but three times as much.

I: So, an average breakfast for instance would contain what?

JR: Maybe six eggs, some bacon, some fruit, some fresh fruit, maybe a little toast or a little bran.

I: What about your main meal of the day? What quantities? What would that contain about?

JR: The main meal of the day for me would be taken around 8 o'clock at night after training. I maybe train around 7 then eat around 8 which would be maybe fish, potatoes, rice, chicken, greens and some milk.

I: Any special foods though you need particularly, say, when you go in for a competition? Any foods for strength?

JR: Not really. Strength's built throughout the year. The food I would maybe eat before competitions or lifting would be such as spaghetti or pasta, rice for carbohydrates for a lot of energy on that day, so I know that physically I was performing to the best of me ability. Use a lot of nutritional products, from a lot of protein drinks and high supplements . . . a lot of high protein drinks, things like that.

I: Any foods you have to avoid?

JR: Not really. Before a competition I always cut out a lot of fats for maybe two months, I avoid fats with eating so much to keep me cholesterol level down and keep pretty healthy. So, yeah, fats I avoid more or less.

I: You're a pretty good athlete as well though.

JR: I've run the 100 metres, I've been timed in under 12 seconds, at around 11.97, and I've also been timed on the 400 at 56.

I: What about tips for ordinary people and the training they can do to be fit?

JR: I think whether it's fitness or power-lifting or strength or just general aerobics or whatever, it's very important to start off properly, to start off very light and then work your way up nice and steady, nothing too strenuous to avoid injury and then progress from there.

I: I don't suppose there are many people come up to you in a pub and pick a fight, are there?

JR: No, only very silly ones.

genetically gifted: born with big bones
biceps: the large muscle in the upper arm
deltoid: the large muscle that covers the shoulder joint (used for raising the arm to the side)

RECORDING 2

Could you get me some eggs, some fish, a few potatoes and a pint of milk?

RECORDING 3

file, light

a) I'll b) tell c) lunch d) please e) school f) careful

RECORDING 4

DIANE: Yes. There are dozens of bottles of wine left. White wine? Ah! No, there's no white wine, none at all - well, there wasn't much in the first place. Certainly not enough for a party. Most of the red wine is quite drinkable, though.

Food in the freezer? No, there's not a great deal left. The children have eaten nearly everything. There are a couple of cakes which they haven't touched. I'd better put them aside or they'll both be gone before long.

Salad . . . ah! No, all of that's disappeared too. Lucy gave it to the rabbit. No doubt if you want a sandwich Ben will make you one. Oh, no, I've just remembered! I don't think there's any bread left. Come to think of it, there aren't many things we could put in it anyway.

Fruit? There might be half a melon left. Not a whole one, I'm afraid. We had some of it last week. And several packets of biscuits perhaps. I know for certain there are lots of packets of crisps. Possibly some cheese but none of it's any good. What! What do you mean you're going to eat out?! I was only joking!

Key

LISTENING

Listening

2

a) His parents were *big* people and he has always been big. He eats *three times* as many calories as the average person and he eats *every three hours*. He can run the 100 metres in *just under 12 seconds* and the 400 metres in *56 seconds*. He splits his exercise routine into *three days*. He *includes* other sports like *swimming, running, sprinting and football.*

b) He eats more spaghetti or rice as well as a lot of high-protein drinks and supplements. He also cuts out fats for two months before a competition.

3

1 six eggs, some bacon, some fruit, maybe a little toast or a little bran
2 fish, potatoes, rice, chicken, greens and some milk

4

a) competition b) strength c) sprint d) fitness
e) injury

VOCABULARY

Homonyms

1

[See Exercise 2.]

2

a

WORD	MEANING 1	MEANING 2
port /pɔː/	place where ships can load (n)	strong Portuguese wine (n)
fox /fɒks/	wild animal (n)	deceive (v)
safe /seɪf/	not dangerous (adj)	box used for protecting valuables (n)
match /mætʃ/	competition (n)	be suitable (v)
can /kæn/	be able to (v)	metal container (n)
miss /mɪs/	fail to hit (v)	feel sad at the absence of (v)
file /faɪl/	march one behind the other (v)	container for keeping papers (n)
spot /spɒt/	a small mark (n)	notice (v)
tap /tæp/	strike lightly (v)	device for controlling flow of liquid (n)
sink /sɪŋk/	go slowly down below surface (v)	container for washing (n)
park /pɑːk/	public piece of land used for enjoyment (n)	place a car for a time (v)
light /laɪt/	not heavy (adj)	lamp (n)
flat /flæt/	apartment (n)	level (adj)
book /bʊk/	something we read (n)	arrange in advance to have (v)
kind /kaɪnd/	sort (n)	friendly and generous (adj)
swallow /swɒləʊ/	small bird (n)	move food from mouth to stomach (v)
bat /bæt/	type of flying animal (n)	stick used in sport for hitting balls (n)
pick /pɪk/	choose (v)	type of tool (n)
chest /tʃest/	upper half of body (n)	large strong box (n)
fine /faɪn/	bright and clear (adj)	money paid as punishment (n)
play /pleɪ/	take part in a game (v)	work performed by actors (n)

Sounds: /l/

a) A b) A c) B d) B e) A f) A
(A) sounds usually occur at (or towards) the end of a word.

A selection of idioms

a) 5 b) 3 c) b d) 8 e) 1 f) 7 g) 4 h) 2

REVISION

Quantity

1
Countable: eggs, people, cornflakes, oranges
Uncountable: damage, bread, salt, news, soap, sugar, milk

2
Example answers:
b) bread c) news d) damage e) chocolate/soap
f) sugar g) milk h) cake

3
1 dozens 2 no 3 none 4 much 5 enough 6 Most
7 great deal 8 couple 9 both 10 all

4
a
Countable: a (n), many, few / a few, one / both, several, (a) whole, a couple (of), dozens (of)
Uncountable: little, a little (bit of), much, a great deal (of) more / less
Both: some, any, a lot (of) / lots (of), hardly any, no / none enough, most, all / half (of the), more

b
1 a
2 one (some)
3 any / much
4 many
5 half
6 whole
7 several (a few)
8 lots of / several / dozens of
9 some / a little
10 none

5 Example conversation:
B: Are there any bottles of white wine left?
A: Yes, there is a whole box of white wine.
B: Is there any food in the freezer?
A: Yes, there's a lot of food in the freezer.
B: Is there any salad?
A: Yes, there is a lettuce, some tomatoes and a cucumber.
B: Is there any bread?
A: Yes, there's some bread in the bin and several loaves in the freezer.
B: What about some cheese?
A: There's a nice piece of cheese in the fridge.

Diane was joking.

EXTENSION

Compounds of *some, any, no* and *every*

a) You're cleverer than everyone/anyone I know.
b) Everybody else was on time.
c) Everything in the garden looked lovely.
d) There was nowhere else to go.
e) Somebody else has parked in my parking space.
f) There was nothing else she could do.
g) I heard that story somewhere else.

Each, another, both, either, etc.

1
Example answers:
Each of the people we interviewed thinks that people work better in the mornings.
Simon doesn't think that most people are the right weight for their height. Julia doesn't either.
Julia thinks that on one day we should swim or play tennis and that on another day we should go to aerobics.
None of them thinks that people are the right weight for their height.
Neither Simon nor Julia think people should sleep more than 8 hours.
Both Simon and Julia think people should go swimming at least once a week.
Simon and Julia believe in exercise. The other person doesn't.

WRITING

Attitude words

1
Most likely answers:
1 I suppose 2 Personally 3 unfortunately
4 Presumably 5 At least 6 Surprisingly 7 Surely
8 Actually 9 To be honest 10 probably

2
Example answers:
a) as far as I'm concerned
b) as a matter of fact
c) funnily enough

A deafening noise

Students' Book

General theme: sport.
Unit topic: spectators and sport.

READING: newspaper article on an unfair attempt to influence the result of a horse-race; reference words.
VOCABULARY: sport (e.g. *tennis racket, tennis court, to play tennis*); homophones; phonemic transcriptions.

EXTENSION: deduction in the present (*must be, can't be,* etc.).
REVISION: mixed modals.

SPEAKING: debate on dangerous sports.
WRITING: letter of complaint (including 'reference' words such as *it, the ones, he,* etc.).

Workbook

LISTENING: people talking about the sports they like watching; vocabulary in context.
VOCABULARY: word building (adjectives, adverbs, nouns and verbs); similes; foreign words and phrases.
GRAMMAR: modals; 'reference' words.
WRITING: dialogue of complaint.

Language

This unit revises the use of modals in general and introduces ways of making deductions in the present using such modal constructions as *must be* and *can't be.* (Note that past forms come up in Unit 19.) At this level SS will already be familiar with *must* for obligation, *can* for ability, *might* for possibility, etc. and might find it confusing to be told that we also use *must* to say something we feel sure about because we have the evidence for it. (*He* ***must*** *be out. His coat's not here.*) Note the contrast between *He's out.* - I know for a fact, and *I don't know where he is. He* ***must*** *be out.* – that's the logical conclusion based on the known facts. It needs to be pointed out that when making deductions *must* usually associates with *be* and can be used with the continuous form (*He* ***must be having*** *a bath.*).

Common problems

Modals

1 Although there are modal equivalents in most languages except Arabic, modals are used more extensively in English and have a range of different nuances, particularly in polite forms.

2 SS at this level may still have problems with form (**I might to come. / *Do you must...? /* She cans...*) and the pronunciation of the weak forms, such as /məs/ instead of /mʌst/ in *I must go.* However, the main problems are ones of use (**I must go to Cambridge yesterday.*) and avoiding modals when it would be natural and more polite to use them (*Hurry up, please.* instead of *Would you hurry up, please?*).

Modals of deduction

1 There is a tendency for SS to avoid modals when making deductions (*Perhaps he's washing his hair.* instead of *He might be washing his hair.*).

2 SS need to know that the negative of *must be* is *can't be* (*He can't be out.* not **He mustn't be out.*) and when asking a question we say *Couldn't / Mightn't he be out?* or *Might he not be out?* not **Mustn't he be out?*

3 In front of most verbs *must* is pronounced weakly to allow the stress to fall on the main verb (*I must* /məs/ *'go.*). However, before *be* the word *must* often carries more stress to allow for the word after *be* to carry stress (*He must* /mʌs/ *be 'out.* – with *out* carrying the stress).

4 In American English, *has to be* / *has got to be* is more commonly used than *must be* (*He* ***has to be*** / ***has got to be*** *out.*).

5 SS often use *can* instead of *might* or *could* to talk about possibility in affirmative sentences (**Jill can be in Paris now.*).

READING

Before reading

• **Exercise 1** This exercise warms SS up to the topic of corruption in sport. Ask them about any recent events in the news. Possibly elicit the words *bribe* and *betting* through other examples: bribing football referees, bribing sportsmen to lose where spectators gamble on the result (e.g. *What's the word we use when money is offered to make somebody do something illegal?*) or a personalised example (*If I give a policeman money,...*).

• **Exercise 2** Elicit guesses about what's happening in the pictures as well as some important vocabulary: *jockey, horseracing, binoculars, racecourse, the favourite* (i.e. the horse that is expected to win). Then ask SS in pairs to make predictions based on the headlines and caption. Get SS to make guesses about the more difficult vocabulary in the headlines and caption before checking in the dictionary or you telling them what they mean, e.g. *firework, drug dealer, ultra-sonic* (beyond the range of human hearing), *veered, bruised, my colours* (the colours worn by jockeys), *ripped off.*

READING

• **Exercise 1** Some of the words in the text are exploited in Exercises 5 and 6. Words that SS might need help with are: *Royal Ascot* (an annual horse-racing meeting in Britain attended by the royal family), *high-tech* (the most modern technology), *back-street inventor* (someone who invents things secretly for dishonest reasons), *bookmaking* (taking money risked on the results of races), *Ile de Chypre* (the name of a horse), *King George V Handicap* (the name of a race), *drug conspiracy, drug baron* (a drug dealer with a lot of power), *terraced house* (house which is one of a row of houses), *greyhound* (a dog used for racing). It might be worth stressing that the story was a true story, not science fiction.

• **Exercise 2** Compare notes in pairs or groups.

• **Exercise 3** This exercise revises question forms. It is important that the questions are answerable from the text. You could make the exercise into a game by SS giving their partner a mark of 1-5 for each answer – 5 for correct English. Partners can challenge the mark if they think it is unfair but a reason must be given.

• **Exercise 4** Light guns were used in the film *Star Wars* and both sound and light guns are used in science fiction. Some 'advantages' of these kinds of weapons are the precision with which a strike can be made and the continuous beam which can be adjusted towards the target.

• **Exercise 5** Make sure SS use elements in the context to help them make their guesses (e.g. ***devised by*** *... What is it that inventors normally do?*).

• **Exercise 6** Encourage SS to write down any useful vocabulary in their vocabulary records.

• **Exercises 7 and 8** These exercises focus on 'referencing' (the use of words such as pronouns to refer to things already mentioned in the text). See also Units 8 and 11. This is an important part of natural, native-speaker discourse. Exercise 7 focuses on recognition of referencing in the text. Exercise 8 gets SS to practise it. There is also an exercise on this in the WRITING section.

VOCABULARY

Sport

• **Exercises 1 and 2** These exercises move away from racing and make SS aware of the vocabulary associated with different sports. Before Exercise 1 perhaps get SS to write down their favourite sport and all the words they associate with it. If available, use visuals to liven up the activity. Or, in groups, after Exercise 2, brainstorm words associated with the names of sports you write on the board. You could ask SS who are familiar with the sports in Exercise 1 to explain what the terms mean.

• **Exercise 3** Elicit what sort of person the people in the pictures are and what kind of lifestyle they lead (sedentary, active, fun-loving, etc.). This should help you to diagnose how well SS can use *may/must be*, which are focused on later in the unit. As an extra activity ask SS to guess what sports other SS are interested in, giving a reason. One way of doing this would be for everyone to write down the names of all SS in the class, with the name of a sport next to each and a reason. SS could then exchange lists to see if they agree.

Homophones

• **Exercises 1-3** These exercises focus on words which have the same pronunciation but different spelling and meaning. (Homonyms, words with the same spelling but different meanings, are dealt with in Unit 15.) Both homophones and homonyms are very common in English and form the basis of many English jokes (e.g. *What sort of robbery is the easiest? A safe robbery!*). In practical terms, when they listen, SS have problems working out which word is being said in words with more than one meaning. You could ask SS to think of some more homophones and do a quick dictation to include confusing words.

• **Exercise 4** Together with Exercise 3 this exercise helps SS become more sensitive towards pronunciation through revision of the phonemic transcript. In some more advanced classes you could dictate some sports words to SS and see if they can write them down in phonemics, possibly using the *Pronunciation* chart on SB page 149 to help them.

EXTENSION

Deduction in the present

• **Exercise 1** This exercise gives examples of *must be, can't be* and *may be* in context and asks SS to work out the meaning. *Must be* and *can't be* indicate a degree of certainty; *may be* indicates possibility.

• **Exercise 2** This exercise focuses on use and shows that *may* and *might* are interchangeable in the affirmative; that *might* and *could* are not interchangeable in the negative; that the negative of *must* is *can't* in modals of deduction.

• **Exercise 3** This focuses on the pronunciation of modals when making deductions in the present. (See *Common problems,* 3). In *can't be,* notice the weak /bi/ for *be* and the assimilation of the *n't* to /m/ (/ca:mbi/).

• **Exercises 4-6** These give controlled practice (Exercise 4), semi-controlled practice (Exercise 5) and freer practice (Exercise 6), where SS have to make the correct choice of form according to the communicative purpose. For optional alternative activities ask SS to empty their pockets and see what other SS can deduce about their lifestyles; bring in pictures of furnished rooms and get SS to make deductions about the people who live there; get SS to bring in pictures of their family doing things and ask other SS to make deductions about their character and lifestyle; bring in pictures of people and get SS to make deductions about them from the way they look, dress, etc.

REVISION

Mixed modals

• **Exercise 1** Get SS to read the texts first and make guesses about the context (e.g. *Who might be speaking to whom? Why might things be getting bad? Who do you think Starling is?*, etc.).
The Silence of the Lambs is a novel about a psychopathic killer, Dr Hannibal Lecter, and a woman police officer, Starling. (Buffalo Bill is the nickname of another killer.) In this extract Starling is talking to Dr Lecter.
After the Show is a short story about a young seventeen year-old boy, Maurice, who starts a relationship with Sylvia, his Uncle Victor's mistress.

You could get SS to say what 'function' each modal has before they try to match them to the categories given. Note that there is one modal of deduction used to express the speaker's feeling of certainty (He ***must be*** *sitting...*). It should be stressed that these categories are only a rough guide since it is possible to argue that in some contexts a modal belongs in another category than the one allocated here. For example, you could argue that *must* expresses that the person is not certain but *almost* certain. This also applies to the chart in Section 1 of the *Language reference.*

• **Exercise 2** Make sure SS understand the terminology (*permission,* etc.).

• **Exercise 3** These sentences reflect the kind of things SS say to avoid using modals. You could elicit other ways of saying them using different modals (e.g. ***Could*** *you lend me £50?*) and ask whether there are any differences in meaning (i.e. *Could you...* is less direct and therefore usually more polite than *Will you...*).

SPEAKING

Debating

Many SS are unfamiliar with the idea of debating. Debates have the following characteristics:

- There is a motion on which a vote is taken.
- Opposing parties try to convince an audience of their point of view. (As in a court of law, it is not always necessary to believe your own arguments!)
- They are formal and organised: usually there is a set time and there is one person acts as 'chair' (the chairperson).

Tell SS that the best debaters are humorous, forceful and talk to their audience rather than read from notes. They make a few points clearly, with strong arguments and, if possible, quote evidence. They also try to finish their argument with a strong summarising sentence.

You could elicit some of the key points about debates listed above. Alternatively, do this after Exercise 4. Note that in formal debates the opposing sides do not usually interrupt each other. However, in the interests of the English language classroom this has been allowed here! Also, in this debate, unlike in public debates, there is no separate audience.

You might prefer to change the order of the exercises and start with Exercise 4.

• **Exercise 1** Other dangerous sports include: mountain climbing, bullfighting, motor racing, skiing, flying, hang-gliding, parachuting.

• **Exercise 2** Note that the headline *Finish to the fight* is a play on words. The usual expression *fight to the finish* means to fight someone until one or the other is killed.

• **Exercise 3** Some arguments in favour of boxing are: it gives poor kids the chance to get rich and famous; it helps us get rid of our own naturally aggressive instincts indirectly; you can't ban it, because that would mean denying us freedom of choice. Some arguments against the sport are: it's not the boxers who profit but the people who organise boxing; it is immoral that people should try to hurt each other for sport; it can cause permanent brain damage, etc.

• **Exercise 4** You could write these headings on the board and ask SS to give you an expression under each heading before referring to the *Speaking functions* on SB page 150.

• **Exercise 5** Start by getting SS to discuss how the classroom should be organised and, if necessary, discuss what a debate is (see above). Make sure you appoint (or SS appoint) a strong 'chair' (chairperson) or things can go wrong. Make sure SS plan the debate properly and try to be disciplined when they carry it out, e.g.

- the class, should understand the 'rules';
- groups should decide in advance who will say what, ideally a different person taking a different point of view;
- each speaker should be introduced by the 'chair' and given a time limit;
- the 'chair' should ensure that interruptions are disciplined and that speakers are allowed to speak;

Having said that, let SS have fun! The main aim is still to give SS maximum practice in speaking fluently.

WRITING

Letter of complaint

Letters of complaint are often required in exams (perhaps more often than in real life). In complaint letters it is important to say what the problem is and what we want done about it (e.g. a repair, a refund or an apology). In most Western cultures if we want to be taken seriously it is better to be brief, firm, well organised and polite rather than rude. It is important too to give precise information, like dates of purchase of a product, where something was bought, etc.

• **Exercise 1** Possibly elicit a list of types of shops and places and get SS to suggest what the complaints might be.

• **Exercise 2** This gives further practice in 'referencing', focused on in Exercises 7 and 8 of the READING section. Make SS tell you what it is the words refer back to. The exercise also gives a model for a letter of complaint.

• **Exercise 3** Refer SS back to the layout of a formal letter in Unit 6. As indicated above, it is important to get SS to organise their letter in advance. Remind them they should be precise and give exact details and be polite even if they're angry. Their letters must also be brief, business-like and well organised. You could elicit the language of complaint on to the board before you get to b), drawing on any situation in which SS had to make a complaint: *I must object to...; I must complain about...; I can no longer put up with...*, etc. Get SS to write their letter in groups or SS could write drafts and other SS could suggest improvements.

Tapescripts

RECORDING 1

1 A: Have you seen Alan?
B: No. I don't know where he is. I'm not sure if he's here at the moment. He may be out.
A: You don't know much, do you?

2 A: Have you seen Alan?
B: No. I don't know where he is. He must be out. His car keys are missing and his coat's not here.
A: Never mind. I'll catch him tomorrow.

3 A: Have you seen Alan?
B: No, but he can't be out. I heard his voice in the other room just a minute ago.
A: Thanks. I'll see if I can find him.

RECORDING 2

a) They may be late.
b) She must be crazy.
c) You can't be serious.

Key

READING

Reading

2

Direct victim: racehorse Ile de Chypre
Indirect victims: jockey Greville Starkey, the public, bookmakers, etc.
Type of crime: drug conspiracy
Weapon: a high-tech sound gun
Accused: James Laming, a 49-year-old grandfather and South London car dealer
Implications: could be used to destroy the entire system of race-course betting and bookmaking in England

3

STUDENT A

a) What happened when the racehorse got close to the winning post? (The gun was fired causing a deafening noise in the horse's ears; the horse swerved and the jockey was unseated.)
b) Why wasn't it discovered the same day? (Because there was no evidence of its use.)
c) When was it first used? (Last year.)
d) How harmful is it to horses? (There is no permanent damage.)

STUDENT B

a) How does the gun work? (It was built into a pair of binoculars and fired at the horse's ears as it galloped past.)
b) When did the jockey come off? (Just before the end of the race).
c) Why did James Laming do it? (He was supposed to be helping a drug baron win large bets).
d) What kind of bet did the criminals make? (They bet that the favourite or the second favourite would lose.)

5
a) 3 b) 4 c) 2 d) 6 e) 5 f) 1

6
a) fired b) potential c) fortune d) device
e) temperamental f) swerve g) permanent

7
a) the sound gun
b) the King George V Handicap
c) the astonishing story
d) the sound gun
e) the race binoculars
f) the deafening noise
g) the horse Ile de Chypre
h) the drug baron and other conspirators

8
a) These vehicles
b) to the country / to that country / there
c) in the restaurant / in that restaurant / there

VOCABULARY

Sport

1
Example answers:

SPORT	EQUIPMENT	PLACE	VERB
tennis	racket	court	play tennis
swimming	trunks/costume	pool	swim
boxing	gloves	ring	box
golf	clubs	course	play golf
football	boots/ball	pitch	play football
skiing	skis	mountain slopes	ski

2

SPORT	EQUIPMENT	PLACE	VERB
weightlifting	weights	gym	train
table tennis	bat	table	play table tennis
surfing	surfboard	sea	go surfing
athletics	running shoes	track	run

Homophones

1
a) pause b) weight c) principle d) hire
e) seize f) steal g) mourning h) tales

2
b), c), f), h), j)

3
a) where / wear
b) aren't / aunt
c) guest / guessed
d) stares / stairs
e) meat / meet
f) waist / waste
g) whole / hole
h) peace / piece

4
netball, penalty, fishing, foul, rider, chess, pitch, goal, shoot, race, field, pass, amateur, referee, squash

EXTENSION

Deduction in the present

1
a) He can't be out. b) He may be out. c) He must be out.

2
a) might / could
b) He might not be out.
c) Keith can't be out.

3
a) They, late; She, crazy; You, serious
b) /bi/
c) The *t* disappears and the *n't* changes to /m/.

4
a) Yes, he must be her son.
b) It can't be Tom; it's too early.
c) They can't be English; they're speaking Spanish.
d) I don't really know. It might be next week.
e) It can't be his wife. She's abroad.
f) Yes, there must be somebody at the door.
g) I don't know. There may / might / could be a party.
h) It can't be Sue's; hers is a red one.

REVISION

Mixed modals

1
a) I *might* if . . .; It *may* be sooner . . .; It *may* be tonight
b) He *must* be sitting . . .; You *won't* have...
c) I *can't* go on . . .
d) *Can* I call on . . .

2
a) can, may, might, could
b) can, could, would, will
c) must, should, ought to

3
a) You *should / ought to* take malaria tablets but you *must* have a cholera injection.
b) Things *may / might / could* / (*can*) get better.
c) A lot of the people *couldn't* read or write.
d) *Can / May / Might / Could* I take off my coat?
e) . . . It *must* (*should*) be Bill.
f) *Could / Can / Would / Will* you lend me £50?
g) I'm certain Steve *won't / will / would* never help.
h) *May / Can / Could* / (*Might*) I use your computer?

WRITING

Letter of complaint

2
a
a) there, them
b) this, ones
c) them, them, it
d) the problem, the, he
e) the, he, it
f) it, you
g) you, he, he
h) the

b
Sentences a) and h) could be separate paragraphs. Sentences b)-g) could be one paragraph or divided: b), c) + d)-g) or b)-e) + f), g).

Staying alive

Students' Book

General theme: issues of life and death.
Unit topic: 'life' issues.

READING: magazine text about cryonics.
VOCABULARY: forming adjectives with suffixes; word stress; pronunciation of the letter *a*; prepositional phrases.

REVISION: reported speech.
EXTENSION 1: reporting verbs.
EXTENSION 2: reporting tones of voice.

SPEAKING: discussion of 'life' issues.
WRITING: presenting an argument.

Workbook

LISTENING: radio phone-in programme on hunting; vocabulary in context.
GRAMMAR: reporting direct speech; reporting indirect speech; reporting verbs.
VOCABULARY: adjectives and nouns; synonyms and antonyms; phrasal verbs.
WRITING: personal letter.

Language

This unit revises reported speech and extends into looking at reporting verbs, including reporting tones of voice.

At this level, being able to report speech accurately is very important, particularly if SS are intending to do written examinations which include narratives, etc. In general they will already be aware of the 'tense backshift' rule, but will often be restricted in the number of reporting verbs they use, and usually make a lot of mistakes with the word order of sentences. The principal problems tend to be those of form rather than of meaning.

Common problems

Reported speech

1 Remembering to 'backshift' can cause problems, and some languages do not use this device (e.g. Japanese, Arabic and Greek). But, backshifting doesn't always matter, e.g. when statements are still true (*She told me she's got a new car.*).

2 Remembering which modals change their form is also a problem (e.g. *can* becomes *could* but *must* becomes *had to*, and *would* stays the same).

3 The word order of sentences can cause problems, e.g. *say* is not followed by a personal indirect object (**I said him I was ready.*). However, *tell/ask* are followed by a personal indirect object when reporting statements or questions (**I told to her the bus was late. *I asked to her where the bus stopped.*). In most other languages *tell* and *say* are the same word.

4 *Tell* and *ask* are also confusing because they can both be used to report imperatives, e.g. *I told her to phone me.* The word order of imperatives is a problem for many SS. Whereas English uses a verb + personal indirect object + *to* + base form, some languages use *that* (**He asked that I phone her.*).

5 Questions are difficult to report because the word order is different from the statement. Many SS still keep *do/did* (**I asked him where did he live.*) or the inversion (**I asked him where was he going.*). The negative forms cause a problem too, especially for Scandinavians, because of the position of *not*, e.g. *I asked her not to smoke.*

6 SS often forget to make other relevant changes (such as pronouns and adverbials) when reporting speech (e.g. '*Let's meet* ***tomorrow morning.***' becomes *He suggested meeting* ***the following morning***.).

Reporting verbs

1 SS often find it difficult to think of a verb which conveys what the person is trying to say. This is particularly difficult when the meaning depends on the context and/or intonation, e.g. '*I'll see you later.*' can become (among other things) *He* ***promised*** *to see me later.* or *He* ***threatened*** *to see me later.*

2 The sentence structure varies according to the verb (*He apologised* ***for being*** *late. She warned* ***me not to call*** *the police.*). SS tend to transfer their L1 rules (**He wanted that I came.*).

READING

Before reading

• **Exercise 1** Explain briefly what cryonics is (i.e. the science of body freezing) and ask SS to think of the pros and cons of this new science before they read the extracts. Alternatively, SS read the extracts first, then ask them whether they agree with what is said. Tell them they are going to read a magazine article about this new science. The idea may, to many, be controversial.

Reading

• **Exercise 1** This requires SS to read quickly just to identify the content of each paragraph. You could give a time limit to encourage faster reading. Discourage too much attention to new words, since there is a vocabulary exercise based on the text later.

• **Exercise 2** PW? Get SS to justify their answers with evidence from the text.

• **Exercise 3** PW or GW. This is a speaking activity based on statements from the text.

• **Exercise 4** This exercise requires SS to look carefully at the context. PW? SS could use a dictionary to check the answers themselves.

VOCABULARY

Suffixes

Before doing Exercise 1, an alternative approach would be to elicit from SS as many adjective endings as possible and then compare what they suggest with what is written in the box.

• **Exercise 1** PW? Get SS to read quickly for comprehension before they work on the formation of adjectives. Make sure SS do not use dictionaries to check their work as the follow-up listening activity will give them the answers.

Word stress

• **Exercise 1** This is an activity to make SS aware of syllable stress. Do not let SS check in their dictionaries before they have listened to the recording.

• **Exercise 2** Stop the tape after each word and get SS to count out the number of syllables in the word and identify the stressed one. An alternative activity is to give each SS one of the words and to get them to 'mingle' with each other and match 'their' word with someone else's (i.e. to find another word which has, for example, the stress on the first syllable).

The pronunciation of the letter *a*

• **Exercises 1-3** The letter *a* can be pronounced in many ways. Ask SS to say the words before checking in the dictionary. Ask them to identify the vowel sound in the *Pronunciation* chart, SB page 149, and practise reading the sounds at the top of the chart in Exercise 2.

Prepositional phrases

• **Exercises 1-2** These exercises practise prepositions which commonly go with specific nouns. Before doing Exercise 2 go over the answers to Exercise 1. An alternative approach is to play 'Prepositions Bingo'. Give SS cards with prepositions written on them, such as the one following. (Note that two prepositions, *in* and *by* are repeated.) Then read out the nouns which correspond to the prepositions. (Include some nouns which do not go with any of these prepositions, as distractors.) SS have to write the noun below the preposition which they think it goes with. (See the example on the card.) When they have completed a line, either horizontally, vertically or diagonally, they shout 'Bingo'. In order to win the game they have to give correct sentences using the prepositional phrases (e.g. *I think I have got that song **on tape***.). The game could also be played in teams. In this case the Bingo card is put on the blackboard and the class divided into two teams. After each noun is read out the teams take turns to decide where the noun should go on the board. The other team is allowed to challenge them. If the team is correct they can put, for example, a cross (X) in 'their square' and when the other team is correct they could put a nought (0). The winning team is the one that first completes a line, vertically, horizontally or diagonally.

Example Bingo 'card'

at	by	for
in	off	on *tape*
under	in	by

REVISION

Reported speech

Make sure that SS understand the meaning of *whales* and *life raft*. Tell them that this is a true story from a book called *Survive the Savage Sea*.

• **Exercise 1** The aim of this exercise is to transform indirect to direct speech as an awareness raising activity. Make sure SS can identify who all the people are (i.e. what the pictures are showing) before getting them to complete the speech bubbles. During feedback you could jump to Exercise 3 to focus on the grammatical form.

In the WB there is more practice on reporting direct and indirect speech. You could also integrate work on the punctuation of direct speech.

EXTENSION 1

Reporting verbs

• **Exercise 1** Before getting on to the main objective of this exercise (practising indirect speech and different sentence structures with a variety of reporting verbs) you could go over the meaning of the words in the box and get SS to make sentences with them, so that problems of sentence structure can be highlighted. Also check comprehension of the answerphone messages before SS try to report them. Encourage SS to use as many reporting words as they can, trying to avoid *say*, *ask* and *tell* in the interests of variety and 'colour'. (The verbs need not necessarily be ones from the box.). Make it clear that 'partners' in this case means, e.g. boyfriend or wife.

• **Exercise 2** GW? Make it clear that SS can use whatever reporting words they want to, not just the ones in the box. Encourage them to be as imaginative as they can about the story. Get each group to read their story out.

• **Exercise 3** This is a jigsaw activity, with one group working on a reading and one on a listening text. Get SS to work individually before comparing their notes in pairs or groups.

• **Exercise 4** Divide the two groups into pairs so that each person from Group A works with someone from Group B. Tell them to compare their stories and find as many differences as they can. This should result in SS using reported speech quite naturally.

If a jigsaw activity is difficult to do, an alternative activity is for the whole class to read the text as well as listening to the tape, and then compare the differences.

There is more work on different sentence patterns for reporting verbs in the WB.

EXTENSION 2

Reporting tones of voice

• **Exercise 1** You could demonstrate the words in the box first and get SS to guess which ones you are demonstrating. Alternatively, get individual SS to act out each of the sentences before another S replaces the words in italics.

• **Exercise 2** Attention needs to be paid to the prepositions following some of these verbs, e.g. *grumble* ***about***, *scream* ***in/with*** *horror.*

SPEAKING

Discussion

• **Exercise 1** This activity aims to get SS to express their views on controversial issues, and the topics reflect the theme of serious 'life issues', such as cryonics, in this unit and the next. Avoid any which may not be suitable for your particular situation, and add others as appropriate. You could get each group to report their views back to the class, which would also give extra practice in reported speech. Alternatively, this activity could be done as a formal debate, with small groups taking a position either for or against one of the statements. Another idea would be to have a kind of 'Question Time' forum, modelled on the British TV current affairs programme, where an audience is given an opportunity to question politicians and public figures on topical issues that have recently come up in the news. To do this, elect a small panel of people (four people?) and give them roles (e.g. a Conservative MP in favour of compulsory military service and against 'moral objectors' to war, who is also in favour of bloodsports; a left-wing politician who is anti-war and pro animal rights; a feminist, who feels that a childless woman has the right to have a child by whatever means she can, etc.). Elect a chairperson to keep the panel in order, and to give time limits.

In small groups, the rest of the class should think of two topics per group they would like to comment on or ask questions about. They then decide on the exact questions, and which member of the panel they will address the questions to.

The chairperson should then ask each of the groups to ask a question, and give the panel member a time limit in which to reply. The person who asked the question should then have an opportunity to give their own opinion.

Note that there is an extract from a radio programme on hunting in the WB, which could be brought in here.

WRITING

Presenting an argument

Being able to write an argumentative essay, putting the points for and against something, is very important for many SS at this level. This section gives them an outline to follow and provides integrated revision of linking words.

• **Exercise 3** You could get SS to do a draft of an essay on cryonics in class as a 'process-writing' activity. By doing this they could, in groups, discuss which ideas they would include and how they would organise it, but not worry too much about producing a perfectly written essay. They could then write another essay at home based on one of the arguments in the SPEAKING section earlier.

Tapescripts

RECORDING 1

The man who worked here over the summer seemed nice enough. He was always reliable as regards timekeeping and so on and, although rather moody and not very talkative, he had a very imaginative and yet systematic approach to his work. He was quite popular with the rest of the staff as well, because he was very attractive, with quite a babyish face. He was artistic and was very helpful to people who were in trouble, so we were quite shocked when the police told us he was a professional criminal.

RECORDING 2

back, although, America, harder, place, attempt, answer, thaw, happen, space

RECORDING 3

a) what b) many c) want

RECORDING 4

1 Hi, this is Bob. I'm phoning from the States to tell you that Pat and I will finally be getting married in Britain on August 10th, so keep that date free. We'd like you to come to the wedding if you can. Cheers!
2 Fred here. Just to warn you that the motorway is still choc-a-bloc with cars - bumper to bumper. It took us nearly four hours to get home. So if you're still thinking of doing this journey tomorrow it would be better to take the A120 road. Good luck!
3 This is the Mr Andrews from the library. Just to jog your memory about the book you ordered from us. It's been here for a week and I'm afraid if you don't collect it soon we'll have to let someone else have it. There's quite a long waiting list because it's just come out.

4 Hello, this is Janice Weston. I never seem to be able to get you these days but I simply must have that translation by Monday at the very latest. I'm sorry to put you under so much pressure but it's really important.
5 Hello, Tim darling. It's Mummy here. Please try to get down for lunch on Sunday. I know you and Pam are so busy but I'll make you a special meal if you come. I'll phone again when you're in - I hate this machine!

RECORDING 5

MARTIN: Yes, the barman said, 'Damned hunters! Shoot 'em. There's plenty of places to bury them.' We could hardly believe our ears! 'Make sure you don't bury them right by the Orinoco river. When the rains come, the river'll wash the bodies down here and the tourists don't like that.'
TANIS: Luckily we never actually came face-to-face with these awful hunters, though I'm pretty sure we were followed on occasions.
M: Yes, do you remember walking along that beach and seeing that beautiful lizard? I tried to catch it and as I was chasing it into some long grass, I saw a man hurry away. We became really nervous after that.
T: We survived in the jungle - by trial and error, I guess. We hadn't brought much from home, just a tent and a medical kit. Everything else we got on arrival.
M: The one thing we never seemed to have enough of, though, was mosquito cream. Do you remember Peru? That was the worst place for mosquitoes. When we went to bed there were so many on our net that we couldn't see out.

Key

READING

Reading

1
a) paragraph 4 (+2) b) paragraph 5 c) paragraph 3
d) paragraph 1 e) paragraph 6

2
a) True b) False c) True d) False e) True
f) False

4
Suggested answers:
a) taken off
b) frozen
c) put on, do freeze
d) fashion
e) normal
f) new and different
g) very sure
h) possible

VOCABULARY

Suffixes

1
1 reliable 2 moody 3 talkative 4 imaginative
5 systematic 6 attractive 7 babyish 8 artistic
9 helpful 10 professional

Word stress

1

TWO SYLLABLES	THREE SYLLABLES	FOUR SYLLABLES	FIVE SYLLABLES
'moody	'talkative	re'liable	i'maginative
'helpful	a'ttractive	syste'matic	
	'babyish	pro'fessional	
	ar'tistic		

The pronunciation of the letter *a*

1
a) /ətræktɪv/ b) /tɔːkətɪv/ c) /ɑːtɪstɪk/ d) /beɪbi-ɪʃ/

2

/ɑː/	/æ/	/ɔː/	/ə/	/eɪ/
harder	back	although	America	place
answer	happen	thaw	attempt	space

3
a) /wɒt/ b) many /meni/ c) want /wɒnt/

Prepositional phrases

1

AT	BY	FOR	IN	OFF	ON	UNDER
war	chance	fun	a bad mood	duty	purpose	control
	mistake	rent	common			
		a change	charge		tape	
			writing		duty	
			fun			
			control			

2
a) on purpose b) for a change c) on tape d) in writing
e) under control f) by chance

REVISION

Reported speech

1
a) Picture 1: 'It's a ship!'
b) Picture 2: 'Will they be able to see us?'
c) Picture 3: 'Get out the flares!'
d) Picture 4: 'I'm going to use our last rocket flare.

2
a) *Don't come!* (Mrs Young told them not to come.)
b) *I can't swim.* (I remember Alan told me (said to me) that he can't (couldn't) swim.)
c) *What'll you do tomorrow?* (Julian asked me what I would do the next day / tomorrow.
d) *Have you just bought a new car? No, I haven't.* (Alison asked me if I had just bought a new car. I said I hadn't).
e) *I have been living here for two years.* (Simon told me that he has been / had been living here/there for two years.)

3

a) They 'shift back' into the past.
b) *Tell* is normally followed by an indirect object; *say* is followed by an object with *to*.
c) They have the same word order as a statement.

EXTENSION 1

Reporting verbs

1

b)

Example answers:

1 Bob phoned to tell us he was getting married in August, and to invite us to the wedding.
2 Fred warned us that the motorway was still very crowded. He said it took them nearly four hours to get home and he advised us to take the A120 road.
3 Mr Andrews phoned from the library. He rang to remind you that you had ordered a book and warned you that if you didn't collect it they'd have to let someone else have it.
4 Janice Weston phoned, insisting that she had to have the translation by Monday at the latest. She apologised for putting you under pressure, but insisted that it was really important.
5 Your mother phoned, to persuade us to go to lunch on Sunday. She promised to make us a special meal and said she'd phone again when you were in.

3

GROUP A

What the barman said: 'Shoot them and throw them in the Orinoco as a warning to other hunters'.
Almost meeting the hunters: 'We were running away from a large snake. They threatened us, but we managed to escape.'
Survival in the jungle: 'We never really learned how to survive.'
Provisions: 'We brought all our provisions from home.'
Peru: 'Peru was the best because the air was clear and fresh.'

GROUP B

What the barman said: He told them to shoot them, but to make sure they didn't bury them by the Orinoco river. When the rains came the river would wash the bodies down there and the tourists didn't like that.
Almost meeting the hunters: Martin was chasing a lizard along the beach and he saw a man hurry away.
Survival in the jungle: They survived in the jungle by trial and error.
Provisions: They didn't bring much, just a tent and a medical kit. All the rest they got on arrival.
Peru: Martin said that Peru was the worst place for mosquitoes.

EXTENSION 2

Reporting tones of voice

1

a) exclaimed b) stammered c) screamed
d) whispered/muttered e) muttered/whispered
f) grumbled g) swore

2

Example answers:

a) English people grumble about the weather because it rains all the time.
b) He screamed in horror when he saw the knife.
c) Jane whispered/muttered something in my ear and winked at me.
d) I heard her mutter a threat under her breath.
e) Roy stammered nervously when he gave the man's name to the police.
f) She swore/grumbled at her boss because she/he (had) made her stay late.
g) He exclaimed in delight when he saw his new car.

WRITING

Presenting an argument

2

Introductory paragraph b) is the better opening paragraph because it introduces the topic first and gives some background, rather than going straight in with the writer's opinion.

Presenting the argument

b)

There are three main arguments against animal experimentation. Firstly, and perhaps most importantly, it causes a great deal of suffering, which cannot be justified in the name of research and also makes one ask what right humans have to treat animals in this way. Secondly, drugs tried out on animals are not necessarily successful on humans. In fact there have been many cases where humans have been very ill or died as a result of using such drugs, as in the case of the 'thalidomide babies'. In addition to this it is becoming increasingly clear that many serious illnesses are cured not so much by drugs as by social reform such as better food, hygiene etc. Finally, many drugs are being produced where others already exist, in the name of profit.

Presenting the counter argument

c)

Example answers:

On the other hand; Despite / In spite of; Nevertheless

Conclusion

a) In conclusion b) I think; I feel that

Rites of passage

Students' Book

General theme: issues of life and death.
Unit topic: ceremonies.

LISTENING 1: radio programme about 'rites of passage' ceremonies.
VOCABULARY: word formation; euphemisms and idioms.

REVISION AND EXTENSION: defining relative clauses; non-defining relative clauses; intonation of relative clauses.
LISTENING 2: a talk about funeral customs in China; word stress with *-ion* words.
EXTENSION 2: participle clauses.

SPEAKING: designing a monument; choosing an epitaph.
WRITING: description of a scene.

Workbook

READING: magazine article about a pets' cemetery.
GRAMMAR: defining relative clauses; defining and non-defining relative clauses; participle clauses; adjectives ending in *-ing* and *-ed*.
VOCABULARY: word building, prepositional phrases; confusing words.
PRONUNCIATION: vowel sounds.
WRITING: joining sentences.

Language

This unit revises defining relative clauses and introduces non-defining relative clauses and participle clauses. All of these are useful to SS at this level because of their importance in writing, particularly when describing something. However, many SS tend to avoid using them.

The main problems with relative clauses are usually associated with form, punctuation and intonation. SS need to decide whether to use a defining or non-defining clause and when the pronouns can be dropped. Although SS will probably be familiar with the form of participles they often find it difficult to use them correctly. They should realise that participles placed after the noun serve the same function as a relative clause, but are a more abbreviated form.

Common problems

1 In some languages (e.g. Spanish, Dutch) there is only one relative pronoun for things and people.

2 In some languages (e.g. Spanish) the relative pronoun can never be deleted.

3 In some languages (e.g. Turkish) relative clauses come before the noun.

4 In some languages (e.g. Greek and Arabic) the object must be included (**The dog which I saw it yesterday.*).

5 Many SS have problems with where to position the preposition, and often miss it out (**That's the boy (from) who I bought the car.*).

6 Some languages (e.g. Dutch) do not differentiate between defining and non-defining relative clauses.

7 SS often try to use a relative participle clause for a non-progressive meaning (**I am quite friendly with the bloke working in the shop on Saturdays.*).

LISTENING 1

Before listening

SS may be able to guess what is happening in the different photographs and what links them together (they are all ceremonies which mark going from one stage of life to another). However, they will probably not know the names of most of the ceremonies. Don't tell them the answers at this stage as they will find out from the listening text.

Listening

• **Exercise 1** The tape could be played twice, first just to check that SS have guessed the names of the ceremonies correctly; the second time to find out what each ceremony is about. Make it clear that answers in b) only need to be brief. There are more detailed questions in Exercise 2.

• **Exercises 2 and 3** SS could try doing Exercise 2 based on what they remember or what they can predict, and then listen to the tape. Stop at the end of each extract to elicit answers to the questions.

VOCABULARY

Word formation

• **Exercises 1 and 2** These exercises practise forms of the verbs which always seem to cause SS problems. In Exercise 1, SS frequently confuse *died* and *dead* and say *I am born in* ... In Exercise 2 SS have great problems with the *lay/lie* distinction (**I am laying on the bed.*) and it is probably worth writing the verb forms on the board (e.g. ***to lie***, *lying, lay, lain;* ***to lay***, *laying, laid, laid*).

Euphemisms and idioms

• **Exercise 1** A euphemism is an expression which is used to avoid being direct about something thought to be unpleasant or embarrassing. Death is one situation lots of euphemisms are used for (e.g. *pass away, kick the bucket,* etc.) and there is a sketch by Monty Python, available on tape or video tape (the 'Parrot sketch') which is based on many such euphemisms. This could be integrated very well here. (In Unit 9, *Listening,* Michael Palin refers to this famous sketch.) Work on euphemisms could be extended to give SS other examples, e.g. *in his birthday suit* (naked), *it fell off the back of a lorry* (it was stolen), *gay* (homosexual), *a coloured woman* (a black woman), *to powder one's nose* (to go to the toilet), etc.

• **Exercise 2** This provides revision of idiomatic expressions. If SS have not done Unit 9, discuss how to find the meaning of an idiom in a dictionary (i.e. identify the key word and look it up).

• **Exercise 3** This could be done as a written rather than an oral activity.

REVISION AND EXTENSION

Defining relative clauses

• **Exercise 1** The aim of the listening extract is to get SS to use defining relative clauses and then to focus their attention on how they are used. First, get SS to listen to the tape and take notes on what the photographs show (e.g. picture 1: boat – Galapagos Islands last year). They can then work on writing complete sentences in pairs. Many of the problems with form, such as correct choice of a relative pronoun, position of adjectives, etc. will probably come up in the feedback phase.

• **Exercise 2** Part a) of this exercise focuses on the form of relative clauses and part c) gets SS to choose the correct form in a controlled exercise.

• **Exercise 4** Do this as a dictionary activity or as revision of vocabulary studied recently. SS could give other SS words to define. There are examples of such words in P. Ur, *Grammar Practice Activities* (see *Bibliography*).

Extra work on defining relative clauses can be found in the WB.

Non-defining relative clauses

• **Exercise 1** Make sure that SS understand the difference between the two sentences, i.e. in b) ***That*** *woman* means she has already been defined, so the information in commas is optional.

• **Exercise 3** Discuss with SS possible situations in which these sentences could be defining clauses, and how they might be changed to make more sense (i.e. a) would make more sense if it were to become ***The*** *new boss.*).

Intonation of relative clauses

• **Exercises 1 and 2** These exercises give practice in both the recognition and production of relative clauses. In Exercise 1 help SS to practise the sentences, making sure that they pause where the commas would be in a non-defining relative clause, and get them to contrast this with a defining relative clause, where there are no pauses. It is important that SS practise the intonation when they are doing Exercise 2.

LISTENING 2

Before listening

The photograph shows a funeral procession in China, and could be used to stimulate discussion about different traditions for funerals, such as the colour of clothes worn for mourning.

Listening

• **Exercises 1-3** Exercise 1 focuses on global comprehension, Exercise 2 requires more detailed listening and Exercise 3 is an intensive gapped summary. Exercise 2 gives an opportunity for revising contrastive stress (e.g. *China has* ***a quarter*** *of the world's population, not 40 per cent.*) Answers to Exercise 3 could also be checked with the tapescript.

• **Exercise 4** This discussion may be of particular interest in a multinational class because SS can compare their cultures with each other. Some Ts may prefer to avoid any discussion of funeral ceremonies, or at least keep them non-personal. You may in any case prefer to go directly to the *Word stress* exercise and leave any discussion until the SPEAKING section.

Word stress

The example words are taken from the *Listening* text. Make sure SS include the 'schwa' (/ə/) sound as well as the /ʃ/ sound and that they put the stress on the penultimate syllable. Other ideas for words: *nation, tension, decision.*

EXTENSION 2

Participle clauses

Reduction of the relative clause by using participles is very common in spoken English, but SS are often not used to using them.

• **Exercise 1** You could replace or supplement this exercise by finding photographs yourself which incorporate minimal differences and which will elicit participle clauses. This exercise also gives an opportunity to practise contrastive stress (e.g. *In my picture the woman's wearing a* ***blue*** *jumper, not a yellow one.*).

Base form of the verb or *-ing*?

Make it clear that in many of the sentences in Exercise 2 (e.g. a), c), f), g)) both alternatives are possible with a slightly different meaning. (In a) the choice of *crawl* would mean that you flicked the insect off immediately, whereas *crawling* gives the impression it remained there for longer).

SPEAKING

Designing a monument

Tutankhamen was an Egyptian king living in around 1350 BC, whose tomb was discovered almost intact in 1922. You might want to show photos of his tomb and what was found there, and discuss what it tells us about the times he lived in. Get SS to think of some things used or worn in the 1990s that people might be surprised by in the future (e.g. an electric toothbrush, a CD player, mini-skirts).

You could brainstorm a list of famous people to choose from (e.g. Elizabeth Taylor, Princess Diana, Mother Teresa) before splitting into groups. Give a limit on the number of things to be buried (ten?).

Choosing an epitaph

You could give SS a wider range of epitaphs to look at, including some which don't rhyme (e.g. *Rest in peace – until we meet again* (from a widow to her husband), *Here lies an honest lawyer / And that is Strange* (for the lawyer, John Strange).

Try to keep the activity light-hearted! Again, perhaps brainstorm famous people who have an unusual name or are particularly notorious.

WRITING

Description of a scene

The main aim of this writing activity is to encourage SS to be creative. The focus is on the process of writing rather than on the final product and is intended to be fun. However, it is a good idea to get the person who begins each story to see how they can improve it before reading it out, and there may be an opportunity to include relative and participle clauses.

Tell SS that the picture is of a Sri Lankan Buddhist festival, which happens every year and lasts for ten days. People bring elephants into the town of Kandy, paint them in bright patterns and lead them through the streets in a procession. There is music and dancing, sometimes by torchlight. You could lead on to a general discussion of festivals which are held in SS' own country/countries (e.g. the Day of the Dead in Mexico, or the Carnival in Trinidad). Optional follow-up homework could be to write about such a festival and possibly illustrate it with photos.

Tapescripts

RECORDING 1

Nearly all societies hold 'rites of passage' ceremonies, which observe a person's entry into a new stage of life. The most common rites of passage are occasions such as birth, marriage and death. Most rites help people to understand and accept their new roles in society and help others to learn to treat them in new ways. And now we're going to hear about five different ceremonies.

Muslims hold a ceremony a week after a baby is born, which is known as an Aqiqa. The ceremony is intended to protect the baby from dangers in its life, and it has several parts. The child's head is first shaved so that it's completely clean, and then the weight of the cut hair is given in gold or silver to the poor. This is the baby's first act of charity towards others. After this, the baby is named, and the ceremony is followed by a feast. Goats and sheep are cooked and sweetened, as it's believed that sweet food will make the child good-natured. Two thirds of the meat is given to the poor.

Another religious ceremony which babies often go through is called baptism. This practice involves a symbolic washing with water to indicate the washing away of sins and the start of a renewed life. Most churches consider baptism to be the main ceremony which signifies a person's entry into the Christian community. Children are often given their first name at this ceremony, and there is usually some kind of party afterwards.

A jewish *bar mitzvah* celebrates the reaching of spiritual adulthood, which is, for a Jewish boy, at the age of thirteen. A crucial aspect of the bar mitzvah experience is when the father lets his son go, accepting that he is now his own person, responsible for his own actions. The father is thanking God for his son's manhood when he says: 'Blessed is he who has released me from responsibility for this child.' From the following day the boy is expected to observe all the relevant commandments and to be responsible for his own behaviour.

Nearly all religions include the belief that human beings survive death in some form. For many people, such as the Balinese, a funeral symbolises the passage from one life to another, rather than an end of a person's existence. In Bali, a cremation is therefore a time of joy and celebration. On the morning of the cremation, friends and relatives gather to pay their last respects and to eat and drink with the family. There is then a procession to the cremation ground, some men carrying the corpse in a tower built of bamboo and paper, and other men carrying a special container called a sarcophagus, which may be in the shape of a cow or a bull. At the cremation ground the body is transferred to the sarcophagus and when it has been reduced to ashes and the soul released there is a happy noisy procession to the sea, where the ashes are scattered. This last ceremony represents cleansing and purification.

Not all 'rites of passage' are religious, and other kinds of 'rites' in modern times would include the 'key of the door' which young people get at the age of eighteen or twenty-one, the right to vote, or a driving licence. People often pass through rites as a group. In graduation ceremonies in the United States, for example, students first stand together in a special area, away from their friends and relatives. Then they walk across a stage to symbolise the transition, and change the tassels from one side of the cap to the other to indicate entry into society as graduates. The graduation gowns symbolise their temporary separation from society.

RECORDING 2

TIM: That's nice. Why have you got a photo of a boat in your album?

IMOGEN: Ah yes, that's the boat which we went round the Galapagos Islands on last year. It was wonderful - really comfortable.

T: What a lovely cat!

I: That's Basil. I'd forgotten about him! He was our first cat, the one that won a prize at the local cat show.

T: Who's the woman in this photo?

I: Ah, that's Suzanne. She's a girl - one of many! - who used to be engaged to my brother.

T: I see. And is that the flat where you used to live?

I: That's right - in Rome. And the last picture is of a really great Portuguese family whose house we rented one summer.

RECORDING 3

a) My new boss, who I spoke to after work, agreed to give me time off.
b) The French students who had failed badly decided not to resit the exams.
c) My uncle, who lives in Manchester, is retiring next week.
d) That singer whose record is currently top of the charts is doing a concert next month.

RECORDING 4

The Shanghai crematorium might almost be called a model institution in the Chinese leadership's new drive to spread the practice of cremation from China's cities to its rural areas. The altogether plausible argument is that, with a quarter of the world's population but only seven per cent of its arable land, China just hasn't got room for graves. The new regulations specifically ban burials on agricultural land or scenic spots and, although burials are still to be allowed in certain circumstances - for instance, for national minorities - there must, the government says, be no use of what it calls superstitious burial objects. The problem is that it's not an easy matter to persuade the intensely superstitious Chinese to accept cremation as an alternative to burial. Since Mao Tse Tung's first pronouncement on cremation thirty years ago the cremation rate - as the Chinese call it - has risen to 80 per cent in the cities. However, in the countryside, even where there are crematoria, it's still only thirty per cent. Mao, in his own death, scarcely helped - his embalmed uncremated body lies on display in a mausoleum in Peking.

The way the Chinese have traditionally seen it, a dead man can never rest in peace until he's properly buried under ground. The right spot has to be found with what's termed in Chinese the right *feng-shui*, or combination of water and wind, and that can be literally anywhere.

Whatever the government's stand on such things it's many a time travelling around China that I've already come across what one might call fresh 'wild cat graves' by the road or field-side, complete with exquisite wreaths of white paper flowers. In China, white, not black, is the colour of mourning.

But it's not enough just to find the right spot for burial - the deceased has, in Chinese custom, to be given the goods he'll supposedly need in the afterlife - specially printed paper money for petty bribes in the nether world and sometimes, in this electronic age, paper television sets, cassette recorders, even paper cars, bikes and sewing machines.

It's feudal superstitions like these that appear, much to the disquiet of the powers-that-be, to be making something of a comeback in China.

RECORDING 5

The Shanghai crematorium might almost be called a model institution in the Chinese leadership's new drive to spread the practice of cremation from China's cities to its rural areas. The altogether plausible argument is that, with a quarter of the world's population but only seven per cent of its arable land, China just hasn't got room for graves. The new regulations specifically ban burials on agricultural land or scenic spots and, although burials are still to be allowed in certain circumstances - for instance, for national minorities - there must, the government says, be no use of what it calls superstitious burial objects. The problem is that it's not an easy matter to persuade the intensely superstitious Chinese to accept cremation as an alternative to burial. Since Mao Tse Tung's first pronouncement on cremation thirty years ago the cremation rate - as the Chinese call it - has risen to 80 per cent in the cities. However, in the countryside, even where there are crematoria, it's still only thirty per cent. Mao, in his own death, scarcely helped - his embalmed uncremated body lies on display in a mausoleum in Peking

RECORDING 6

The way the Chinese have traditionally seen it, a dead man can never rest in peace until he's properly buried under ground. The right spot has to be found with what's termed in Chinese the right *feng-shui*, or combination of water and wind, and that can be literally anywhere.

Whatever the government's stand on such things it's many a time travelling around China that I've already come across what one might call fresh 'wild cat graves' by the road or field-side, complete with exquisite wreaths of white paper flowers. In China, white, not black, is the colour of mourning.

But it's not enough just to find the right spot for burial - the deceased has, in Chinese custom, to be given the goods he'll supposedly need in the afterlife - specially printed paper money for petty bribes in the nether world and sometimes, in this electronic age, paper television sets, cassette recorders, even paper cars, bikes and sewing machines.

It's feudal superstitions like these that appear, much to the disquiet of the powers-that-be, to be making something of a comeback in China.

RECORDING 7

institution, cremation

Key

LISTENING 1

Before listening

1

They are all connected to 'rites of passage' (i.e. a new stage in a person's life).

2

a) bar mitzvah
b) graduation
c) cremation
d) Aqiqa
e) baptism

Listening

1

a)

2 e) 3 a) 4 c) 5 b)

b)

i) The entry of a person into a new stage of life.
ii) An Aqiqa ceremony is intended to protect a child from the dangers in its life.
Baptism signifies a person's entry into the Christian community.
Bar mitzvah is when a Jewish boy becomes a man.
A Balinese cremation symbolises the passage from one life to another.
Graduation indicates entry to society as a graduate student.

2

a) A week after birth.
b) The equivalent weight of gold or silver is given to the poor.
c) To make the child good-natured.
d) Washing away of sins and the start of a renewed life.
e) Thirteen.
f) In the sea. This represents cleansing and purification.
g) Transition.
h) To symbolise separation from society.

VOCABULARY

Word formation

a) dead b) dying c) was born d) died e) birthday
f) death g) birth

2

a) lying b) unhelpful c) announcement
d) inconvenience e) enjoyable f) lay g) failure h) daily

Euphemisms and idioms

1

a) *'I've been feeling under the weather recently.'* means 'I've been feeling ill.'
'Senior citizens half price'. Senior citizens is another way of talking about old people.
'. . . thin on top' means 'going bald'.

2

Example answers:

a) . . . he's going to bed.
b) . . . come round and see me.
c) . . . I'd better buy another one.
d) . . . he told them the joke.
e) . . . he dresses as if he was a teenager.
f) . . . I think we will be happier.
g) . . . whether to stay or not.

REVISION AND EXTENSION

Defining relative clauses

1

a) Picture 2 shows Basil, her first cat, the one that/which won a prize at the local cat show.
Picture 3 shows Suzanne, one of the many girls who used to be engaged to her brother.
Picture 4 shows the flat in Rome where she used to live.
Picture 5 shows the Portuguese family whose house she rented one summer.

2

c)

i) that / which
ii) that / which
iii) -
iv) whose
v) where

3

a) a corkscrew b) a thermometer c) a widow
d) a robin e) a comedy f) a will g) a jury

Non-defining relative clauses

1

b)

2

a) The relative pronouns *can be* / *can't be* left out.
b) Non-defining relative clauses are *more common* / *less common* in writing than in speaking.
c) *Which* is used for *people* / *things*.
d) *Who* is used for *people* / *things*.

3

a) My new boss, who I spoke to after work, agreed to give me time off.
b) The French students, who had failed badly, decided not to resit the exam.
c) My uncle, who lives in Manchester, is retiring next week.
d) That singer, whose record is currently top of the charts, is doing a concert next month.
e) Our best friend, who nobody had expected to settle down, got married last year.

b) Could also be defining but would mean that only some of the French students had failed the exam.
c) Could also be defining, but would mean that there was more than one uncle.
d) Could also be defining but would mean that the singer had not been referred to before.
e) This sentence would be unlikely as a defining clause as there is likely to be only one best friend.

Intonation of relative clauses

1

a)

a) ND b) D c) ND d) D

2

a) Joan, whose car had broken down, asked my husband for a lift to work.
b) Phil, who'd been ill the previous week, lost the tennis match.
c) The postman, who came from Wales, had a lovely accent.
d) Pat was in Scotland, where her grandparents live, when it happened.
e) She showed me her pet snake, which frightened me very much.
f) I left my favourite jacket, which I'd bought on holiday, on the bus.

LISTENING 2

Listening

1

a) Burial ceremonies.
b) Cremate the dead.

2

1) China has a quarter of the world's population.
2) It has only 7 per cent of its arable land.
3) Burials are not allowed on agricultural land (or scenic spots).
4) The Chinese are intensely superstitious.
5) The cremation rate is 80 per cent in the cities.
6) It is 30 per cent in the countryside.
7) There are some crematoria in the countryside.
8) Mao was not cremated - he was embalmed.

3

1 are properly buried under the ground
2 water and wind
3 anywhere
4 by the road or fieldside
5 white
6 wreaths of white paper flowers
7 paper money
8 paper electronic goods

Word stress

1

a) It is pronounced as a schwa.
b) On the syllable before '*tion*'.
c) popu'lation
regu'lation
combi'nation
super'stition
tele'vision

EXTENSION 2

Participle clauses

1

In Picture 2 the woman is talking to a man (not watching a tennis match); there is a dog (not a horse) tied to a tree; there is a man drinking a cup of coffee (not holding it) and holding a newspaper. There is a car parked in front of a *No Parking* sign.

2

a) The houses designed in Victorian times were quite solid.
b) There's a fast road leading to the motorway.
c) Trains leaving from platform 5 go to Warsaw only.
d) Is there a man called Tim here?
e) I eventually found the letter posted to me yesterday.
f) People caught shoplifting will be sent to prison.

Base form of the verb or *-ing?*

1

go into the house refers to a complete action, while *opening the door* refers to a part of it.

2

a) crawling b) quarrelling c) take off d) talking
e) building f) catch g) happen h) burning

A mystery!

Students' Book

Unit topic: mysteries.

READING: first part of a mystery story; vocabulary.
REVISION AND EXTENSION: deduction in the past (*must have, can't have, might / may / could have*); connected speech (*may, have* etc.).
LISTENING: second part of mystery story; vocabulary.

READING AND WRITING: last part of story; writing a newspaper report.
VOCABULARY: different sounds (*squawk, roar,* etc.); idiomatic expressions (e.g. *spark off*).
SPEAKING: roleplay: a press conference.

PRACTICE: past modals of deduction.
WRITING: a newspaper article using participle clauses.

Workbook

All the activities in this unit are based on a short story,'*Skeleton in the cupboard*' by Tony Wilmot. The emphasis is on skills practice, although there is also vocabulary work and revision of past modals of deduction.

READING 1: first part of short story; vocabulary in context.
LISTENING 1: second part of story; vocabulary.
READING 2: third part of story; vocabulary.
LISTENING 2: fourth part of story; revision of modals of deduction.
READING 3: last part of story.
WRITING: continue the story.

Language

The language focus in this unit is on modals of deduction in the past. This includes *must have done / been doing; can't have done / been doing; may / might / could have done / been doing.*

SS will already be familiar with the meaning of *may, might* and *could* for possibility in the present but may not have used the constructions when talking about the past.

The use of *must* and *can't* in the present for deductions based on 'evidence' in the situation was introduced in Unit 16. In this unit it is extended to talk about deduction in the past.

The form of past modals was introduced briefly in Unit 6 (e.g. *needn't have*) and also with *should have* in Unit 12. Although specific controlled practice exercises do not occur until later in the unit, SS are encouraged to use modals of deduction from the beginning to talk about their deductions based on the account of an unsolved crime.

Common problems

1 The form of past modals (to include the Perfect Continuous infinitive) is quite difficult for SS to use spontaneously. They prefer to say *Maybe he went.* or *I'm sure he didn't go.*

2 The pronunciation of the form is often a problem, both to understand and produce, as *have* is usually weak, as is *been* in the continuous form (*He could have been* (/kʊdəvbɪn/) *living in Mexico.*).

READING

• **Exercise 1** It is important that SS understand the first part of the story, because it is continued in the LISTENING section. In addition, the language point of the unit comes out of the text. The three questions, a) – c), focus on the main detail of the text and b) and c) give an opportunity for use of the target language before it is introduced. This is useful for diagnostic purposes.

'Concept' questions to focus on the meaning of modals of deduction in the past could include: *Did Cooper blow up the plane? Where is he living now? Is he still alive? Where did he get the bomb from?*

• **Exercise 2** Other words in the text which could either be guessed by SS or explained to SS are: *calculating, cruised, bargained, pirate, inpenetrable.*

REVISION AND EXTENSION

Deduction in the past

• **Exercise 1** Instead of SS reading the sentences, you could write the sentences on the board, with gaps for SS to complete (e.g. *D.B. Cooper is remembered as a hero, so he ___ blown up the plane.*). In this way, if you cannot elicit the target structure, you can introduce it in context. SS should refer to the *Language reference* section after completing the rules which follow the sentences. Work could be done at this stage on the weak forms of *have* and *been*, to help SS practise pronunciation of the constructions. However, there is specific focus on the pronunciation of *must have*, etc. in *Connected speech* later in the section. Make it clear that after *have* the past participle, or *been* + base form + *-ing* can often be used.

• **Exercise 2** You could get SS to work in pairs and think of two things Cooper *must, can't* and *may have done*.

Connected speech

• **Exercises 1-3** These exercises aim to help SS to recognise and give practice in the weak and contracted forms of modals of deduction in the past. Don't tell SS how many words there are in the sentences until they have completed the dictation in Exercise 2.

If you want to do more controlled practice of modals of deduction in the past, there is a PRACTICE section later in the unit which could be slotted in at this point. However, if SS seem reasonably confident using it, it is probably better not to interrupt the flow of the story.

LISTENING

• **Exercises 1 and 2** These exercises require SS to listen for detail as well as make inferences. You may need to play each extract more than once.

• **Exercise 4** SS could look at the tapescript to check their answers, perhaps after comparing with other SS.

READING AND WRITING

• **Exercise 1** Give SS a time limit to read the text and decide on their answers. Discourage use of dictionaries for the moment. In any case, some of the idiomatic language is focused on in the VOCABULARY section.

• **Exercise 2** There is plenty of scope here for use of modals of deduction in the past (e.g. *Anyone could have written the note. It may not have been Cooper.*). If SS avoid using them (e.g. *Perhaps someone else wrote the note.*), try to get them to rephrase their answers so that they do use them.

• **Exercise 3** This is an opportunity for some creative writing, and the discussion before SS write should help them to generate ideas about what happened to Cooper. Instead of writing a newspaper report, SS could write Cooper's diary or a letter from him to a friend. If it is to be a newspaper report, remind SS of the features of different kinds of newspapers (perhaps referring back to Units 11 and 12). The actual writing could be done either as a collaborative activity in pairs or groups, or on an individual basis.

VOCABULARY

Different sounds

• **Exercise 1** This exercise is for fun, although SS can, of course, also be encouraged to use such expressions in their writing. Point out that *hiss* is used metaphorically to show anger: real hissing involves continuous use of the *s* sound. For fun, SS could try saying one sentence (e.g. *Where is he?*) in a variety of different ways.

• **Exercise 3** You could ask SS to brainstorm other animals and sounds, and compare them with animal sounds in their own language(s).

Idiomatic expressions

All these expressions come from the reading text and all are used metaphorically. Warn SS that the drawings (a man in a hole and a man combing a mountain) are meant as a joke! SS might be interested in learning more metaphors in English, and they might be able to translate some from their own language(s), although they should be warned that most do not translate literally.

SPEAKING

A press conference

This activity is a fluency activity, and is good for question practice. It could be done either as a class activity, which would involve a lot of journalists, or in groups of about eight or nine.

After giving roles to the SS, allow them time to look back at the texts and tapescript to recall details about what happened. If this is being done in groups, it would be useful for all the 'Tinas', all the 'pilots', etc. to compare notes on what they are going to say.

Tell the journalists what kind of paper they are writing for so that you have a mix of quality and tabloid newspapers. This is a good opportunity for the journalists to practise question forms, and for follow-up remedial work.

As a follow-up to the roleplay, perhaps as homework, SS could write a summary of the press conference. This would also provide useful revision of reported speech (see Unit 17).

PRACTICE

SS have been using past modals throughout the unit - this is an opportunity to go back and focus their attention on the rules. However, note that some of the examples refer to the present, not the past, so are revision of Unit 16. The exercises could be preceded by looking at the *Language reference.*

• **Exercise 1** While you are monitoring SS working in pairs try to get them to use weak forms, as practised earlier in the REVISION AND EXTENSION section, *Connected speech.*

• **Exercise 2** These two short dialogues are intended to encourage SS to speculate about what is happening and who the people are. Further examples of dialogues like this can be found in C. Mortimer, *Dramatic Monologues for Listening Comprehension* and A. Maley and A. Duff, *Variations on a Theme* (see *Bibliography*).

• **Exercise 3** There are more puzzles like this in C. Frank, M. Rinvolucri and M.Behrer, *Challenge to Think* (see *Bibliography*).You may need to keep reminding SS to use modals.

• **Exercise 4** There is an opportunity here to do more work in the area of puns. Although most of the discussion will probably not involve the use of past deductions, when groups are reporting back try to encourage them to use *must have been / may have been about* ... The discussion links to a writing activity in the next section.

WRITING

Newspaper article

The exercises in this section aim to help SS to think about how to organise a short article, as well as writing sentences economically by using participle clauses.

• **Exercise 1** Get SS to work out the rationale behind the organisation of the article (i.e. how an article might open, where the main information comes, and how it can conclude).

• **Exercise 2** This provides revision of work done on participle clauses in the previous unit. Remind SS that participle clauses can only be used when the subject remains the same.

Tapescripts

RECORDING 1

a) A: He can't've gone by car because if he'd driven he'd've taken his glasses.
   B: He may've gone by bus.
b) A: He might've gone for a run, or he may've popped out to the shops.
   B: It's after five so he can't've gone to the shops.
c) A: Steve must've come back because the window's been opened.
   B: Yes, but he might've left it open last night.
d) A: Jane can't've phoned or she'd've left a message.
   B: She may've decided to call back later.

RECORDING 2

The first time D. B. Cooper was seen was in the departure lounge at Portland Airport, Oregon, where he bought his one-way ticket and checked in for the 400-mile journey to Seattle, Washington. It was 24 November 1971.

The slim, quiet middle-aged man with dark-tinted glasses carrying a canvas carrier bag and a raincoat and wearing a lightweight suit and flimsy shoes paid cash for his ticket and gave his name as 'D. B. Cooper'. After a forty-five minute wait in the lounge, where no one looked at him twice, he boarded the plane when the flight was called and the jet roared off into the darkening skies.

Shortly after take-off Cooper pushed the button in the overhead panel to summon one of the cabin crew to his seat. Stewardess Tina Mucklow approached with a tray, ready to take his order for a drink.

Cooper simply thrust a crumpled note into her hand and then reached under his seat to pull the canvas bag on to his lap. He waited for a few seconds for the flight attendant to read the note. It warned: 'I have a bomb with me. If I don't get $200,000 and two parachutes I will blow us all to bits.'

As the terrified woman tried to control her panic, Cooper calmly opened the bag to let her glimpse the dynamite and detonator inside. While she walked slowly up to the flight deck, Cooper settled back in his seat and peered out at the storm clouds below.

RECORDING 3

Within seconds a special transmitter on the flight deck of the Boeing was 'squawking' its coded electronic message over the radio frequencies: 'Hijack . . . Hijack . . . Hijack'.

At Seattle Airport a team of FBI agents, local police sharpshooters, hostage negotiation experts and airline officials were hastily gathered as the plane prepared to land. The passengers were still unaware of the drama when the jet touched down and stopped at the end of the runway.

There was a groan of annoyance from the travellers when the captain made the terse announcement: 'Ladies and gentlemen, there will be a slight delay in disembarking. Please remain in your seats until we're ready to taxi to the terminal building.'

Only one passenger ignored the announcement. Cooper unfastened his seatbelt and, clutching his bag, walked swiftly up the flight deck and positioned himself behind the crew. 'Now gentlemen,' he said softly, 'don't bother to look round.'

In twenty minutes of unyielding demands over the ground control radio from the flight deck of the airliner Cooper stuck to his original threat and nobody dared to call his bluff.

As the passengers began to grow more and more restless the door of the Boeing slid open and the flight engineers in overalls - undercover FBI men - came aboard with a trolley of 'catering equipment'. Under radio instructions they then withdrew.

The trolley was wheeled up to the flight deck by a flight attendant and Cooper studied its contents. It contained a tough white sack with $200,000 and four parachutes.

Finally Cooper allowed the complaining passengers to file off the aircraft. The jet was refuelled and Cooper told the pilot to head for Mexico. He told him to fly with the flaps lowered and the landing gear down, the speed below ninety metres a second, to fly at 2,000m, and open the rear door.

Before leaving the flight deck, locking the door behind him, he made a point of retrieving his ransom note. Four hours later, as the plane was approaching Reno Nevada Airport to refuel, the co-pilot unlocked the door of the flight deck and found the passenger cabin deserted. Cooper and the money had gone, leaving two parachutes behind - one of them ripped to shreds. Inspection of the flight recorder black box later measured a tiny change in the plane's altitude, which showed a loss of weight thirty-two minutes after leaving Seattle.

The danger of mid-air death and destruction had passed. The hunt to find D. B. Cooper was on.

RECORDING 4

a) 'Get out'
b) 'I suppose so.'
c) 'It's amazing!'
d) 'Don't do it!'
e) 'Not again.'
f) 'Come here!'
g) 'It's over there.'
h) 'Did you hear what she said?'
i) 'Hello, Pooh.'

RECORDING 5

A: Have you got the parcel?
B: Yes, it's in the bag under the table.
A: How much?
B: Ten thousand pounds.
A: OK. Were you followed?
B: I don't think so.
A: Tell Bill I'll hand her over tomorrow.

RECORDING 6

A: Has she seen him yet?
B: Yes, she went this morning. He's quite bad, apparently.
A: When did it happen?
B: Yesterday evening - about seven, I think.
A: Were there any witnesses?
B: I don't know. I just hope he wasn't over the limit, that's all.

Key

READING

1

a) He threatened to blow up the plane he was on.

2

a) detonator
b) vanished into thin air
c) commandeered
d) gloating
e) lucrative
f) ruthless
g) pulled off

REVISION AND EXTENSION

Deduction in the past

a) *must* + *have* + past participle or *must* + *have* + *been* + base form + *-ing*
b) *Can't* + *have* + past participle
c) *May, might* or *could have* + past participle

Connected speech

1

a) A: 18 B: 6
b) A: 16 B: 13
c) A: 11 B: 10
d) A: 12 B: 8

2

a) A: He *can't have gone by* car because *if he'd* driven *he'd have taken his* glasses.
B: *He may have* gone *by* bus.
b) A: *He might have gone for a* run, *or he may have* popped out *to the* shops.
B: It's after five *so he can't have gone to the* shops.
c) A: Steve *must have come back because the* window*'s been* opened.
B: Yes, *but he might have* left *it open last* night.
d) A: Jane *can't have* phoned *or she'd have left a* message.
B: *She may have* decided *to call back* later.

LISTENING

1

Date: 24 November 1971
Place of departure: Portland Airport, Oregon
Cooper's destination: Seattle, Washington
Description: slim; quiet; middle-aged
Wearing: dark tinted glasses, a lightweight suit, flimsy shoes
Carrying: a canvas carrier bag and a raincoat
What his note said: 'I have a bomb with me. If I don't get $200,000 and two parachutes I will blow us all to bits.'
Who he gave the note to: Stewardess Tina Mucklow
What happened next: He opened the bag and showed the stewardess the dynamite and detonator and she went to the flight deck.

2

Example answers:

a) They were waiting at the airport when the plane landed and dressed up as flight engineers to go on the plane with the money and parachutes.
b) This, in fact, was a trolley with the money and parachutes that were brought on board for Cooper.
c) The money and parachutes were in a white sack.
d) Cooper told the pilot to fly to Mexico after the passengers had disembarked.
e) The black box was the flight recorder, and showed that Cooper must have jumped out 32 minutes after leaving Seattle.

4

b)

1 checked in
2 departure lounge
3 boarding
4 take-off
5 cabin crew
6 touched down
7 taxied
8 runway
9 flight deck
10 crew
11 disembark
12 terminal

READING AND WRITING

1

a) False b) True c) True d) False e) False f) True g) True

VOCABULARY

Different sounds

2

a) hiss b) grunt c) gasp d) scream e) groan f) roar g) murmur h) whisper i) squeak

3

Example answers:

b) grunts c) squeaks d) roars e) hisses f) hisses g) murmurs h) roars / whispers / murmurs i) roars

Idiomatic expressions

Example answers:

a) unlikely / remote
b) hiding away
c) gave the impetus for / provoked
d) searched very carefully
e) caught
f) lose impetus / lose enthusiasm

PRACTICE

1

a) Yes, she must have been on holiday.
b) She must have had a perm.
c) He must be ill.
d) She might be playing tennis.
e) She can't have gone abroad because her passport is here.
f) They must have copied.
g) It may have run out of petrol.
h) There must be someone at the door.

2
Example answers:
a)
1 Kidnappers.
2 The ransom money.
3 The leader of the gang.
4 The kidnapped woman or girl.
5 They are worried about the police.
b)
1 The hospital.
2 Husband and wife / partners / father and daughter.
3 There was an accident (*badly hurt; witnesses; over the limit*).

3
Possible answers:
a) Because he's not tall enough to reach the twentieth button.
b) A man or woman in the next room, because the woman was snoring.

4
Example answers:
Three battered in fish shop (batter which fish is fried in, or batter meaning *hit*)
Police found drunk in shop window (A policeman found a drunk man or someone found a drunk policeman.)
Body in garden was a plant, says wife (It was a garden plant, or a body which someone put there.)
New shock on electricity bills (surprise, or electric shock)
Meat shortage; Prime Minister attacked (He was attacked physically – to eat – or in words.)
British bird men held by Turkey (the country or the bird)

WRITING

1
The first paragraph gives a summary of what has happened; the second gives more details; and the third says what happened in the end.

2
a) Asked what he thought of the present economic situation the Prime Minister said…
b) Admitting that unemployment needed to come down he pointed out that …
c) Speaking to the press today after spending seven years in captivity Mr Fred Linton talked about…
d) After welcoming the guests and giving his speech the Mayor…

Revision

Students' Book

READING: magazine article about Dorothea Shaw's life in the jungle.
VOCABULARY 1: revision (word puzzle).

LISTENING: song, *I will survive*, by Gloria Gaynor.
VOCABULARY 2: vocabulary review (word fields; idioms).
GRAMMAR: verb forms.

WRITING: correcting errors.
INTEGRATED SKILLS: poem, *Happiness*, by Raymond Carver; speaking and writing.

Workbook

GRAMMAR: review of verb forms; conditionals and *wish*; modals; spot the errors; which language item is correct?
VOCABULARY: colloquial language; test your vocabulary.
WRITING: linking expressions; spelling; punctuation.

Organisation and aims

The last unit of the book is a skills-based unit containing revision of the language practised in the previous units. The main themes are: living alone, survival and happiness.

The unit is divided into three main sections: a reading text, which also revises grammar; a listening text and verb review; and an integrated skills section which is preceded by some writing exercises which focus on the mechanics of writing. Including the WB, there are exercises on the main verb forms as well as conditionals and modals, and exercises covering most of the vocabulary.

The main texts (the magazine article, the song and the poem) are probably best dealt with in separate lessons but the other exercises can be fitted in wherever appropriate. The vocabulary, grammar and writing exercises (both SB and WB) can be set for homework or they can be used as tests. The *Verb forms* exercise in the SB is particularly suitable as a test. Another strategy is to get SS to do the language exercises in class in pairs.

READING

Before reading

• **Exercise 1** Ask SS what they think the headline means, using the picture and caption to help them. (When SS read the text they will see that the word *interior* could refer to the jungle or it could refer to the inner life of Dorothea and other living things.) Some SS may not know that Belize is a country in Central America and was a British colony (British Honduras) until 1981. (This information could be useful when SS read the text and discuss Dorothea's background – in fact, she was born in Belize, went 'home' to England at 17 and returned in later life.) Check SS know what a *short-wave radio* is.

• **Exercise 2** This provides revision of question forms.

Reading

• **Exercise 1** Notice that the gaps are to be filled with a number of clauses practised in other units (relative, addition, contrast, etc.). If necessary, elicit clues in the context to help SS make their choices. Complete the first one with SS and then give as PW? Notice that although Dorothea is 71 and nearly blind she is basically happy. Introduce the words *telepathy* (the sending of thoughts from one person's mind to another)/*telepathic* and *empathy* (the ability to imagine yourself in the position of other living things and share their feelings). SS might need help with some of the words (*posse, hammock, encampment, kerosene lamp, unbearably*) but try to avoid giving the meaning of the words practised in the deduction in context exercise which follows (Exercise 3).

• **Exercise 2** This is a comprehension exercise. (Some SS may have problems with the word *insensitive*.)

• **Exercise 3** This deduction in context exercise revises an important learning skill.

• **Exercise 4** Complete the first one with SS and then set as PW/GW? Notice that the words in italics are important grammatical items practised in the book. There are many possible answers and the alternatives can be discussed and the reasons for wrong answers elicited. Not all the information needed will be found in the text so SS will need to use their imaginations.

VOCABULARY 1

This section revises word formation (affixes, compounds), as well as homonyms and homophones. The word puzzle could be done as a game, by putting SS in teams and giving a time-limit. The winner is the first team to finish with all the answers correct. Note that the correct suffix for *generous* is *-osity* (not just *-ity*).

There is an exercise on colloquial language in the WB.

LISTENING

This is a powerful song about a woman who survived a broken heart and is determined to go on and live independently of her former lover or husband.

• **Exercise 1** Do this creative prediction exercise as GW? Get SS to use their imaginations to compose some possible lines for the song. (It doesn't matter if they are completely different from the actual words.) To start them off remind them of the title and possibly elicit a range of possibilities for the first line (e.g. *Why was she afraid? What did she keep thinking?*). It might be more challenging *not* to tell SS what the song is about.

• **Exercise 2** To answer all these questions SS need to be able not only to understand the words of the song but to make inferences about what happened.

• **Exercise 3** This is a pronunciation and comprehension exercise. First SS match words according to their sound and then match them to the context according to their meaning. SS might not know what *crumble* means (i.e. collapse)

• **Exercise 5** This may best be done with SS reading the tapescript to help them.

• **Exercise 6** This is a creative writing exercise, perhaps best done in groups if there is time. You could display the letters for everyone to read. (Another option is to get SS to write letters which follow the events of the song.)

VOCABULARY 2

• **Exercise 1** Focus on vocabulary as linked to topic. The five topics are: weddings, cars, travel, employment and crime. They are all topics from the SB. Do as PW? Note that there is another exercise in the WB.

• **Exercise 2** This exercise revises particles (both adverbs and prepositions) as used in idiomatic expressions.

• **Exercise 3** This is an important 'round-up' for the learner-development part of the SB related to vocabulary.

GRAMMAR

Verb forms

• **Exercise 1** This is a prediction exercise. Do as PW? Establish that what the cartoons have in common is electricity and the effect that either the electricity is having on Pauline or Pauline is having on the electricity. (In fact, it is the latter.) Note there is another exercise in the WB.

• **Exercise 2** This could be used as a test. Get SS to read the text quickly once and answer one or two comprehension questions first (e.g. *Why is Pauline's problem 'shocking'? Explain the double meaning of the word 'shocking'. What things have gone wrong? Why is her problem expensive? When did the problem start?*). SS might need help with one or two words first: *static, to blow (the TV), tumble drier, countless, a guarantee, sparks, thermostat.* Either tell them the meaning or allow them to use dictionaries. Do the gap-fill as PW or individually. Use the opportunity to do some revision on any problem areas.

• **Exercise 3** If necessary, do some further revision of problem areas.

• **Exercise 4** This is a roleplay which revises question forms and making notes.

WRITING

Correcting errors

PW? Possibly do as a kind of 'Grammar auction', where SS 'bid' for the sentences which they think are correct (see M. Rinvolucri, *Grammar Games* – details in the *Bibliography*).

INTEGRATED SKILLS

This series of exercises involves SS using all four language skills: listening, speaking, reading and writing.

• **Exercise 1** Elicit what the poem is about from clues in the picture (e.g. *What time of day is it? What do you think the boys are doing? What is one of them carrying? What do you think their mood is? Who do you think the man is? What is his mood?*). The theme is the quiet happiness of the two boys which impresses itself on the narrator and for a moment makes everything else in life seem unimportant. Raymond Carver (1939–1988) was an American poet and short story writer famous for making ordinary people and ordinary scenes seem extraordinary. You could ask SS what they would include in a poem on happiness and if they know any other poems on happiness.

• **Exercise 2** Do as PW. In a weak class you could write the actual words on the board in jumbled order before getting SS to complete the gaps. (See the Key or the tapescript.)

• **Exercise 4** You might prefer SS to read the tapescript while listening. The questions focus on comprehension of detail and inference. Question a) invites a personal answer.

• **Exercise 5** This extends the theme of happiness through a newspaper article. Maybe get SS to look up the words *extrovert* and *introvert* in the dictionary (as well as *stable* and *impulsive*, if necessary). They could then decide which they think other SS in the class are (extrovert or introvert) and discuss their answers in pairs. (Most people are a mixture of both in different degrees.) They could also make a list of famous people under each heading or you could give out a list of names and get the SS to divide them. In c) you could add social status, class and sex.

• **Exercise 6** At this stage of the course, probably keep the writing completely free and unguided. However, if necessary, you could integrate the more controlled writing exercises from the WB. Get SS to share their poems or diary entries with each other.

Tapescripts

RECORDING 1

(First two verses of Recording 2).

RECORDING 2

'I Will Survive' sung by Gloria Gaynor.
At first I was afraid, I was petrified
Kept thinking I could never live without you by my side
But then I spent so many nights thinking how you did me wrong
And I grew strong - And I learned how to get along

And so you're back, from out of space
I just walked in to find you here with that sad look upon your face
I should have changed that stupid lock, I should have made you leave your key
If I'd have known for just one second you'd be back to bother me

Go on now go, walk out the door
Just turn around now cos you're not welcome anymore
Weren't you the one who tried to hurt me with goodbye
Did you think I'd crumble. Did you think I'd lay down and die

Oh no not I
I will survive
Oh as long as I know how to love
I know I'll stay alive
I've got all my life to live
I've got all my love to give
And I'll survive
I will survive

It took all the strength I had not to fall apart
Kept trying hard to mend the pieces of my broken heart
And I spent oh so many nights just feeling sorry for myself
I used to cry, but now I hold my head up high

And you see me, somebody new
I'm not that chained up little person still in love with you
And so you felt like dropping in and just expect me to be free
But now I'm saving all my loving for someone who's loving me

RECORDING 3

HAPPINESS
So early it's still almost dark out.
I'm near the window with coffee,
and the usual early morning stuff
that passes for thought.
When I see the boy and his friend
walking up the road
to deliver the newspaper.
They wear caps and sweaters,
and one boy has a bag over his shoulder.
They are so happy
they aren't saying anything, these boys.
I think if they could, they would take
each other's arm.
It's early in the morning,
and they are doing this thing together.
They come on, slowly.
The sky is taking on light,
though the moon still hangs pale over the water.
Such beauty that for a minute
death and ambition, even love,
doesn't enter into this.
Happiness. It comes on
unexpectedly. And goes beyond, really,
any early morning talk about it.

Key

READING

Reading

1

a) 3 b) 1 c) 7 d) 2 e) 6 f) 5 g) 4

2

a) No. 'She lives happily and totally alone' (line 6); 'Sometimes she gets lonely but most of the time the animals and radio are company enough.' (lines 19–21); 'You cannot be miserable here if you look and listen' (lines 31–2).
b) Yes. She 'listens for hours to any Spanish, English, German or French broadcasts she can find on her short-wave radio' (lines 16–19).
c) No. 'When someone was angry, or in pain, she felt that anger, she suffered their actual pain.' (lines 50–2).
d) No, she was an empath then too and was 'a strange girl ... solitary to the point of reclusion' (lines 39–41).
e) It seems so. There is a 'roar of bulldozers not many miles away' (lines 68–9).
f) It seems not. She 'went out each time [she] heard it [the jaguar] approaching and banged saucepan lids' (lines 81–2).

3

Example answers:
a) taking care of
b) supplies of food
c) filled with hate or other unpleasant feelings
d) crazy
e) loud noise

4

Examples answers:
a) should have run away / must have been very frightened
b) much human life / many people
c) must have been very strange / can't have been very happy
d) insisted that the journalist didn't make her out to be a lonely old embittered lady, / urged the journalist not to make her out to be...
e) have to be careful in case wild animals attack you / you don't need to worry about the cold
f) few people she can trust / lots of dangerous wild animals around
g) stop living in the jungle one day / regret living in the jungle
h) either reads a book or listens to the radio / neither watches TV nor goes to the cinema

VOCABULARY 1

1

Across	*Down*
1 SAFE	1 SPOT
3 MEAT	2 ED
7 TRAY	3 MAIL
8 AL	4 AUTO
9 OSITY	5 CURLY
	6 WAIST
	8 ACHE

LISTENING

2

Example answers:

a) Her boyfriend or her husband.
b) He left her.
c) Because she thought she could never live without the person.
d) She is stronger and knows she can live without him.
e) She realised the person had behaved badly towards her.
f) She regretted not having changed the lock or having made him leave his key behind.

3

3 goodbye 4 die 5 survive 6 alive 7 live 8 give
9 apart 10 heart 11 new 12 you 13 free 14 me

5

Example answers:

a) Probably not because she talks about 'that chained up little person'.
b) Probably because she says, 'but now I'm saving all my loving for someone who's loving me'.
c) He probably doesn't because she says, 'so you felt like dropping in and expected me to be free'. However, he might just be desperate.
d) Probably not because she says, 'I'm saving all my loving for someone who's loving me'.

VOCABULARY 2

1

reception, honeymoon, ceremony, licence
globetrotter, trip, explorer, stopover
appoint, employer, applicant, recruit
clutch, overtake, gears, slow down
burglary, bail, arrest, prosecution

2

a) up b) in c) up with d) round in e) on f) out of
g) at h) in i) in j) up with / of k) on l) of

GRAMMAR

Verb forms

1

a) Pauline is an 'electrical sensitive' who gives off ten times the normal amount of static electricity which causes chaos with electrical equipment.

2

1 gives 2 has blown 3 be switched off 4 to work
5 was opened 6 get mended (mend) 7 have
8 was working 9 go 10 would fly 11 embracing
12 had caused 13 to overheat 14 has been struck
15 to give up 16 went 17 would be blamed
18 shaking 19 don't shower 20 'll start

3

a) I'll help
b) you are going to set up / you're setting up (*plan*); you'll be setting up (*planned event - no intention*)
c) will have run out (*future in the past – focus on the state at the end of the week with no money);* will run *(focus on the whole action of running out);* will be running (*In the process of running out – will run out later*)
d) lasts (*regular, fixed event*), will last (*confident prediction*); is going to last six days (*prediction based on previous knowledge*); will have lasted (*by the end of a certain time*)
e) will play (*intention*); will be playing (*in the process of*); are playing / are going to play (*plan / starting to play*)

WRITING

Correct the errors

a) Katherine wrote her a lovely letter. / a lovely letter to her.
b) The motorbike I bought... /. which I bought last year.
c) Do you know anyone who has seen her?
d) Although he's not...; He's not very good at his job but / even though he earns ...
e) What awful weather!
f) Elizabeth suddenly dropped the cup. (...dropped the cup suddenly / Suddenly Elizabeth...)
g) We're looking for the place...
h) Planes which leave / leaving from...
i) Let's meet next week if...
j) My wife, who works in New York, is ...

INTEGRATED SKILLS

2

1 dark 2 coffee 3 boy 4 newspaper 5 sweaters
6 bag 7 happy 8 sky 9 moon 10 water

4

b) The poem suggests a lot of natural intimacy, affection and happiness but (perhaps) being American it is not socially acceptable for two young boys to show physical affection.
c) i) 'this thing'
ii) the early morning sky / the scene with the two boys
iii) '*It* comes on', 'talk about *it*'

Irregular verbs

Note that some of these verbs have different Past Simple forms in American English.
For these variations see the *Longman Dictionary of Contemporary English*.

VERB	PAST SIMPLE	PAST PARTICIPLE
be	was	been
beat	beat	beaten
become	became	become
begin	began	begun
bend	bent	bent
bite	bit	bitten
bleed	bled	bled
blow	blew	blown
break	broke	broken
bring	brought	brought
build	built	built
burn	burned, burnt	burned, burnt
burst	burst	burst
buy	bought	bought
catch	caught	caught
choose	chose	chosen
come	came	come
cost	cost	cost
cut	cut	cut
do	did	done
draw	drew	drawn
dream	dreamed, dreamt	dreamed, dreamt
drink	drank	drunk
drive	drove	driven
eat	ate	eaten
fall	fell	fallen
feed	fed	fed
feel	felt	felt
fight	fought	fought
find	found	found
fly	flew	flown
forget	forgot	forgotten
forgive	forgave	forgiven
freeze	froze	frozen
get	got	got
give	gave	given
go	went	gone, been
grow	grew	grown
hang	hung, hanged	hung, hanged
have	had	had
hear	heard	heard
hide	hid	hidden
hit	hit	hit
hold	held	held
hurt	hurt	hurt
keep	kept	kept
kneel	knelt	knelt
know	knew	known
lay	laid	laid
lead	led	led
lean	leaned, leant	leaned, leant
learn	learned, learnt	learned, learnt
leave	left	left
lend	lent	lent
let	let	let
lie	lay	lain
light	lit	lit
lose	lost	lost
make	made	made
mean	meant	meant
meet	met	met
mistake	mistook	mistaken
pay	paid	paid
prove	proved	proved, proven
put	put	put
read	read	read
ride	rode	ridden
ring	rang	rung
rise	rose	risen
run	ran	run
say	said	said
see	saw	seen
sell	sold	sold
send	sent	sent
set	set	set
shake	shook	shaken
show	showed	shown, showed
shut	shut	shut
sing	sang	sung
sink	sank, sunk	sunk
sit	sat	sat
sleep	slept	slept
slide	slid	slid
speak	spoke	spoken
spell	spelt	spelt
spend	spent	spent
spill	spilt, spilled	spilt, spilled
spoil	spoiled, spoilt	spoiled, spoilt
spread	spread	spread
spring	sprang	sprung
stand	stood	stood
steal	stole	stolen
stick	stuck	stuck
sting	stung	stung
sweep	swept	swept
swell	swelled	swollen, swelled
swim	swam	swum
swing	swung	swung
take	took	taken
teach	taught	taught
tear	tore	torn
tell	told	told
think	thought	thought
throw	threw	thrown
understand	understood	understood
wake	woke	woken
wear	wore	worn
weep	wept	wept
wet	wet	wet
win	won	won
wind	wound	wound
write	wrote	written

Language index (Students' Book)

Language index (Workbook)

INSTITUTE FOR APPLIED LANGUAGE STUDIES
UNIVERSITY OF EDINBURGH
21 Hill Place
Edinburgh EH8 9DP

Bibliography

Some of the following books are referred to in the Teacher's Book. All have been a useful source of information and ideas to us and we recommend them to teachers for their own reference.

ALEXANDER, L.G. *Longman English Grammar* (Longman, 1988)

BAKER, A. *Ship or Sheep?* (Cambridge University Press, 1977)

DAVIS, P. and RINVOLUCRI, M. *Dictation* (Cambridge University Press, 1988)

ELLIS, G. and SINCLAIR, B. *Learning to Learn English* (Cambridge University Press, 1989)

FRANK, C. and RINVOLUCRI, M. *Grammar in Action* (Pergamon, 1983)

FRANK, C., RINVOLUCRI, M. and BEHRER, M. *Challenge to Think* (Oxford University Press, 1982)

GAIRNS, R. and REDMAN, S. *Working with Words* (Cambridge University Press, 1986)

HEDGE, T. *Writing* (Oxford University Press, 1988)

KENWORTHY, J. *Teaching English Pronunciation* (Longman, 1987)

KLIPPEL, F. *Keep Talking* (Cambridge University Press, 1984)

LEECH, G. *An A–Z of English Grammar & Usage* (Edward Arnold, 1989)

LEWIS, M. *The English Verb* (Language Teaching Publications, 1986)

Longman Active Study Dictionary of English (Longman, 1983)

Longman Dictionary of Contemporary English (Longman, New edition – 1987)

McALPIN, J. *Longman Dictionary Skills Handbook* (Longman, 1988)

McARTHUR, T. *Longman Lexicon of Contemporary English* (Longman, 1981)

MALEY, A and DUFF, A, *Variations on a Theme* (Cambridge University Press, 1978)

MORGAN, J. and RINVOLUCRI, M. *Once Upon a Time* (Cambridge University Press, 1983)

MORGAN, J. and RINVOLUCRI, M. *Vocabulary* (Oxford University Press, 1986)

MORGAN, J. and RINVOLUCRI, M. *The Q Book* (Longman, 1988)

MORTIMER, C. *Dramatic Monologues for Listening Comprehension* (Cambridge University Press, 1980)

O'CONNOR, J.D. and FLETCHER, C. *Sounds English* (Longman, 1989)

RINVOLUCRI, M. *Grammar Games* (Cambridge University Press, 1984)

ROGERSON, P. and GILBERT, J.B. *Speaking Clearly* (Cambridge University Press, 1990)

SWAN, M. *Practical English Usage* (Oxford University Press, 1980)

SWAN, M. and SMITH, B. *Learner English* (Cambridge University Press, 1987)

UR, P. *Discussions that Work* (Cambridge University Press, 1981)

UR, P. *Grammar Practice Activities* (Cambridge University Press, 1988)

WHITE, R. and ARNDT, V. *Process Writing* (Longman, 1992)